Citizenship

Personal Lives and Social Policy

WINCHESTE

WITHDRAWN FROM
THE LIBRARY
UNIVERSITY OF
WINCHESTER

Personal Lives and Social Policy
Series Editor: Janet Fink

This book forms part of a series published by The Policy Press in association with The Open University. The complete list of books in the series is as follows:

Sexualities: Personal Lives and Social Policy, edited by Jean Carabine
Care: Personal Lives and Social Policy, edited by Janet Fink
Work: Personal Lives and Social Policy, edited by Gerry Mooney
Citizenship: Personal Lives and Social Policy, edited by Gail Lewis

Notes on contributors to *Citizenship: Personal Lives and Social Policy*

Gail Lewis is a Senior Lecturer in Social Policy in the Faculty of Social Sciences at The Open University. Her research interests focus on the constitution and intersection of gendered and racialized processes and identities in policy discourses and welfare practices. Recent publications include 'Racialising emotional labour and emotionalising racialised labour: anger, fear and shame in social welfare' (with Y. Gunaratnam) in *Journal of Social Work Practice* (2001); and 'Racialising culture is ordinary' in *Contemporary Culture and Everyday Life* (edited by E.B. Silva and T. Bennett; Sociology Press, 2004).

Janet Fink is a Lecturer in Social Policy in the Faculty of Social Sciences at The Open University. Her research interests are centred on the cultural turn in contemporary social policy and the intersections of family life and child welfare discourses during the second half of the twentieth century. Her recent publications include *Rethinking European Welfare* (co-edited with G. Lewis and J. Clarke; Sage, 2001); 'Private lives, public issues: moral panics and the "family"' in *Journal for the Study of British Cultures* (2002); and 'Europe's cold shoulder: migration and the constraints of welfare in Fortress Europe' in *Soundings* (2002).

Helen Lucey is a Lecturer in Social Psychology in the Faculty of Social Sciences at The Open University. Her area of interest is the formation of contemporary subjectivities, with particular reference to gender and social class. She takes an interdisciplinary, psychosocial approach to explore the interrelationship between emotional and structural processes in the lives of individuals, families, communities and institutions. She is author of the book *Democracy in the Kitchen* (with V. Walkerdine; Virago, 1989) and, more recently, *Growing Up Girl: Psychosocial Explorations of Gender and Class* (with J. Melody and V. Walkerdine; Palgrave, 2001).

Esther Saraga is a Staff Tutor in Social Sciences at The Open University in London. She is currently engaged in biographical research around her parents' flight from Nazi Germany and their early experiences in the UK. She is author of 'Dangerous places: the family as a site of crime' in *The Problem of Crime* (edited by J. Muncie and E. McLaughlin; Sage, 2001); 'Abnormal, unnatural and immoral? The social construction of sexualities' in *Embodying the Social: Constructions of Difference* (edited by E. Saraga; Routledge, 1998); and 'Children's needs: who decides?' in *Welfare: Needs, Rights and Risks* (edited by M. Langan; Routledge, 1998).

Citizenship

Personal Lives and Social Policy

Edited by Gail Lewis

This publication forms part of the Open University course DD305 *Personal Lives and Social Policy*. Details of this and other Open University courses can be obtained from the Course Information and Advice Centre, PO Box 724, The Open University, Milton Keynes MK7 6ZS, United Kingdom: tel. +44 (0)1908 653231; e-mail general-enquiries@open.ac.uk. Alternatively, you may visit the Open University website at http://www.open.ac.uk where you can learn more about the wide range of courses and packs offered at all levels by The Open University.

To purchase a selection of Open University course materials visit the webshop at www.ouw.co.uk, or contact Open University Worldwide, Michael Young Building, Walton Hall, Milton Keynes MK7 6AA, United Kingdom, for a brochure: tel. +44 (0)1908 858785; fax +44 (0)1908 858787; e-mail ouwenq@open.ac.uk

Copyright © 2004 The Open University

First published 2004 by The Policy Press in association with The Open University

The Open University
Walton Hall
Milton Keynes
MK7 6AA
United Kingdom
www.open.ac.uk

The Policy Press
Fourth Floor, Beacon House
Clifton
Bristol
BS8 1QU
United Kingdom
www.policypress.org.uk

The opinions expressed are not necessarily those of the Course Team or of The Open University.

All rights reserved. No part of this publication may be reproduced, stored in a retrieval system, transmitted or utilized in any form or by any means, electronic, mechanical, photocopying, recording or otherwise, without written permission from the publisher or a licence from the Copyright Licensing Agency Ltd. Details of such licences (for reprographic reproduction) may be obtained from the Copyright Licensing Agency Ltd of 90 Tottenham Court Road, London W1T 4LP.

Open University course materials may also be made available in electronic formats for use by students of the University. All rights, including copyright and related rights and database rights, in electronic course materials and their contents are owned by or licensed to The Open University, or otherwise used by The Open University as permitted by applicable law. In using electronic course materials and their contents you agree that your use will be solely for the purposes of following an Open University course of study or otherwise as licensed by The Open University or its assigns. Except as permitted above, you undertake not to copy, store in any medium (including electronic storage or use in a website), distribute, transmit or re-transmit, broadcast, modify or show in public such electronic materials in whole or in part without the prior written consent of The Open University or in accordance with the Copyright, Designs and Patents Act 1988.

British Library Cataloguing-in-Publication Data
A catalogue record for this book is available from the British Library.

Library of Congress Cataloguing-in-Publication Data
A catalogue record for this book has been requested.

Edited, designed and typeset by The Open University.

Printed and bound in Great Britain by The Bath Press, CPI Group.

ISBN 1 86134 521 6

1.1

Contents

UNIVERSITY COLLEGE
WINCHESTER
02887371
323.6
LEW

Preface

Citizenship: Personal Lives and Social Policy is the final book in a new series published by The Policy Press in association with The Open University. The series takes an interdisciplinary and theoretically informed approach to the study of social policy in order to examine the ways in which the two domains of *personal lives* and *social policy and welfare practice* are each partially shaped and given meaning by the other. This process of mutual constitution is explored in the books through core practices of the everyday. Such an approach is both exciting and innovative. It is also indicative of a growing recognition within the social sciences that 'the personal' is a valuable lens of analysis. More generally, the series is concerned not only with debates and questions that are highly visible in social policy, but also with those that tend to be marginalized or silenced and how these might be interpreted through the use of different theoretical perspectives, conceptual tools and research evidence. Overall, therefore, the books move beyond what are usually considered to be the parameters of social policy and its study.

The four books make up the core texts of an Open University course entitled *Personal Lives and Social Policy*. The first book, *Sexualities: Personal Lives and Social Policy*, considers why questions of sex and sexuality matter for the study of social policy and, in turn, illustrates how such questions provide important insights into the relationship between personal lives and social policy. Its concerns with the normative and taken-for-granted assumptions about sexuality, that inform social policy and welfare practices, establish the central interest of the series – the dynamics by which social policy and personal lives intersect and become entangled.

The second book, *Care: Personal Lives and Social Policy*, focuses on the meanings and definitions attributed to care and examines the norms and values associated with care relationships that are embedded in welfare policy and practice. The book illustrates the highly charged and often contradictory nature of care relations by exploring issues of power, conflict and control and considering the different spaces and places where questions about care have been lived out, debated and struggled over.

The third book, *Work: Personal Lives and Social Policy*, traces the central place that work has been afforded, historically, in policy-making and the extent to which it has remained an unproblematic category not only for policy-makers but also in the study of social policy. The book foregrounds the contingent relationship between work and welfare in order to examine the ways in which this arena of policy practices and discourses has developed around particular constructions of personal lives.

This fourth and final book, *Citizenship: Personal Lives and Social Policy*, looks at ideas and meanings associated with citizenship in order to broaden and problematize the term. In particular, it emphasizes the importance of moving away from associating citizenship with rights and obligations within nation-states towards recognizing how a consideration of multiple belongings and practices of the everyday opens up the study of social policy to new and challenging questions.

Although these books are edited volumes, each chapter has been specially written to contribute not only to the exploration of the mutual constitution of personal lives and social policy, but also to the process of student learning. The books have, therefore, been constructed as interactive teaching texts which encourage engagement with and further reflection on the themes, issues and arguments presented in the chapters. The process of interaction is organized around:

- *activities* – variously made up of exercises, tasks and questions, highlighted in colour, which have been designed to extend or consolidate understanding of particular aspects of the chapters;
- *comments* – interpretations and discussions of the activities, which provide opportunities for readers to compare their own responses with those of the author(s);
- *in-text questions* – short questions, again in colour, that build into the chapter opportunities for consideration of core points or arguments;
- *key words* – terms and concepts, highlighted in colour in the text and in the margins, which are central to the arguments, theoretical perspectives and research questions being used and interrogated by the author(s).

In addition, the opening chapter of each book has been written to provide a critical introduction to key issues, ideas, theories and concepts associated with the book's field of interest. The individual books are self-contained but there are references to other chapters and other books in the series. Such references help readers not only to make connections between the books, but also to understand and reflect on the themes and debates that run across the series overall.

The series has been shaped and informed by discussions within the Open University Course Team. Each member of the Team brought to these discussions their own interests, enthusiasms and fields of expertise, but never lost sight of the overall aims of the series and their commitment to those aims. The series is, therefore, the product of a genuinely interdisciplinary and collaborative process. This also means that contributions have been made to all the chapters of the books within this series by people who are not explicitly named as authors. The process of collaboration extends further, however, than the production of materials by academics. In writing chapters, the Course Team and consultant authors have been advised and guided by an external assessor, a tutor panel and a developmental testing panel. The wide-ranging involvement and assistance from the editors, designers and picture researchers have been invaluable in the production of these accessible and attractive texts. Course managers have used their knowledge and skills to resolve the many questions and difficulties that arose during the course's development. Secretaries brought their expertise to the styling and organization of seemingly endless manuscript drafts – and did so with admirable good humour. We thank them all for their work and support which are reflected throughout this book, the series and the course as a whole.

Janet Fink

CHAPTER 1

'Do Not Go Gently ... ': Terrains of Citizenship and Landscapes of the Personal

by Gail Lewis

Contents

1 Introduction

Since the 1980s the question of citizenship and what it means to be a citizen has risen to the top of the political, social and cultural agenda both in the UK and globally. Linked to questions of nationality and political and social rights within a given nation-state, the urgency with which discussions of citizenship are conducted is also a product of the breadth and depth of unrest and realignment within and between states and regions that characterized the last quarter of the twentieth century. The causes, dimensions and consequences of these processes of change are neither fully determined nor without disputation. Yet we can identify some of the factors that combined to place citizenship at the forefront of official and popular concern at the beginning of the twenty-first century. Among these factors are the end of the Cold War and the reconfiguration of national and international borders in what was once Eastern Europe and in the expansion of the European Union.

In parallel, this period has seen the (re)assertion of national identity, alongside a proliferation of ethnic and/or religious identities, and both these have occurred in the context of the challenges to national sovereignty posed by global capital flows and the strategies of transnational corporations. Similarly, the increase in the movement of people has reached unprecedented heights, and, while we should take seriously Massey's (1999) warning not to overstate this, such movement has tested the commitment of many states in the overdeveloped North to the free movement of people and the offer of protection from persecution to those who need it. On the one hand, this movement of people across internationally recognized borders, together with the strains on the sovereignty of nation-states, has nurtured the rise of a discourse of human rights in which 'personhood' (that is, the mere fact of being a human) rather than 'nationhood' (that is, having legitimate nationality) (Soysal, 1994, pp.163–4) is positioned as the criterion legitimating claims to welfare resources and other 'public goods'. On the other hand, we have witnessed a more strident policing of international borders and an increased demonization and criminalization of asylum seekers and refugees. At the same time we can note the proliferation of social struggles over effective membership in a community of citizens (often defined as coterminous with the borders of a nation-state). These struggles have been expressed in the claims to legitimate entitlement to services *and* for recognition of social particularity, leading to what Cornel West (1993, p.11) has called a 'politics of cultural difference'. And finally, welfare states such as the UK have given far greater emphasis to self-reliance, obligation, duty and conditionality in welfare policy, attempting to tighten the link between entitlement and the behaviour and moral outlook of the recipients of welfare services and benefits (Deacon, 1994; Dwyer, 2000; **Fergusson, 2004**). In their overlapping but distinct ways it is these (and many other) factors that have forced citizenship and the notion of the citizen to the top of the global agenda.

Thus, in addressing questions of citizenship, this book is about one of the most taken-for-granted yet contested identities and relationships in the contemporary UK. As Frazer and Gordon remind us, 'citizens' and citizenship are two words notable for their power:

> They speak of respect, of rights, of dignity ... in a welfare state citizenship carries entitlements to social provision. It ... brings social provision within an aura of dignity surrounding 'citizenship' and 'rights'. People who enjoy 'social citizenship' [are] entitled to 'equal respect' [and] share a common set of institutions and services designed for all citizens, the use of which constitutes the practice of social citizenship.
>
> (Frazer and Gordon, 1994, p.90)

If we look more closely at this short statement from Frazer and Gordon we begin to see that social citizenship (which we will look at again in section 2):

- locates us in a relationship to the state whereby we can make *legitimate* claims;
- locates us in an institutional infrastructure through which we are *connected* to others – that is, to those with whom we share citizenship;
- accords to us a *status* from which we can gain a sense of self-worth and dignity;
- provides a conduit to *resources* – that is, to welfare services and benefits.

It is from this conceptual density that we take our cue in thinking about some of the dimensions of citizenship in the UK today. Rather than view citizenship as an absolute – that is, as something that one does or does not have – our approach to citizenship is to see it as a *relation* – between state and citizen, between citizen and citizen and between citizen and non-citizen. In this sense it is what Dean and Melrose (1999, p.82) refer to as 'associative'. We shall use vignettes and extracts taken from individuals' narratives about parts of their lives in an attempt to grasp something of how this relation is lived out. This will help us to see a second key point in our approach to citizenship which is to view it as a *process* – in which there is an ebb and flow of degrees of citizenship across the life-course, within and between specific social groups and through historical time.

citizenship/ anti-citizenship

One useful way in which to think about citizenship as relational and as a process is provided by David Matless (1998) who refers to a dynamic tension between **citizenship/anti-citizenship**. Matless develops this notion in relation to struggles in the 1940s over the use of the countryside as a source of outdoor leisure activity. Nevertheless, the idea of citizenship/anti-citizenship is a powerful one for us precisely because of its ability to extend beyond the particular focus on recreational struggles and cast light on the multi-dimensional character of citizenship. Thus citizenship is not only about rights to make claims against the state, important as these are, it also includes 'behavioural obligations' in which 'particular types of *conduct* ... promote good citizenship via mental, moral, physical and spiritual' (Matless, 1998, p.182, emphasis added) practices and orientations. Where these orientations are lacking so too are the normative qualities that define citizenship. Thus 'citizenship [becomes] defined in relation to an "anti-citizenship"' (Matless, 1998, p.182).

The theme of citizenship/anti-citizenship runs throughout each of the following chapters in this book and we will return to it in various ways later in this introductory chapter. Before we do, however, we want to state again what this book is about. For while citizenship is central to our focus, it is only so because we think it can tell us something about the relation between personal lives and social policy – a relation that we suggest is mutually constitutive.

Does this raise for you the question that social citizenship and social policy are in fact also in some way linked? And what are we to understand by the reference to personal lives? What do you think this might mean in the context here?

The *Shorter Oxford English Dictionary* definition of 'personal' is that it relates to something (an object, an emotion, a viewpoint, a piece of biographical information, etc.) concerning or affecting the individual person or self. The definition also links 'personal' with 'private'. While maintaining some of this meaning of personal, in this book we treat the idea of '*the* personal' as itself something that is to be explored and interrogated (see also **Carabine, 2004b; Fink, 2004; Mooney, 2004**). So rather than take its meaning for granted, we want to try to use the theme of citizenship to unpack the notion of 'the personal'. In doing this, we will explore not only how the contents of 'the personal' (in personal lives) are constituted, but also how 'the personal' of an individual's life changes across the life-course. We will also explore how an individual's personal life is in some senses 'collective' in that the content is similar to and shared with that of many other people. Finally, we will see that our personal lives might provide the basis from which we, individually and collectively, challenge normative ideas about what it means to be a citizen.

This means that our starting-point is to treat the content of an individual's life as having been formed from a complex mix of external (social, cultural, economic, political and institutional) influences and internal (emotional and psychic) ones. '**The personal**' in this context is the point of conjunction between external and internal worlds so that it is on the terrain of 'the personal' that things thought and felt as 'belonging to me', the individual, meld with wider societal processes, thus marking out an individual biography. When thinking about the **mutually constitutive relation** between personal lives and social policy we can therefore identify the following points:

the personal

mutually constitutive relation

- Social policy involves policy discourses and debates about the nature of people's lives and circumstances from which criteria of access and types of service provision will be identified (see, for example, Chapter 2).
- This means that policy discourses tend to involve normative assumptions about personal lives.
- Social policy influences the distribution of 'public goods' or resources among individuals, social groups and geographical locations, thus contributing to the content of people's personal lives through their access to and experience of welfare services, benefits and practices, and the consequences of these (see, for example, Chapter 4).
- Professional practices and the cultures of welfare organizations shape how social policy becomes entangled with and constitutive of personal lives (see, for example, Chapter 3).

Figure 1.1 Post-Second World War citizens in the making?

social policy

These are some of the ways in which **social policy** – that is, the cluster of agencies, professions, services and benefits, professional practices and administrative systems – helps to shape the content of personal lives. But this process of mutual constitution works the other way too, so that personal lives in their turn help to shape social policy. From this perspective we can identify three further points:

- The approaches, values and experiences of welfare professionals are influenced by the content of their personal lives.
- Individuals and social groups have varied understandings of social policy interventions and services and this shapes their actions towards and relationships with welfare practitioners.
- Welfare users, practitioners and providers comply with, reject or actively seek existing or new kinds of policy intervention and/or service provision and in doing so legitimate or contest existing policy and practice regimes and cultures and/or make claims as citizens for new kinds of provision or practice.

It is from this standpoint that we think of the mutual constitution of personal lives and social policy. Activity 1.1 uses an example from my own personal life to encourage you to think about 'personal lives and social policy' while at the same time keeping in mind issues of citizenship.

ACTIVITY 1.1

Conjure up in your mind's eye the phrase 'personal lives and social policy' and, without giving it any further consideration, *immediately* write down the ideas, images, thoughts and/or feelings that come to you.

COMMENT

My mother came to my mind – well, a scene in 1983 involving my mother and the local authority housing department. My mum is white and English and she is in hospital with cancer and she needs to go to the Council to sort out something about her tenancy. I, of course, could go – am desperate to go because she might die (as in fact she did) and I'm trying to do any, everything I can for her. But I feel rather than hear her pause, her hesitancy – and I know exactly what she is thinking. It is this. That if I, her black daughter, go for her then I might get a Council Officer who will:

(a) treat me in a racist way;

(b) therefore indirectly but powerfully punish her by not sorting out that which needs to be sorted out. So:

(c) what we need is to have someone else go, someone who is white, so that she (we?) can pass as a white family.

So we're in the NHS hospital where she proudly claims me as her daughter, thinking about the Council's housing department, where she is frightened to do so, and negotiating a very painful dynamic that structures our mother/daughter relationship in powerful, but not unloving, ways.

The content of this very particular family story is in part historical in that my mum's fear was the result of the numerous experiences she and my father had had in the 1950s, 1960s and 1970s of racist treatment from private and local authority landlords. In 1983 it was also very current though, in that this historical legacy was made to *live* in the present by the way it entered into and structured the interaction between me and my mum on that day. I use this example from my own 'personal' life and particular family biography for a number of reasons. First, it is, I think, a very potent illustration of the way in which we 'live' our relationships in the *context* of our connections to the institutional infrastructures of the welfare state, as Frazer and Gordon (1994) suggest. Second, and developing directly from the first, we can see that actual or feared practices of welfare institutions have the power to shape the *content* of our personal lives and the dynamic of interpersonal relations. Third, it shows that part of this content is the *inner life* of emotionality – welfare practices both help to craft and resonate with the inner world of the emotions. Fourth, it shows how deeply intertwined welfare institutions and their actual, remembered or feared practices are with the inequalities of *social power* (see section 2.1). Fifth, it illustrates that, despite benefiting from the right as a citizen to a share of welfare resources (in this case, the National Health Service and social housing), the effects of the unequal distribution of social power help to craft the *experience* of citizenship as a form of belonging. And finally, I use an example from my own life/biography both to illustrate the kind of terrain that is encompassed by the phrase the 'personal lives/social policy relation' and to say that, while I along with the other authors in this book am inviting you to traverse this terrain, we do so having done it ourselves.

Did you notice the shift to the use of 'I' in the Comment to Activity 1.1, rather than the 'we' that is used in the rest of this chapter? Why do you think this happened?

Figure 1.2 Mother and daughter: complex negotiations of citizenship

Aims

In general terms, then, the aims of this book are:

- To explore the mutually constitutive relation between personal lives and social policy through the analytical lens of 'citizenship'.
- To explore the provenance of citizenship through the analytical lens of personal lives/social policy.

Chapters 2, 3 and 4 examine this two-way relation in varying ways, using different theoretical perspectives and diverse subject matter, and with differing degrees of emphasis on dimensions of 'the personal'. In Chapter 5, we look back across the three chapters and consider how these different theoretical perspectives open up the personal lives/social policy relation in distinct but overlapping ways. Notwithstanding the variations between them, each chapter utilizes the lens of citizenship to analyse and illustrate the mutually constitutive relation between personal lives and social policy.

Aims Starting from an approach that sees citizenship as a process embedded in the dynamics and tensions of everyday life, the aims of this introductory chapter are:

- To introduce you to a range of debates about citizenship.
- To utilize the concepts or categories of rights, obligations and responsibilities; belongings; and practices of the everyday as a way to examine the question of citizenship. These concepts or categories may be explained as follows:
  (a) *Rights, obligations and responsibilities:* this considers citizenship as an abstract status in which formal equality to make claims against the state (and to comply with obligations to it) masks forms of inequality that are linked to social divisions and inequalities of social power.
  (b) *Belongings:* this refers to the associational dimensions of citizenship in terms of membership and identity. It points both to the claims to and exclusions from national belonging and identity that result from citizenship as a juridical (legal) status, and to the ebb and flow, or 'density', of citizenship rights that often occur on the basis of particular identities and forms of belonging – for example, identities of class, sexuality, gender, ethnicity or religion.
  (c) *Practices of the everyday:* this refers to two overlapping but competing dimensions. On the one hand, there are the ways in which hegemonic discourses of citizenship have embedded within them ideas about the 'best' and most appropriate ways of organizing domestic, sexual, work or leisure activities. On the other hand, there are the actual practices of everyday life in these and other spheres of activity and how these might either be deployed in opposition to hegemonic conceptions and/or be the basis of claims for an extended or deepened citizenship. Examples of this would include claims made by gay, lesbian or queer people for citizenship rights on the basis of the legitimacy of their forms of daily life, or claims made by working-class communities for full citizenship in the face of state attempts to erode their rights.
- To consider some of the questions that our approach raises in relation to citizenship as both discourse and practice.

This chapter is, then, an attempt to orientate your engagement with the chapters that follow. The rest of the chapter is organized into three main sections. It has become common – almost compulsory – to begin any discussion of 'citizenship' through an engagement with the work of T.H. Marshall, who in 1950 offered a definition of citizenship, and in section 2 we spend some time exploring his approach. Yet while Marshall provides the starting-point for most contemporary debates about the meanings, dimensions and limits of citizenship, many commentators have not been content with his definition. They have sought to interrogate the meanings of citizenship both as an idea and as a social relation in the light of the unequal distribution of social power across the highly differentiated populations that characterize many societies in the contemporary world. In keeping with this spirit of interrogation, we spend a little time analysing the idea and limitations of 'rights'. In section 3 we use the ideas of 'belongings' and 'practices of the everyday' to consider further the possibilities and limitations of citizenship and also how these open a window on to the personal lives/social policy relation. In section 4 we look briefly at the culture of suspicion, generated in part by the notion of belonging, which has come to the fore in practices of citizenship.

2 Marshall, rights and social power

In formal terms citizenship refers to a legal status conferred by an internationally recognized nation-state. This status accords a nationality (via the right to carry a passport issued by a particular nation-state) and the right to make claims against the state and receive a share of the public goods. Having a nationality means that the individual is understood as having membership of or as 'belonging' to the state that issues the passport and thus citizenship also contains within it the notion of national identity. Citizenship in many parts of the contemporary world also carries with it the right to participate in the political process through formal electoral procedures – for example, local, national and cross-national regional elections such as those for the parliament of the European Union. As well as according certain rights – to vote, to hold a passport and have a designated nationality status, to protection by the state when overseas, and so on – citizenship carries with it certain duties or responsibilities. Among these are the duties to observe the law, to pay taxes, to ensure the education of any children one may have, and to participate in juries unless excused under specific conditions. In abstract legal terms, all citizens are formally equal and their civil rights, themselves guaranteed by rule of law, protect their safety and freedom.

These features are the core of citizenship as a juridical or legal and political status. However, in overdeveloped liberal democratic states citizenship has, since the post-Second World War period, come to signal a link between the individual citizen and welfare rights, mutuality and responsibilities to the community for the 'collective good'. Thus citizenship implies a link between the individual, his or her fellow citizens, the state and social welfare. This is what is referred to by T.H. Marshall as **social citizenship**, which in his view equalled an attempt to erase 'one invidious mark of class distinction and creating for the community as a whole a mutual benefit society' (Marshall, 1981, pp.130–1). First writing in the late 1940s and early 1950s, Marshall, referring to the British context, had defined citizenship as having three elements:

social citizenship

> I shall call these three parts, or elements civil, political and social. The *civil* element is composed of the rights necessary for individual freedom/liberty of the person, freedom of speech, thought and faith, the right to own property and to conclude valid contracts, and the right to justice. This last is of a different order from the others, because it is the right to defend and assert all one's rights on terms of equality with others and by due process of law. This shows us that the

> institutions most directly associated with civil rights are the courts of justice. By the *political* element I mean the right to participate in the exercise of political power, as a member of a body invested with political authority or as an elector of the members of such a body. The corresponding institutions are parliament and councils of local government. By the *social* element I mean the whole range from the right to a modicum of economic welfare and security to the right to share the social heritage and to live the life of a civilised being according to the standards prevailing in the society. The institutions most closely connected with it are the educational system and the social services.
>
> (Marshall, 1992, p.8, emphases added)

For Marshall, just as these dimensions or elements of citizenship had their concrete manifestation in specific institutional frameworks (for example, the legal system, parliament and other agencies of the political process, and institutions and professions of the welfare state), so too was their development linked to particular centuries, with civil rights associated with the eighteenth century, political rights with the nineteenth and social rights with the twentieth. Thus the emergence of a fully rounded citizenship was, according to this view, a developmental process, unfolding in line with the movement of modernization and progress.

While this developmental schema points to an ever-increasing place for the public provision of welfare, income maintenance and the creation of opportunity, it is important not to forget the significance accorded to individual enterprise and responsibility and the role of the voluntary or non-statutory sector in facilitating such self-reliance. Indeed, as Gail Lewis and Janet Fink show in Chapter 2, the importance of these aspects of social democratic citizenship was a point emphasized by William Beveridge in his arguments for a new relation between state and citizen after the Second World War. Presented in this way, the expansion of citizenship rights to encompass more and more areas of life might seem a benign, uncontested process. Thus, while it is useful to look at questions of the *practice* of citizenship through the analytical lens provided by Marshall, we need to think of the civil, political and social elements as bound together in an unstable unity, with social rights occupying the position of the irreducible core of citizenship. As we shall see, however, this is itself dependent on the distribution of symbolic (for example, respect, legitimacy or dignity) and material resources and social power. Precisely because symbolic and material resources and social power are *unevenly* distributed, citizenship is one of the most contested ideas in social policy and sociological and political theory. For some, citizenship continues to define the parameters of rights and responsibilities, guaranteeing a base line of equality of opportunity and respect within the context of differential potential and achievement. For others, citizenship as a social relation (as opposed to an ideal) is among the most exclusionary of discourses and practices – this exclusionary effect itself being an outcome of the inequalities of social power linked to divisions of class, ethnicity, gender, age, sexuality and disability.

We will return to some of the limits or exclusionary effects of hegemonic discourses and practices of citizenship below, but before doing so let us take a moment to think about how the social citizenship that was encapsulated in the welfare reforms that followed the Second World War, helped to shape the content of one woman's personal life.

ACTIVITY 1.2

Read carefully through Extract 1.1 below and make notes on:

- the range of welfare services potentially available to the family discussed;
- the areas of service provision that were not available and their links to the gendered division of labour within the household;
- any evidence of an emotional dimension to the response by family members to social welfare, and therefore ambivalence regarding aspects of social citizenship;
- what this personal narrative tells us about the relationship between personal lives and social policy.

Extract 1.1 The vagaries of social citizenship: Liz's story

I was born two days after the end of the Second World War, in 1945. This was a moment of national euphoria and confidence, but one blighted by hardship, poverty, poor housing and other severe social problems. It was the moment when the post war welfare settlement was actively being settled – somewhere between the Beveridge Report and the founding of the NHS. I was born at home – or rather at my maternal grandmother's home since at that time care for women during and after childbirth was provided by their mothers or by women in the local neighbourhood, with visiting doctors who were paid for their services by the patient.

The post war housing shortage – caused partly by bomb damage and partly by slum clearance programmes – meant that we lived with my other grandparents along with an aunt in their (privately) rented house. It was not till I was six that we had a house of our own – this was the first generation in my family to become owner-occupiers, and we were very proud of it. We were, if you like, 'respectable' working class, with my father moving into professional then managerial work, and my mother staying at home as a mark of this new family status.

Both of my grandmothers were very important to me, and their lives show something of the ways in which social policy influenced personal lives in the 1950s. Grandma Ross, who carried out most of my early upbringing, became blind, and received, as far as I know, no support from any health or welfare service. She by no means thought of herself as disabled but was fiercely independent, placing huge demands on my aunt to care for her in a way that did not challenge that independence. My other grandmother suffered from (undisclosed) mental health problems and 'went away' for short periods of time, receiving ECT [electroconvulsive therapy] treatment that affected her very adversely. I was not aware, as a child, of what was going on – it was hushed up in the family and treated as matter of shame. Her two daughters lived in constant fear, as they aged, of 'going the same way' and their brother, who subsequently had what was termed a 'nervous breakdown', was more or less ostracised. Both grandmothers were cared for by their daughters at home until their deaths, and the message that this was what was expected of me was transmitted very powerfully. Receiving state care of any kind was viewed as the equivalent of going onto social security. My mother adamantly (and I sometimes thought deliberately) failed to distinguish between social security and social services even when she was receiving considerable support from the latter in her last years. The stigma attached to receiving state care was linked, for her, to images of the kinds of relief available to the poor in the depression of the 1920s and 30s.

I had childhood asthma and, at the age of seven, was sent to a special school – an 'open air' school said to be for 'delicate' children. It turned out that children with poor health in those days – those who had had polio or diphtheria, who suffered from epilepsy, asthma etc – were not expected to achieve much academically. Although the care was good, the education was poor. But I suddenly gained the attention of one teacher – Miss Williams – who began to encourage me and then persuaded the school to put me in for the 11+ exam (only the second child to have been entered for this in the school's history). Her individual determination was able to counter the structural constraints of the system she worked within, and I owe her an enormous debt.

I was one of that generation of women who benefited enormously from the linked expansion of HE [higher education] and the growth of public sector employment opportunities in the expanding welfare state of the 1960s. On leaving school I went to work for the local council, gained a professional qualification and then studied for my degree with the Open University. ...

I also became active politically in the late 1960s and early 1970s, in the women's movement, the peace movement and other developments. We went on demonstrations – against anti-immigration legislation, the Vietnam war and much else – set up anti-psychiatry groups, a free university and other alternatives to state institutions. I was part of a network of various collective endeavours, including collective living. We sought to influence social policy by shaping agendas and redefining the terms of debate. But we – but ... a very white 'we' – were also attempting to create alternatives of our own, setting up new models of everything from childcare to housing. It was a hugely exciting and optimistic period, and the experience of many of those involved in this kind of informal politics subsequently influenced more mainstream policy developments.

In my 40s I became an academic, researching and writing about public and social policy and its impact. I was involved in programmes for public service professionals and managers during the Thatcher and Major years, and ... under the [first] New Labour administration. This work has helped me to understand their [public sector professionals'] experience of delivering the social policy agenda and the way in which they deal with the impossible demands of public management under successive programmes of radical change. Their experience continues to influence my understanding of the relationship between personal lives and social policy.

(Liz [pseudonym], 2004, unpublished autobiography: reproduced with kind permission of the author)

COMMENT

This personal narrative is interesting for what it tells us about the uneven effects and responses to the social citizenship inaugurated by the post-Second World War welfare state. In part this is related to the birth of Liz at the time when the welfare state was being established, so that the level of service delivery was more about promise than actual provision. Yet, she talks about the benefits – albeit uneven as these appear to have been – of state schooling and her access to higher education through The Open University when she was an adult. Receipt by family members of mental health services was in keeping with the ethos of the time, marked by deep stigma and not always apparently beneficial. What is equally clear is a profound reluctance on the part of some members of the older generation to take up those services that were available, illustrating the pre-war subjectivities which resulted in a particular, and widespread, emotional response to the provision of state welfare. For many of this generation the reconfiguration of the state/citizen relation, in which rights rather than charity provided the conduit to services, was not something that made emotional sense and thus could not provide the basis for a new sense of self. In part this inability to enter the new discourse of social citizenship resulted in either a refusal of or resentment for services that were available. Moreover, this seems to have contributed to an expectation of a traditional gendered division of household labour. Indeed, the social, emotional and psychic relations of gender have long been, and continue to be, ingrained in the organization of care both practically and symbolically (**Fink, 2004**). At the same time there is some hint that Liz's own gendered subjectivity – as granddaughter – had shifted in subtle ways.

More broadly, the narrative illustrates some of the points made earlier about the dimensions of the personal lives/social policy relation. For example, we see that the nature of this relation shifts across time – compare the grandmothers and the granddaughter. It also shows something of the way in which the already existing content of an individual's personal life can influence their response to social policy – here helping to shape the take-up or otherwise of certain services since the grandmother's immersion in a different cultural moment of citizenship (when use meant charity and shame) inhibited her from making an internal rearrangement of her emotional responses to social citizenship. In the figure of Miss Williams we see something of the way in which the practice of individual welfare professionals also helps to shape the content of the user's (and indeed their own) 'personal life'. And the reference to the attempts by feminists and other constituencies of welfare users – acting as politically conscious citizens – to resist certain kinds of service provision and craft alternatives to them, illustrates the ways in which welfare users can provoke changes in social policy.

The narrative in Extract 1.1 shows us something of the civil element of citizenship in the form of property rights (owner-occupation) and the political element in terms of the activism in which Liz became involved during the 1970s and 1980s. In addition, it helps us to see something of the blockages to dispersion of the ethos of social citizenship that the welfare state was meant to embody. In doing so it indicates that there was more to the welfare state than an attempt to ameliorate excessive inequality and material deprivation: it was also attempting to create both a new relation between state and citizen *and* men and women with new subjectivities, identities and practices of belonging.

BRITANNIA IN WONDERLAND

"It was still very uncomfortable . . ."

Figure 1.3

This was to be achieved, however, without fundamentally undermining the logic or imperatives of a patriarchal, heteronormative, racially inscribed and capitalist society and this had profound implications for the form of social citizenship that developed. It meant that 'a system of [formal] equality was to be built upon a structure of inequality' (Marshall, 1992). As is evident from this quotation, Marshall was acutely aware of the inequalities that a capitalist society could generate, yet he also believed that the emergence of a welfare principle (and the social citizenship it inscribed) at the core of society fundamentally altered the problem. This led him to develop the notion of the 'hyphenated society' to extend his argument about the potential of such a structure to deliver equality of citizenship. Starting from a designation of the post-war UK as a mixed economy as opposed to an unfettered capitalism, the component parts of the **hyphenated society** are 'Democracy – Welfare – Capitalism'. Its distinguishing feature is that each of these areas operates according to its own principle, but all contribute in equal but specific ways to the overall societal dynamic. It is the operation of each domain, working to its own principles, that ensures the stability and continual development of the society so hyphenated:

hyphenated society

> The hyphen links ... different and contrasted elements together to create a new entity whose character is a product of the combination, but not the fusion of the components, whose separate identities are preserved intact and are of equal contributory status ... the differences strengthen the structure because they are complementary not divisive.
>
> (Marshall, 1981, pp.124–5)

The specific 'principles' of the three elements stress different things or imperatives: the *democratic principle* stresses majority rule and the duty to participate; the *welfare principle* is a social ethic and stresses the right to receive; while the *capitalist principle* stresses the imperatives of the market. For Marshall what is key is that none of these can be subordinated to the other, none can become the sole driver of the modern society, and each is essential to the enrichment of life. Perhaps more fundamentally, both the welfare principle and that of the mixed economy 'are contributing to the creation of welfare in the broad, non-technical sense of the word' (Marshall, 1981, p.131) and thus: 'It is legitimate, and also profitable, to regard welfare and the market as embodying two different ways of performing the same task, that of satisfying the needs and wants of the population' (Marshall, 1981, p.133).

Here it is clear that Marshall's argument about citizenship and its ever-widening extension into the societal fabric is premised upon the beneficial effects resulting from the tensions between the three major principles of the hyphenated society. This is an argument about the functional effects of systemic tension between the three domains of the 'hyphenated society'. This systemic tension arises from the different logics or imperatives of each domain that we identified above. Moreover, this tension maps on to Marshall's tripartite model of citizenship. Civil rights provide a vital foundation for capitalist forms of wealth production; political rights, via the guarantee of freedoms of association and formal participation, open up a space for contestation of inequalities; and social rights, by their capacity to ensure access to material and symbolic goods, 'provide a basis on which all citizens ought to be equally able to participate in the spheres of civil and political society' (Dean and Melrose, 1999, p.84). Thus just as the tension between the principles of the hyphenated society maintain the overall structure of social democracy, so too the tensions between the three elements of citizenship ensure that the citizenry have equal opportunity to engage in and benefit from such a society. The measure of this is social mobility and the provision of equality of opportunity (as opposed to equality of outcome) it demonstrates.

2.1 Social power and the inequalities of citizenship

But to what extent does this analysis of the structure of citizenship accurately reflect the current social relations of welfare and distribution of symbolic and material resources across the highly differentiated population of the UK? How are we to square this approach with the inequalities linked to class, religion, gender, ethnicity, sexuality, nationality, age, disability and region that produce multiple fractures across the social body? The chapters that follow address some of these issues in their discussions of class, housing and representation in the period following the Second World War (Chapter 2), the psychosocial dynamics of the transition between primary and secondary school (Chapter 3) and the shifting boundaries of exclusion faced by asylum seekers and refugees (Chapter 4). What they show is that focusing on the inequalities embedded in discourses and practices of citizenship means that formal juridical or legal status, and the rights that accrue to that status, is only *one* of the dimensions through which citizenship can be analysed. However, it is an important dimension for a number of reasons, all of which relate to the exclusions produced by regimes of citizenship as well as its inclusive aspects. For example, juridical status helps us to assess the extent to which the claims made by a state about its commitment to democratic principles, its respect for and protection of the dignity and autonomy of its people, and its promotion of equality and opportunity for all, are lived up to in practice. Similarly, the criteria for the attribution of juridical status of citizen (and, by extension, of nationality and rights of abode) are central not just to the opportunities afforded those deemed to be members of the citizenry, but also to the exclusions faced by those, such as refugees and asylum seekers, deemed to be outside the parameters of citizenship.

In this way, then, 'rights' can alert us to the limits of citizenship as well as helping us to identify the entitlements they underwrite. However, citizenship also involves the dynamic relations between different social groups and individuals; between these and specific institutional processes and forms of organization; and between the images of which people comprise the citizenry and the kinds of behaviour and values constituted as normative. In other words, citizenship as a social relation is mediated and experienced through the workings of social power.

ACTIVITY 1.3

Read through Extract 1.2, taken from an article by David Taylor in which he discusses the importance of incorporating into discussions of citizenship an analysis of social power. As you do so, make sure you understand and can respond to the following two questions:

- What does Taylor mean when he says that 'an appeal to *universalism* has ignored the particular reality of power'?
- Why is it important to consider the issue of social power when evaluating different approaches to citizenship?

Extract 1.2 Approaching social power

Some authors (most notably Keane, 1988a, 1988b) have faith in the 'best elements' of the liberal tradition to provide us with a foundation for a theory of citizenship, while others are happy to rework [T.H.] Herbert Marshall's (1950) classic views on welfare. A different approach is suggested here, however. If the concept of citizenship is to be of any use to progressive politics in Britain, it must be taken out of its liberal history and inserted into a very different set of theorisations and political practices. Indeed, the liberal tradition of citizenship, resting on an abstract notion of rights and an appeal to *universalism* has ignored the particular reality of power. In this context, social relations of power are seen as taking historically varying forms, but most notably those associated with class, gender and 'race'. These historically specific power relations have undermined attempts to realise the liberal ideal of citizenship through either the false collectivism of state welfare or the consumerist 'democracy' of the market. Both these ways of attempting to meet citizenship rights have led to the marginalisation of those excluded from the 'collective' nature of state welfare provision on the one hand, and of those unable to compete as market consumers on the other. Abstract conceptions of rights and entitlements attached to citizenship, then, must come to terms with the underlying structural power relations which underscore practices of *both* state and market mechanisms.

In addition, the political history of citizenship rights is inextricably linked to the history of Western European nationalism, which in turn must be situated in its world historical context. This history is one in which the consolidation of national states to which citizens belong and against which they have claims has to be understood in terms of an international division of labour, a particular world distribution of resources and the super-exploitation of human labour and the environment by the capitalist core. Citizenship (in Western Europe) becomes not only a process of the struggle for rights and entitlements in Western European nation states but also a struggle to reject claims of entitlement by those initially residing outside the core, and, subsequently, of migrant and immigrant labour. The 'liberal' history of citizenship, then, must be viewed in the context of a set of *inclusionary* and *exclusionary* practices, aimed at consolidating a particular set of social relations and of rights and entitlements.

References

Keane, J. (1988a) *Democracy and Civil Society*, London, Verso.

Keane, J. (ed.) (1988b) *Civil Society and the State*, London, Verso.

Marshall, T.H. (1950) *Citizenship and Social Class*, Cambridge, Cambridge University Press.

(Taylor, 1996, pp.156–7)

COMMENT

social power

Although Taylor does not specifically define what he means by **social power**, we can infer that he is talking about the relative and unequal ability of different social groups to gain a share of collective resources, to have equal legitimacy in making welfare and wider citizenship claims, or to have equal influence over deciding criteria of access and the terms of membership in the community of citizens. It is this kind of inequality that is occluded by the ethos of universalism that Taylor suggests is only a formal and abstract universalism, more applicable to some than others, and not reflected in the distribution of resources among the citizenry. Thus abstract equality is only made concrete when it can be translated into recognized and legitimated forms of claim-making across all constituencies of welfare users. It is this that makes it vitally important to consider the issue of social power when evaluating different theories of or approaches to citizenship, since without it we seriously inhibit our ability to excavate and analyse the historically specific and shifting inequalities in citizenship as a lived social relation.

To talk of citizenship in the way suggested by Taylor is to shift the focus so that it is no longer solely on status, rights and responsibilities, and to urge a broader analytic canvas in order to reveal the unequal effects of particular discourses and social practices. It has been in relation to these dimensions of social relationships that social movements, including those organized around identities of class, have made claims to citizenship rights and recognition. Indeed, in Extract 1.1 Liz made reference to some examples of this kind of claim-making in her reference to the women's movement and the peace movement. Others include claims by gays, lesbians and queer people for sexual citizenship, by environmental activists for the citizenship rights of future generations, and by disability rights activists for access to resources that foster independent living. By seeking to expand the definition of citizenship, groups such as these have highlighted some of the ways in which hegemonic discourses and practices of citizenship result in forms of exclusion from or subordinated inclusion in the social relations of citizenship. Importantly, these claims have indicated the way in which such exclusions or subordinated inclusions have often resulted from the divergence between the everyday living practices, values and forms of social solidarity and identity of different sections of the population, and the normative behaviours, values and identities embedded in citizenship. In so doing, they have drawn attention to the links between personal lives and social policy. Let us take a moment to explore this idea a little further.

In section 1, in the Comment to Activity 1.1 it was noted that the current, remembered or imagined actions of welfare professionals and/or the institutional norms and cultures of welfare agencies can produce a state of fear in service users and that this can partially structure their interpersonal relations. We will return to this example later, but here let's use it as a way of extending our discussion of the links between social power and citizenship and to think about the ways in which one form that the personal lives/social policy relation can take can be found in the social practice of 'passing'.

Figure 1.4 Collective voices expanding the horizons of citizenship

passing

'**Passing**' can be thought of as a public presentation of self in a way that denies or disguises the identity or membership of a subordinated (and often despised, feared and hated) social group in an attempt to avoid the stigma, discrimination or ridicule that such individuals and groups often receive. In the context of a discussion of citizenship, actions of this sort provide a powerful index not only of the costs to individuals that may result from such denials of full citizenship, but also of the way in which differential social power is made tangible in the context of specific welfare institutions.

Can you recall the two welfare institutions identified in the example given in the Comment to Activity 1.1 and how these seemed to affect the way in which racial difference impacted upon the relationship between mother and daughter?

This idea of 'passing' can also be used in connection with the work of Gill Clarke (1998) who has undertaken research into the ways in which lesbian school teachers of physical education negotiate homophobic and heterosexist assumptions and structures in their working lives. Clarke illustrates well both how sexuality provides a powerful empirical and analytic terrain for exploring the mutually constitutive relation between personal lives and social policy (see also **Carabine, 2004b**) and how 'the personal' is equally a component of the world of paid work (see **Mooney, 2004**) as it is of the world of the household. Clarke shows how paid work, in this case teaching, 'shapes and constrains how lesbian lives are lived out in the environment of the school' (Clarke, 1998, p.65). For example, one of the women Clarke interviewed for her research said:

> When you go into school you know it is different ... I find it very difficult to cope with, because you know my sexuality to me is a very important part of me and then all of a sudden you are faced with here we go, back again to the conservatism of it all and we are covering our tracks by not saying who we live with, who we go out with, what we do at weekends. You are only choosing to tell me bits that aren't going to tell a story. I did find the change very different (compared to the 'freer' environment of college) and I think that's partly why I moved from the school I was in because I couldn't cope with people you know, I felt I was living a bigger lie there and so when the job came up that I could come back to ... where I had all my friends around me it was far better.
>
> (quoted in Clarke, 1998, p.63)

It should be clear that, as in the example from my own personal life, for at least some of Clarke's respondents the issue of 'passing' becomes a way of negotiating the inequalities of citizenship and social power that result from what we might call the hierarchical ordering of difference. Moreover, if we think back to my own example, we can see that sexuality was also one of the unspoken features that it was feared would lead to inequality in my mother's experience of citizenship, because as her daughter I embodied the sexual transgression that racially mixed relationships were deemed to signify in 1950s Britain. In this way, both examples illustrate some of the inequalities of **sexual citizenship** by showing that, in some sense, everyone is a sexual citizen. By this we mean that discourses of family, household and intimacy assume and normalize certain forms of relationship and that these assumptions

sexual citizenship

intervene in institutional and interpersonal dynamics with powerful effects for sexual dissidents. In this way citizenship and what it means to be a citizen are fundamentally entangled with the structures of heteronormativity, leading Bell and Binnie (2000, p.142) to note that: 'We may all be sexual citizens, but we are not *equal* sexual citizens' and whom we make love to, form households with and consider family can become the behavioural markers of 'anti-citizenship' (see also **Carabine, 2004b**).

3 Citizenship, the politics of belonging and practices of the everyday

In section 1, we suggested that the concepts of 'belonging' and 'practices of the everyday' were useful for thinking about citizenship both as relational and as a process and for exploring the mutually constitutive relation between personal lives and social policy. You will remember that, in speaking of 'belonging', we are referring to those aspects of citizenship that designate, or prevent, membership in the polity and social body. 'Belonging' points to the associational and identificatory aspects of being a citizen – that is, to the ways in which we identify and associate *ourselves* and the ways in which *others* identify and feel associated with us. 'Practices of the everyday' refers to the links between citizenship and ways of life – that is, the ordinary, taken-for-granted ways in which people organize their lives as individuals, members of households, work colleagues and members of communities of identity and/or interest.

The concepts of belonging and practices of the everyday help us to explore further the dynamic between 'citizenship and anti-citizenship' (Matless, 1998) which the examples from my own life and that of the lesbian teacher illustrated in relation to racially defined sexual citizenship and sexual citizenship, respectively. When located within this dynamic these two concepts draw explicit attention to the kinds of behaviours, moralities and social outlooks that come to be constructed as normative and thus equated with what it means to be a citizen. They also help us to identify those identities, communities of identity or interest and ways of life deemed antithetical to hegemonic conceptions of citizen practice. As a result, they enable us to identify sites from which contestations to normative citizenship might arise and lead to claims for full inclusion in the social relations of citizenship. This last point alerts us to the existence of multiple identities and cultures within any given polity or social body and thus to a consideration of the sites and processes by which discourses of citizenship effect forms of exclusion. And finally, but of equal importance in the context of our concerns in this book, the concepts of belonging and practices of the everyday provide us with a way to explore the connection between citizenship, personal lives and social policy. Let us now think about these ideas in more detail.

As should by now be clear, the idea of *belonging* has long been central to the question of citizenship. This is because, as an affective connection to or identification with all those deemed to be citizens, a sense of belonging is considered a baseline for the generation of mutual concern among citizens and for both accommodation and sacrifice to the demands of the state. In some ways the idea of belonging in this context is similar to that of '**imagined community**' (Anderson, 1983) in which it is suggested that a sense of nationhood rests upon the possession of an imagined link to and similarity with a host of people whom one will never meet but who are designated as being one homogeneous people. As we shall see, however, belonging has a different purview in that it raises the question of the *processes* by which individuals and groups come to be included or excluded from the polity and social body. In this sense belonging is a concept that makes for a 'thicker' (Crowley, 1999, p.22) account or analysis of processes of inclusion and exclusion. It raises symbolic as well as material aspects of such inclusion or exclusion and, in emphasizing process, it has the capacity to bring to the fore the fluid and unstable character of the *politics* of belonging and the shifting parameters of citizenship. In this 'thick' approach 'the meaning and effect of rights cannot be separated from the concrete social processes that actually distribute the entitlements they [that is, rights] create' (Crowley, 1999, p.22). Thus the vagaries of belonging(ness) are crafted in the context of formal rights and entitlements (for example, having a right to National Health Service treatment, to schooling or to social housing), discursive frameworks that both shape the meanings of inclusion and constitute the people who can be included – dominant ideas about who 'the British' are, for instance, and about the informal or everyday practices of individuals (professionals, users, other agents) operating within institutional norms and procedures: that is, actual experiences of welfare that make one feel one 'belongs'.

imagined community

This approach recasts the question of citizenship by moving away from formal rights and emphasizing the *connection between* belonging and social, institutional and individual practices. This is very different from the approach to questions of belonging, membership and inclusion adopted by supporters of a liberal conception of citizenship. Remember from the discussion in section 2 that, in the liberal approach to citizenship, the emphasis is on formal rights and an abstract, universal equality among those defined as citizens. It is citizenship itself (in the sense of being a passport holder and having a nationality) that designates belonging and thus provides the connective tissue making for a sense of solidarity. Moreover, this is a belongingness and solidarity that transcends any specific solidarity convened around communities of interest or identity. Indeed, for those subscribing to the liberal theory of citizenship it is essential that people have an identity that rises above any specific communities of interest. For example, the political theorist John Porter argues that 'the organization of society on the basis of rights or claims that derive from group membership is *sharply opposed* to the concept of society based on citizenship' (Porter, 1987, p.128, quoted in Kymlicka, 1995, p.174, emphasis added). This is why the liberal state can only legitimate, recognize or tolerate a *certain amount* of cultural diversity, non-normative behaviour or alternative social practice since to do otherwise would be to foster social fracture and dissension. It is also why, especially in a context of increasing cultural diversity, some governments attempt to construct a sense of national identity on the basis of the inculcation of certain **learned behaviours**, moral

learned behaviours

codes, cultural and social commitments and loyalties, rather than assuming that such an identity and moral outlook automatically follow place of birth.

This approach to membership and belonging is illustrated by Extract 1.3, taken from a UK Government White Paper entitled *Secure Borders, Safe Haven: Integration with Diversity in Modern Britain*, presented to Parliament in 2002.

ACTIVITY 1.4

Read through Extract 1.3 and make a note of the following:

- the kinds of action those seeking naturalization will need to demonstrate in order to become British;
- the approach to cultural diversity that is being promoted in the White Paper;
- any tensions between ideas about Britishness, citizenship and respect for cultural diversity.

Extract 1.3 Citizenship and the acquisition of British nationality

2.1 The Government attaches great importance to helping those who settle here gain a fuller appreciation of the civic and political dimensions of British citizenship and, in particular, to understand the rights and responsibilities that come with the acquisition of British citizenship. This will help to strengthen active participation in the democratic process and a sense of belonging to a wider community. We believe that one means of promoting this understanding is to place much greater emphasis than we do at present on the value and significance of becoming a British citizen.

...

2.2 Common citizenship is not about cultural uniformity, nor is it born out of some narrow and out-dated view of what it means to be 'British'. The Government welcomes the richness of the cultural diversity which immigrants have brought to the UK – our society is multi-cultural, and is shaped by its diverse peoples. We want British citizenship positively to embrace the diversity of background, culture and faiths that is one of the hallmarks of Britain in the 21st Century.

2.3 ... The laws, rules and practices which govern our democracy uphold our commitment to the equal worth and dignity of all our citizens. It will sometimes be necessary to confront some cultural practices which conflict with these basic values – such as those which deny women the right to participate as equal citizens. Similarly, it means ensuring that every individual has the wherewithal, such as the ability to speak our common language, to enable them to engage as active citizens in economic, social and political life. And it means tackling racism, discrimination and prejudice wherever we find it.

2.4 ... We have introduced from this year [that is, 2002] in England compulsory teaching of citizenship and democracy in our schools and the promotion of active citizenship. This reinforces the fact that our sense of identity, understanding of our mutuality and interdependence, comes as much from the contribution we make to the world around us as it does from any theoretical entitlements we possess.

2.5 ...

2.6 ... [The Government] believes that becoming a British citizen is a significant step which should mean more than simply obtaining the right to a British passport. ... Importantly British citizenship confers full political rights ... Whatever the specific benefits, British citizenship should bring with it a heightened commitment to full participation in British society and a recognition of the part which new citizens can play in contributing to social cohesion.

(Home Office, 2001, pp.29–30)

COMMENT

It should be clear that this government document is talking about the importance of inculcating a sense of what it means to be British in those who become citizens through naturalization. Such people *become* British not just in a formal sense of holding a passport, but in the more profound way of a transformed sense of belonging, identity and social outlook. Not only will they be committed to participation in and the promotion of social cohesion, they will also distance themselves from practices of the everyday deemed 'un-British'. In many ways this resonates with the position adopted by Porter referred to above and illustrates the importance a liberal approach to citizenship places on a limited tolerance and recognition of cultural diversity. But it is also clear that the Government is stressing the *learnedness* of citizenship, both for those who become citizens by naturalization and those who are born citizens. This is evident in the reference to the introduction of compulsory lessons in citizenship and democracy for schoolchildren in England.

We can see, then, that in contemporary government discourse not only legitimacy and rights but also belongingness are intimately tied to practices of the everyday, including the inculcation of particular kinds of morality. This is an idea that has been championed among communitarians such as Etzioni (1995) and which has made significant inroads into various areas of social welfare. Deacon has noted that communitarians (or what Hughes and Mooney, 1998, call 'moral communitarians') emphasize:

> both the obligations of individuals and the role of the community in ensuring that those obligations are met. ... Indeed, what is most distinctive about communitarianism is its belief in the power of informal social networks and of moral argument to bring about significant and lasting changes in personal behaviour.
>
> (Deacon, 2002, p.66)

To what extent do you think this view of social connection and responsibility has the capacity to foster a more equal distribution of social power?

3.1 Active citizenship, conditionality and practices of the everyday

In this communitarian world, citizenship is defined through the development of a framework of social values; *and* practices of the everyday that are commensurate with these values; *and* with the constitution of individuals whose subjectivities are (at least in part) formed through the introspection, or incorporation into the self, of a certain moral economy, as Deacon points out in the quotation above. It is on this terrain that social welfare has a key role to play because of its ability to define and implement entitlement criteria and thus contribute to the formation of moralized subjects. This is not the social policy of 'nationalized responsibility' that the New Right under the Conservative governments of Margaret Thatcher and John Major believed characterized the post-war welfare state (Lewis, 1998) with its assumed corrosive effect on self-reliant citizenship and responsible behaviour. It is, however, the social policy of *conditionality*, in which entitlement to publicly provided welfare services becomes dependent upon particular patterns of behaviour and duties (Deacon, 1994) – for example, when entitlement to social housing is tied to anti-social behaviour clauses. Moreover, increasing emphasis on conditionality intersects with the discourse of the **active citizen**, the figure who has come to stand for the organization of social welfare less around a notion of universalism and need and more around worthiness, responsibility and residualization (that is, state welfare as the service provider of last resort). Dwyer (2000, p.69) has defined the 'active citizen' as 'someone who is actively engaged in the public giving of private time and resources to others on a charitable basis' – for example, by being active in a Neighbourhood Watch Scheme – and who by this very action becomes an icon of individual and social responsibility. Similarly, the conjunction of this definition of the citizen with the distribution of services and benefits on the basis of conditionality could result in an increased inequality in the meeting of need. Moreover, those who, by the ways in which they organize their lives, fail to live up to the standard of the active citizen are by definition positioned lower down the hierarchy of citizens, and thus materially and symbolically placed at the margins of or beyond the boundaries of belonging.

active citizen

ACTIVITY 1.5

This leads us to ask the following questions:

- How much has this discourse of social welfare and citizenship permeated the consciousness of constituencies of welfare service users?
- How much has it helped to shape their views about acceptable links between social citizenship, practices of the everyday and patterns of entitlement and institutional belonging?

We can glean something of this by referring again to the work of Peter Dwyer (2000) who has drawn on data generated from a series of focus group discussions with service users to explore some of the debates about citizenship and welfare. Read through Extract 1.4 and consider the extent to which it provides answers to the two questions posed above.

Extract 1.4 Living citizenship, negotiating belonging

The relationship between rights and responsibilities is an issue of central importance to any notion of citizenship. ...this relationship is a dynamic one that is open to challenge and renegotiation over time. ...

Recent changes in legislation (eg the Jobseeker's Act, 1995 and the Housing Act, 1996) and many policy statements of the present New Labour government indicate that the issue of conditionality is very much part of contemporary political welfare debates. Although understandably there were on occasions a number of differing views on a particular issue within each group, in more general terms the extent to which users as a whole approved, or disapproved, of the imposition of a more conditional link between rights and responsibilities varies according to the specific area of welfare under consideration.

...

[For example, in relation to *health care*] an overwhelming majority of users stated clearly that they believed that an individual should not lose their right to treatment because they choose to engage in a form of behaviour that may have a negative effect on personal health. ...

...

> 'I think first and foremost it should be a clinical judgement. Any kind of treatment should be a clinical judgement, but I think that we are seeing some doctors with bias creeping into their judgements and I think that should be resisted. I certainly am opposed to refusing to treat someone because they happen to be a smoker. Smokers should fall into the same category as alcoholics and drug abusers.' (Barry, Benefit Claimants Group)

The discussions concerning conditionality and *housing* were designed to assess the extent to which the users felt that it was reasonable for a housing agency to tie the right to a home to both the individual behaviour of tenants and their willingness to accept further welfare responsibilities for the communities that they inhabit. In order to assess this debates [within the focus groups] were focused on three specific areas: anti-social behaviour, Probationary Tenancy Periods (PTPs) and Mutual Aid Clauses (MACs). ... in the cases of both anti-social behaviour and PTPs the most prevalent view shared by the majority of users was that the right to a house should be contingent on tenants behaving themselves. When debating the idea of MACs, this position was reversed, but it is important to note that a substantial minority ... of the users were in favour of their inclusion into tenancy agreements.

...

Support for a more conditional housing regime was, however, often dependent on a number of important qualifications. The manner in which the policy was implemented was a major concern; similarly it was widely believed that a warning should first be issued to enable tenants to alter their behaviour and so avoid eviction.

> 'If they have been notified of the rule and they are a nuisance, yes, I think that the council or housing association has got a right to evict them because they can become a damn nuisance. It depends what they call anti-social. I don't mean for petty things but for anti-social behaviour, people who are always causing bother, always burgularing [sic] people's houses, you know. I think they should get a warning first, not just throw them out. There should be a procedure like.' (Molly, Lone Parents Group)
>
> (Dwyer, 2000, pp.129–30, 132, 136–8, emphases added)

COMMENT

It seems clear from both Dwyer's statements and the quotations from Barry and Molly that users of welfare services are very conscious of the links service providers are making between entitlement and the past or future behaviour of users of services. What is equally clear is that they have complex and shifting opinions about the legitimacy of such connections. They differentiate between areas of service provision, distinguishing between health and housing, with a degree of support for conditionality in housing and none, or very little, in the case of health services. Interestingly, even where there is evidence of support for conditionality, this is qualified by the emphasis placed on *procedure* – that is, an idea that any penalty resulting from a clause deemed to have been breached would have to be imposed only after a set of suitable and transparent steps had been undertaken. In this it seemed both that a sense of fair play was considered important and that people had the right to be given the opportunity to change their behaviour, suggesting that what people are is not fixed by what they do or for all time.

4 Suspicion, exclusion and the 'immigrationization' of citizenship

Our discussion so far has shown that what it means to be a citizen, who is included as being part of the citizenry, and the experience of citizenship varies across generations and the life-course (think back to Liz's story in Extract 1.1, for example), according to particular identities (for instance, the story from the lesbian teacher in section 2.1) and depending on memory, accumulated experience and particular contexts (the story of my mother and me in section 1). In more theoretical terms we can refer to these variations as fluidities (or vagaries as they were referred to in the heading to Extract 1.1) and, in turn, relate them to:

- inequalities in the distribution of social power, linked to social divisions of class, ethnicity, religion, sexuality, age, disability or gender, and the ways in which these inequalities undermine formal rights of entitlement;
- the relational dynamic set in train by the conjunction of specific users (individuals and groups), particular professional knowledges and policy discourses (**Carabine, 2004a; Fergusson, 2004**) that operate in specific institutional sites (for example, the school and local education authority;

the hospital and NHS Trust; or the particular port of entry to the country, and the Home Office).

We have already considered aspects of these two kinds of differentiated and unequal citizenship experience in the personal narratives looked at earlier in this chapter.

Can you recall some of the ways in which our earlier discussions illustrate these fluidities?

The chapters that follow will also provide examples of the unstable and shifting character of citizenship and the forms of belonging that citizenship produces. In Chapter 2 you will consider some of the ways in which the vagaries of citizenship were linked to the gap between expectation and provision of services and the forms of actions people took in an attempt to gain access to what was felt to be a right. In Chapter 3, Helen Lucey explores a key area of 'active citizenship' in relation to periods of transition between primary and secondary school, showing how the ranking of schools results in everyday practices of citizenship that reproduce class inequalities in relation to access to the 'best' schools. At the same time, these very practices of everyday citizenship feed into and help intensify profound anxieties in schoolchildren and parents alike, thus illustrating how the emotional content of these people's personal lives is clearly linked to government educational policy and institutional practices. In Chapter 4 Esther Saraga explores the shifting boundaries of citizenship in relation to asylum seekers and refugees in two historical moments. She points to the continuities and changes, or discontinuities, in the treatment and representation of refugees, showing how the discourses embedded in immigration, nationality and asylum policy constitute asylum seekers and refugees in particular ways. More significantly, she shows both how this policy framework and linked professional and institutional practices profoundly shape the content of the personal lives of asylum seekers and refugees and how, so often, the personal lives of those seeking refuge is discounted or disbelieved. In doing so, she sheds light on the complex entanglement of personal lives and social policy.

In this last section of this chapter, however, we want to explore further one other dimension of the shifting boundaries of citizenship as a relational process and experience. This is the extent to which 'conditionality' and 'belonging' open up a channel to 'suspicion', drawing rights, entitlement and legitimacy into a net of doubt in which inclusion is something never fully or finally achieved but must be continually proved. It could be argued that to pose the issue thus is to emphasize 'process', but in a way that suggests that a person's claim to full citizenship or belonging can decline as well as increase. Indeed, we can quite convincingly characterize the experience of the majority of older and retired people in these terms (see, for example, **Widdowson, 2004**). To cite Crowley again:

> The natural counterpoint of informal, fluid, vague, discretionary criteria [carried in the idea of belonging] for access is differential *suspicion.* Some people's right to be in a place [or, we might add, to make a claim] is challenged – they are trespassers until proved otherwise – whereas others are *prima facie* welcome. Such suspicion, even when it does not prevent access, may affect its meaning. In

addition, if the level of humiliation is viewed disproportionate to the benefits at stake, suspicion may in itself thin the queue, undermining ostensibly equal rights without the discrepancy really being apparent.

(Crowley, 1999, pp.17–18)

We will explore the idea of suspicion within the policy and institutional context further in a moment when we look at John's story in Extract 1.5 below. Before doing so, though, it is worth casting your mind back over our earlier examples to see how traces of 'suspicion' have affected the meaning and experience of social citizenship and thus have helped to shape the content of personal lives. First, there is the example from my own biography where my mother feared a repeat of a suspicion as to her right to social housing on the part of an unknown housing officer. Second, we saw the case of Liz's grandmother and mother where the experience of an earlier system of welfare clouded for ever the meaning of forms of social welfare, illustrating Crowley's point, in the quotation above, about thinning the queue and undermining entitlement. And then there is Gill Clarke's example of the lesbian teacher, illustrating the way in which a culture of suspicion can unfold from normative and normalizing assumptions, thus demarcating boundaries of belonging and inflecting the meaning of what it is to be a professional with a particular sexual identity working in a particular institutional context.

Each of these examples illustrates the ways in which a culture of suspicion can become incorporated into the subjectivity of the service user or welfare professional, affecting their experience of citizenship and belonging. By moulding their behaviour and even their values (in the case of Liz's relatives) in the context of past experiences of welfare, they exemplify one of the points made in the Introduction to this chapter. This is that individuals and social groups have varied understandings of social policy interventions and areas of service provision and these understandings shape their actions towards and relationships with welfare professionals and agencies.

That a culture of suspicion also emanates from the policy arena or institutional context, impacting on the actual or potential user and thereby helping to exclude people from entitlement and/or corroding their feelings of legitimate and full inclusion in the boundaries of citizenship, can be seen particularly in the case of those seeking asylum or refugee status. The conjunction of a culture of suspicion (see, for example, **Fergusson, 2004**) with a concern to erect ever tighter immigration controls and an emphasis on citizenship as a learned practice, gives rise to what we might term an '**immigrationization**' of social welfare and citizenship, as John's story below shows.

immigrationization

ACTIVITY 1.6

All outsiders now?

Read carefully through John's account, in Extract 1.5, of his attempt to sign on for Jobseeker's Allowance and consider the following points:

- the extent to which John's experience demonstrates the existence of a culture of suspicion;
- any signs that it is John's immigration status that is deemed suspect;

- the extent to which John's account suggests that the link between place of birth, entitlement and belonging have been weakened.

Make a note of your responses.

Extract 1.5 Making a claim: John's story

After I finished university in July 2003, I followed the traditional path of a graduate and moved back home with my parents and looked for meaningful, exciting employment which hopefully wouldn't include the words: 'Would you like fries with that?' Looking for graduate employment proved more problematic than I had previously anticipated so I decided to call into my local Jobcentre to make a claim for Jobseeker's Allowance. Upon arrival at the new offices of the JobCentrePlus I was informed that new claimants now had to phone a call centre as the first step in the process in order to receive benefits. I was handed a leaflet which told me the number to call and what information I would need to have ready.

I went home again and phoned. A member of the call centre personnel took down my name, age, National Insurance number, marital status and asked briefly what my circumstances were. The leaflet had informed me that I would have a meeting arranged for me with a personal adviser at the JobCentrePlus: '... within four working days'. However, when I contacted the call centre on Monday 18th August I was given an appointment for Tuesday 2nd September. I was also informed that some forms would be sent to my home which would need to be completed and brought in when I arrived for my interview at my local JobCentrePlus.

I arrived for my interview laden with my various forms, account details, proof of graduation, passport, etc. and proceeded to have my interview with my personal adviser. Worryingly, she confided in me that she'd never worked anywhere with so much paperwork. Whilst reading my forms, my personal adviser became very interested in my application when she noticed that I had lived outside the UK from August 2001 to July 2002. This was part of my degree which enabled me to study in a university overseas for an academic year and do a bit of travelling afterwards. Unfortunately, I was never given the chance to explain my reasons for living outside of the UK in the paperwork nor did my personal adviser allow me the opportunity to highlight my personal circumstances. My educational record, work experience and my preferred type of employment were noted before I was informed that I would need to be interviewed by one of their visiting officers at my home address before my claim could be processed. I was given a starting date and a specific time to come into the JobCentrePlus and sign on each fortnight, but no real indication of when I would receive benefits.

I received a letter a few days later informing me that I was due to be visited on September 11th between 10 and 2 o'clock. Unfortunately, this clashed with the date and specific time I had been told to come in and sign on. I had to phone the visiting officer in charge of my claim and we agreed that she would not visit before and after a certain time on that date. However, on September 10th I received a phone call from the visiting officer asking me if she could pop in that afternoon instead on her way from another visit in her local area.

Later that afternoon, the interview began with the visiting officer and myself sitting around my kitchen table at my home. I was informed that the reason I was being interviewed was due to the concern of the JobCentrePlus that I did not intend to maintain permanent residence in the UK. I thought that this was quite amusing, sitting in my home of 18 years, surrounded with pictures of myself in primary and secondary school, where I had stayed whilst working in the holidays in 6th Form and university and where I had chosen to settle for the foreseeable future. It is clear to anyone (and depressingly clear to me) that my life has been rather parochial. The interview continued and I was asked questions regarding how long I intended to stay in the UK, if I had any overseas properties or bank accounts, how I was supporting myself and crucially, could I explain my prolonged absence from the UK (which could have been explained weeks before). The interview went well, I was finally able to explain my personal circumstances and I was informed that it would take a few days for the information to be processed.

I was quite hopeful when I walked into the JobCentrePlus the next day to sign on for the first time feeling that the problems with my claim had been resolved. Unfortunately, that was before a security guard lost my Giro booklet – but that's another story. However, as an experience of the 'real' world, I would heartily recommend it to any graduate who was struggling to find work and just happened to spend some time abroad as part of their degree.

(John [pseudonym], 2004, unpublished autobiography: reproduced with kind permission of the author)

COMMENT

It is evident throughout John's story that his entitlement to claim Jobseeker's Allowance is suspect. This is evident in, for example, the cessation of his first interview immediately it became clear that he had spent time out of the country when a student and it was illustrated further in the requirement that he have a home visit, the sense being that this was one way in which the adviser could ascertain the legitimacy of his claim. But what is particularly powerful about this example is the way in which it shows that movement across the territorial borders of the UK for periods longer than the average holiday is itself enough to generate suspicion as to entitlement and belonging – even for a white British 'born and bred' young man such as John. This suspicion is there despite the fact that the reason for his absence was that he was availing himself of one of the 'rights' cherished by the discourse of social citizenship – that is, the opportunity to study at higher education level. Thus we see another example of the fluidity of citizenship and belonging as people's relationship to welfare shifts across institutional sites and areas of service provision. As a citizen exercising his 'right' to seize the opportunity of higher education, John is fully encompassed within the parameters of belonging. As a citizen claiming income support he is suspect and cast (even if only temporarily) to the margins of full citizenship and belonging. It is this that illustrates the reconfiguration of the link between place of birth, entitlement and belonging, showing that, although an individual may have been born and

raised and have lived permanently in the UK, this will not guarantee protection from suspicion. The onus to prove and re-prove entitlement and belonging is placed on the individual.

How would you use this example to explain aspects of the relation between personal lives and social policy?

The idea that John's story indicates what we have termed an 'immigrationization' of social policy and citizenship is given added weight if we consider his experience in the context of a wider policy landscape. We have already noted the emergence of a discourse and practice of conditionality in which behaviours (past and future) are tied to the terms of entitlement and inclusion. In parallel with this development, immigration, nationality and asylum have become major issues in a widening policy agenda. On the one hand, the scope of immigration policy has itself been extended from its traditional concern with the admission of people into the country to include now issues of naturalization and integration, as we have seen from our discussion of Extract 1.3 in section 3, and the control of access to welfare services. On the other hand, immigration and asylum policy has become increasingly entangled with legislation aimed at controlling terrorist attacks – an entanglement that predates but was much intensified following the events of 9 September 2001. As Upton states, in 'grafting anti-terrorist provisions onto immigration law ... the checks to the powers of the state in the form of due process, available in the criminal justice system, weakened though they might be in the case of terrorist legislation, do not exist at all under immigration law' (Upton, 2004, p.6). Among these powers of state are removal from the accused of the right to legal aid; long-term detention, without trial, of foreign residents; curtailment of judicial review procedures, thereby preventing challenge to ministerial and other decisions; and policies for the detention of children. Developments such as these have made for a very wide orbit of influence on the content of the personal lives of those seeking asylum and have denied them many of the forms of civil and political rights that we discussed earlier.

At the same time, the period between the mid 1990s and mid 2000s saw a series of laws aimed at curtailing the rights of asylum seekers to access systems of welfare support, many of which are discussed in Chapter 4. Legislation such as this is continually being placed on the statute books and at the time of writing (at the end of 2003) the Asylum and Immigration (Treatment of Claimants, etc.) Bill was moving through its stages. Among its many proposed changes two are relevant to our discussion. These are:

1 penalties for arriving in the UK without documentation; and

2 withdrawal of support from families who have unsuccessfully reached the end of the asylum process.

The first of these, which applies to adults and to children over the age of ten, will result in a person found guilty being liable to a fine and/or imprisonment for up to two years. But, significantly for our concern with the ways in which behaviour can provide the grounds for inclusion or exclusion from legitimate belonging, this clause amounts to what the Refugee Council (2004) has called the punishment of refugees for behaving like refugees and fleeing from persecution without waiting to sort out their documentation.

The second clause withdraws access to basic state support from unsuccessful asylum applicants with dependent children who have exhausted the asylum process. If introduced this will change the situation that was in place at least until the end of 2003 in which support was given to asylum seekers in this situation by the National Asylum Support Service (NASS). Thus the new proposals will mean that children of such families face the possibility of being taken into the care of local authority social services departments.

From this we see both that those seeking asylum have faced ever more stringent control and that the scope for policy and professional influence over the content of their personal lives is continually expanding. In this sense there is a world of difference between John's temporary consignment to the margins of entitlement and belonging and the situation facing those who have felt it necessary – because of the existing content of their personal lives – to leave their own countries and enter the world of citizenship and social policy operating in the UK in the early twenty-first century. Yet the points of disconnection *and* connection between John's story and the unknown person seeking asylum illustrate well the entangled and mutually constitutive relation between personal lives and social policy.

5 Conclusion

In this chapter we have explored aspects of citizenship through an engagement with some of the key themes and issues that beset questions of citizenship in the contemporary UK. However, we have approached these themes and issues using the concept of personal lives as an analytic lens. This has had implications for what we have emphasized and how we have structured our discussion. In particular, our focus on 'the personal' of personal lives has shaped our concerns in two main ways. First, it has allowed us to engage with citizenship as a set of differentiated and shifting lived experiences. While the rights – and responsibilities – that the status of being a citizen bestows provide the foundations upon which entitlement and inclusion are built, we have argued that there is much more to citizenship than this and that the analytic lens of 'the personal' helps us to grasp and understand these wider dimensions of citizenship.

Can you list some of the dimensions that impact upon and help to shape the experience of citizenship?

For example, we saw that inequalities in the distribution of social power can have profound effects on the lived realities of citizenship. Similarly, we saw that shifts in government and other areas of official policy cut into and shape the content of our personal lives and that our accumulated experiences of social policy and/or welfare agencies can affect whether and how we engage with them in the future. Thus 'the personal' of personal lives may provide the springboard from which we engage with social policy.

The second effect of our concern to use the notion of 'the personal' has been to use it as an intellectual resource. In doing so we have attempted to dislodge the identification of 'personal' with 'individual', instead pointing to the collective or social dimensions of 'the personal' of our lives. But we have also wanted to indicate that policies designating or impacting upon our status as citizens (or non-citizens), like other areas of social policy, have emotional effects and that this dimension of personal life should not be regarded as outside the domain of social policy analysis. Our use of personal narratives has illustrated something of this dimension of citizenship and given greater depth to the idea that citizenship can be regarded as lived experience. In sum, then, we have tried to illustrate our claim that citizenship is both relational and a process by structuring our discussion around personal accounts and the notion of 'the personal' of personal lives.

The following chapters take up the ideas discussed here, using different policy areas and moving across different time spans to explore various dimensions of citizenship as lived experience. We move from the 'birth' of the welfare state in the post-Second World War period, through transition from primary to secondary school in the late twentieth/early twenty-first century UK, to asylum and refugee policy and experience in the 1930s/1940s and 1990s. This ensures that, as a whole, the book offers a wide lens on citizenship as it affects diverse social constituencies, thus illustrating its multidimensional character. In exploring these areas of policy and citizenship experience the chapters that follow draw upon a range of theoretical perspectives, using them to uncover and analyse particular aspects of the social – and indeed emotional – relations of citizenship. Chapter 5 picks up the cue offered by this use of diverse theoretical perspectives to focus on a discussion of theory and the contribution specific theoretical frameworks can make to our understanding of the dynamics of citizenship. The chapters that follow, then, demonstrate the multidimensional and complex character of citizenship and how citizenship – as relation, process and experience – is pivotal in the mutually constitutive relationship between personal lives and social policy.

Further resources

There is a vast literature on citizenship exploring its historical development and contemporary forms in specific countries and in the context of global politics and the claims of particular social constituencies. Here we indicate a few that might be of interest for those wishing to begin a process of more extended reading. Richard Weight and Abigail Beach's edited collection *The Right to Belong: Citizenship and National Identity in Britain, 1930–90* (1998) offers an engaging and informative introduction to the struggles for a more inclusive citizenship in one country at this time. Isin and Wood's *Citizenship and National Identity* (1999) is a particularly useful survey and discussion of contemporary debates about citizenship, including those about diasporic, sexual and cultural citizenship. Another edited collection, Cogan and Derricott's *Citizenship for the 21st Century: An International Perspective on Education* (2000) contains a series of essays, including numerous national case studies, which address approaches to, the development and implementation of policy promoting citizenship education, and dilemmas facing policy-makers seeking to endorse such policy. Books focusing on citizenship and particular social constituencies include Bell and Binnie's *The Sexual Citizen* (2000), Pascall's 'Citizenship: a feminist analysis' (1993) and Vertovec and Peach's edited collection *Islam in Europe: The Politics of Religion and Community* (1997). Finally, Miriam Feldblum offers a compelling analysis of the process of the reconstitution of citizenship and its connections to struggles over national identity and inclusion in France in her *Reconstructing Citizenship: The Politics of Nationality Reform and Immigration in Contemporary France* (1999).

References

Anderson, B. (1983) *Imagined Communities,* London, Verso.

Bell, D. and Binnie, J. (2000) *The Sexual Citizen*, Cambridge, Polity.

Carabine, J. (2004a) 'Sexualities, personal lives and social policy' in Carabine (ed.) (2004b).

Carabine, J. (ed.) (2004b) *Sexualities: Personal Lives and Social Policy*, Bristol, The Policy Press in association with The Open University.

Clarke, G. (1998) 'Voices from the margins: regulation and resistance in the lives of lesbian teachers' in Erbens, M. (ed.) *Biography and Education: A Reader*, London, Falmer.

Cogan, J.J. and Derricot, R. (eds) (2000) *Citizenship for the 21st Century: An International Perspective on Education*, London, Kogan Page.

Crowley, J. (1999) 'The politics of belonging: some theoretical considerations' in Geddes, A. and Favell, A. (eds) *The Politics of Belonging: Migrants and Minorities in Contemporary Europe,* Aldershot, Ashgate.

Deacon, A. (1994) 'Justifying workfare: the historical context of the workfare debates' in White, M. (ed.) *Unemployment and Public Policy in a Changing Labour Market*, London, PSI.

Deacon, A. (2002) *Perspectives on Welfare,* Buckingham, Open University Press.

Dean, H. and Melrose, M. (1999) *Poverty, Riches and Social Citizenship*, Basingstoke, Macmillan.

Dwyer, P. (2000) *Welfare, Rights and Responsibilities: Contesting Social Citizenship*, Bristol, The Policy Press.

Etzioni, A. (1995) *The Spirit of Community*, London, Fontana.

Feldblum, M. (1999) *Reconstructing Citizenship: The Politics of Nationality Reform and Immigration in Contemporary France*, Albany, SUNY.

Fergusson, R. (2004) 'Revaluing the relations of work and welfare' in Mooney (ed.) (2004).

Fink, J. (ed.) (2004) *Care: Personal Lives and Social Policy*, Bristol, The Policy Press in association with The Open University.

Frazer, N. and Gordon, L. (1994) 'Civil citizenship against social citizenship? On the ideology of contract-versus-charity' in Van Steenbergen, B. (ed.) *The Condition of Citizenship*, London, Sage.

Home Office (2001) *Secure Borders, Safe Haven: Integration with Diversity in Modern Britain*, CM 5387, London, The Stationery Office.

Hughes, G. and Mooney, G. (1998) 'Community' in Hughes, G. (ed.) *Imagining Welfare Futures,* London, Routledge in association with The Open University.

Isin, E.F. and Wood, P.K. (1999) *Citizenship and Identity*, London, Sage.

Kymlicka, W. (1995) *Multicultural Citizenship*, Oxford, Clarendon.

Lewis, G. (1998) 'Coming apart at the seams: the crises of the welfare state' in Hughes, G. and Lewis, G. (eds) *Unsettling Welfare: The Reconstruction of Social Policy*, London, Routledge in association with The Open University.

Marshall, T.H. (1981) *The Right to Welfare*, London, Heinemann Educational Books.

Marshall, T.H. (1992) *Citizenship and Social Class,* London, Pluto. (First published in 1950.)

Massey, D. (1999) 'Imagining globalization: power geometries of time–space' in Brah, A., Hickman, M.J. and Mac an Ghaill, M. (eds) *Global Futures, Migration, Environment and Globalization*, Basingstoke, Macmillan.

Matless, D. (1998) 'Taking pleasure in England: landscape and citizenship in the 1940s' in Weight and Beach (eds) (1998).

Mooney, G. (ed.) (2004) *Work: Personal Lives and Social Policy*, Bristol, The Policy Press in association with The Open University.

Pascall, G. (1993) 'Citizenship: a feminist analysis' in Drover, G. and Kerans, P. (eds) *New Approaches to Welfare Theory*, Aldershot, Edward Elgar.

Porter, J. (1987) *The Measure of Canadian Society*, Ottawa, Carleton University Press.

Refugee Council (2004) *Asylum and Immigration (Treatment of Claimants, etc.) Bill: Briefing Note*, London, Refugee Council.

Soysal, Y. (1994) *Limits of Citizenship: Migrants and Post-National Membership in Europe,* Chicago, IL, University of Chicago Press.

Taylor, D. (1996) 'Citizenship and social power' in Taylor, D. (ed.) *Critical Social Policy: A Reader*, London, Sage.

Upton, J. (2004) 'In the streets of Londonistan', *London Review of Books*, 22 January, pp.3–14.

Vertovec, S. and Peach, C. (eds) (1997) *Islam in Europe: The Politics of Religion and Community*, Basingstoke, Macmillan.

Weight, R. and Beach, A. (eds) (1998) *The Right to Belong: Citizenship and National Identity in Britain, 1930–90*, London and New York, I.B.Taurus.

West, C. (1993) 'The new cultural politics of difference' in McCarthy, C. and Crichlow, W. (eds) *Race, Identities and Representation in Education*, New York, Routledge.

Widdowson, B. (2004) 'Retiring lives? Old age, work and welfare' in Mooney (ed.) (2004).

CHAPTER 2

'All That Heaven Allows': The Worker-Citizen in the Post-War Welfare State

by Gail Lewis and Janet Fink

Contents

1 Introduction

> Social security must be achieved by co-operation between the state and the individual. The state should not stifle incentives, opportunity and responsibility; in establishing a national minimum, it should leave room and encouragement for voluntary action by each individual to provide more than that minimum for himself and his family.
>
> (Beveridge, 1942)

> Citizenship is an activity of the soul or the personality concerned to secure certain benefits for the community to which the citizen belongs. ... Here is the case for social service in the broadest sense of that term – a sense of obligation flowing out from each member of the community to embrace every other member. Good citizenship does not consist simply in being ready to undertake this or that particular duty. To inspire it there must be a broad vision of the ideal community for which we have to strive continually ... It is a conscious self-consecration in every department of life, yet a life not of departments but a single integral unity.
>
> (Leeson, 1938, pp.7, 11)

We saw in the previous chapter that questions of citizenship have occupied a central place in official and popular debate for at least six decades. We also noted that more recently concerns about the domain of citizenship have been linked to human rights; social, economic and technological change; increasing religiosity; the global population movement; and the redrawing of political boundaries inside and outside the UK. In this chapter we want to turn our attention to the period between the 1940s and 1960s to explore what might be considered the 'high moment' of social citizenship in the UK. This is the moment when the state explicitly assumed responsibility to ameliorate the worst excesses of inequality while maintaining the system that produced such inequality (Marshall, 1963, p.91). The assumption of this responsibility was expressed in the structures and services of the welfare state and comprised a cluster of agencies, professions and entitlements joined together by a moral ethos captured in the first quotation of this chapter.

Many factors led to the development of the welfare state and were, in part, born of the political, social and indeed recreational struggles of working-class communities up and down the country in the period between 1918 and 1939, and in the aftermath of the Second World War. Equally influential was the extent and costs of the mass unemployment experienced in the late 1920s and throughout the 1930s. Yet another factor was the rise of a particular intellectual configuration in which certain forms of state activity and collectivism attained a position of orthodoxy. The emergence of the welfare state in the 1940s and 1950s represented this intellectual position in which an expansion of the notion of citizenship to include a social dimension alongside its political and civil elements was promoted. The subject at the heart of these developments was the working class – as both a collective subject and an individual, but especially as a white working man, with a dependent wife and children. It was this subject that was more fully incorporated into the democratic state, and emblematic of this incorporation was the guarantee of minimum income and opportunity. It is the emphasis on the working man, on the importance of the state guaranteeing both minimum income *and* opportunity for paid employment that leads us to think of the social figure standing at the heart of this moment of citizenship as 'the worker-citizen'. As we discuss throughout this chapter, more was at stake in the determination of citizenship at this time than the dynamic between workers and employers. It is the citizen as working man – in his relations at work, with family, and in forms of voluntary association – that is directly spoken of, and to, in the major documents inaugurating an extended social citizenship.

Citizenship was to be all-encompassing, to guarantee security – at least of a basic minimum – from 'cradle to grave'. It was to make impossible a return to the deprivation, squalor, inequalities and indignities previously experienced by millions of working-class people in the UK. These were the guarantees of the state to its people. However, this was not all. While the guarantees made by the state to its citizens provided the foundations, individual initiative and responsibility for self and family was to be safeguarded in the new contract between state and citizen. In addition, the new regime of citizenship was to become a way of being, to provoke a sense of self and community belonging fostered by and expressed in the patterns of daily living.

Figure 2.1 White family eating Sunday dinner, 1954

The entangling of state, citizen, morality, everyday practices and senses of self and community in an economy of rights and duties highlights the mutually constitutive relation between personal lives and social policy. This chapter, then, takes its cue from the terrain laid out in the remarks by William Beveridge and Canon Spencer Leeson, a member of the Association for Education in Citizenship, with which we opened the chapter and explores some of the tensions in the system of citizenship inaugurated by the welfare state of the post-war period in Britain. In particular, we look at some of the ways in which working-class people struggled for, and made claim to, the full promise of citizenship.

Aims In doing so this chapter aims to:

- Introduce you briefly to the Gramscian notion of 'the ethical state' as a way of thinking about the reconfiguration of the relation between state and citizen.
- Introduce you to some of the key texts defining the parameters of citizenship – especially social citizenship – in the post Second World War period.
- Bring to light some of the gains and limitations of citizenship as a lived experience in this 'high moment' of social citizenship by considering one area where ordinary people attempted to make real the promise of citizenship made by the newly elected Labour Government of 1945–1951.
- Consider the issue of representation – as a site for the ambivalences and contradictions of citizenship in this period.

In the next section we consider competing conceptions of collectivism, and introduce some of the key texts of the 1940s and 1950s – a period in which what was to become recognized as the then 'dominant paradigm of citizenship' (Roche, 1992) was identified. We show the centrality of the institution of the welfare state in this paradigm and also the notions of collectivism that it institutionalized. In addition, we draw attention to the way in which the relation between the state and citizen was also envisaged as being dependent upon the infrastructures, behaviours and moralities of individuals and groups outside of the state – in voluntary association, leisure and paid employment. This exploration of key texts will allow us to highlight the ways in which '**belongings**' and '**practices of the everyday**' (concepts that were introduced in Chapter 1) were ideas embedded in – albeit at times implicitly – the dominant approach to citizenship at this time.

belongings

practices of the everyday

Section 3 then takes the cue given us about belongings and practices of the everyday and uses them to consider some of the ways in which struggles for housing expressed the political subjectivities of working-class people and their claims to citizenship. We do this by focusing first on the squatters' movement of 1946. It brings us full-square onto the terrain of ordinary everyday practices, and the link between these and struggles to define the parameters of belonging.

Section 4 looks at the issue of cultural representation. By 'representation' we refer not to political representation in the sense of the right to vote and for the representation of collective interests. We mean representation in the cultural sense of **signifying practices** whereby meanings become encoded, produced, circulated and consumed and where some achieve a position of truth and sediment as the common sense. When particular representations achieve a position of truth, making alternative meanings seem nonsensical or even unthinkable, they are said, in Gramscian terms, to be hegemonic. At the same time such hegemonic representations are internally unstable and subject

signifying practices

to contestation as attempts are made to replace them with other counter-hegemonic meanings and/or redefine the meanings of certain symbols, groups or behaviours. Our focus in this section will be on the struggles over cinematic representations of the ambivalences around citizenship, especially in relation to uncertainties about the gains and losses embedded in the new citizenship.

2 The development of the welfare state and discourses of citizenship

As a system of legislative and administrative procedures legitimating and organizing the production and distribution of various benefits and services, what became known as the welfare state *evolved* throughout the first half of the twentieth century. Over this time there were three main periods of activity: the Liberal Government reforms between 1906 and 1914; between the First and Second World Wars; and between 1944 and 1951 when the Labour Government introduced the range of reforms that became associated with social citizenship and the welfare state. (The 1944 Education Act was introduced by the national government headed by Winston Churchill.)

Numerous areas of social reform were institutionalized during these three periods, including those connected to paid employment, formal education, housing, health, and child care and parenting. However, the legislative framework and administrative processes that formed the architecture of the welfare state emerged in a developmental way and should not be taken as an indication of the absence of struggle for such social reforms. We will see that the development of the welfare state is both linked to a politics over the meaning of the social and raises important questions about the subject positions conceived as standing at the ideological heart of discourses of citizenship.

Throughout the first half of the twentieth century there was an important ideological shift in the way that the relation between state and individual was conceptualized. As we have already stated, this shift in thinking was marked by a growing acceptance of a degree of collective responsibility for the standard of living of individual citizens, their life chances *and* moral standards. In the liberal tradition of the nineteenth century, the chief role of the state had been conceived as enabling the practice of laissez-faire in economic and social matters, with intervention into questions of welfare being restricted to the provision of a level of residual care for the deserving poor and punitive measures for the undeserving. In the system of welfare that evolved in the first half of the twentieth century, the state was increasingly to direct its intervention into the maintenance of a minimum standard of living appropriate for the citizenry of a 'civilized society', developing mechanisms for the administration and delivery of services and benefits that were rational and neutral through forms of bureau–professionalism (Hughes and Lewis, 1998), and for fostering a moral attitude that reflected and legitimated a sensibility of constrained collectivism.

The roots of this move towards a form of collectivism stretch back into the nineteenth century when political reform extended the franchise; the proliferation of discourse (Foucault, 1992) led to the emergence of new social subjects deemed socially problematic (for example, the homosexual, the prostitute, the lunatic, see **Carabine, 2004**); and imperial expansion required new forms of governance and a reconceptualization of the state. This confluence of forces was paralleled by a view spreading across the political spectrum that a strong, interventionist state operating in a context of collectivism was necessary. Despite this agreement, differences of political complexion led to division over the character and form of both the collectivism and the state. We can begin to grasp these variations in opinion by looking at Extract 2.1 taken from a piece by Hall and Schwarz (1985).

ACTIVITY 2.1

Read Extract 2.1 which is taken from the Introduction to *State and Society, 1880–1930*. As you do so, you should note the following:

- the main features of each vision of collectivism;
- the general political orientations or positions with which each form of collectivism was associated.

Extract 2.1 What form of collectivism? What form of State?

The political forces of collectivism

Three ... dominant collectivist currents can be identified: imperialist, new liberal and Fabian ...

First, the social-imperialist position. There already existed a long Tory tradition of commitment to a strong state; in this period diehards inside the Conservative Party attempted to resist the 'capitulation' of their party to liberalism, arguing the essential continuity between Tory paternalism and the organic interventionist state. ... [This] resulted in the formation of an authentically Conservative and imperialist collectivism. The politics of imperialist collectivism were most characteristically of the radical right, envisaging drastic solutions, imposed from above, to resolve Britain's ills, and scarcely restrained by the constraints of parliamentary constitutionalism. The language was ... of 'national efficiency' and 'social imperialism' – the former pin-pointing liberalism's inadequacy in facing the task of national renovation, the latter designating a set of policies which, by combining imperialist development abroad with welfare and economic reforms at home, would build up the strength, efficiency and fitness of the British race as an imperial power. ... these collectivists of the right worked energetically to enlist a populist movement in the country. Social imperialism did not so much deny citizenship as recast it in a populist and activist idiom: the new citizen was to be a *participant* absorbed into the larger organic unities of race, empire and nation.

...

The new liberals, a group of highly gifted professional intellectuals, evolved a conception of collectivism which was constitutional and communitarian, ethical rather than utilitarian, and which aimed to preserve individual liberties *through greater state intervention*. New liberalism was a body of thought based on the determination to devise forms of collectivist control which could complement and extend, rather than negate, the inherited ethos of liberalism. Its trajectory was evolutionary, its driving-force idealist and ethical. In this respect and others, it played an inestimable role in the formation of British social democracy. Its concept of citizenship was uncompromisingly constitutional, but principled in its desire to elevate the citizen as a full member of the political nation and the community, as a moral being, with duties as well as rights. The new liberal perspective shared the imperialist belief that citizenship not only conferred legal rights but signalled a *potential* which could be realized in each individual through an educative political participation. ... The significance of the new position within the liberal tradition articulated by the new liberals lies most of all in their advocacy of the provision of *universal* social rights. But this was tempered and qualified by their identification of those whom they deemed were unfit for the purposes of citizenship – an exception to universalism within the discourse of new liberalism which was not perceived as contentious.

...

The third ... collectivist grouping were the Fabians. The Fabians represented the contradictory thrust of collectivism at the very heart of socialism itself ... the most prominent of the Fabians (like Bernard Shaw and Beatrice and Sydney Webb) were socialists: they wanted to destroy the anarchy of the capitalist market and achieve a classless society. But there were many 'socialisms' contending for ascendancy within the working-class movement at this time ... Fabian socialism was the reformist, bureaucratic, anti-democratic and illiberal variety. Their dream was a fully regulated, fully administered collectivist society in which state surveillance would be an essential condition of civic conduct. This variant of socialism was deeply at odds with ... the spirit of self-activism which animated the proletarian socialist organizations of the period. ... the Fabians were not only members of a newly professionalized intelligentsia; they elevated the bureaucrat, the expert and the administrator to the position of the leading *cadre* of their struggle for a new society. ... If the new liberals played a key role in defining the character of the welfare state, it was Fabianism which fashioned the ideology of rational efficiency and administrative neutrality which characterized welfare practice.

(Hall and Schwarz, 1985, pp.21–3)

COMMENT

We can see that one or other vision of collectivism ranged across the political spectrum, from the radical right (social imperialism), through the centre (new liberals), to the left (the Fabians). Each of these had an image of increased state activity and intervention, though they differed over how much, in what spheres and with what aim. So too did their respective images of the citizen. The social imperialists and Fabians imagined a stronger state than the new liberals, with the former supporting the state operating in the field of politics (at home and in the British Empire) and the individual citizen being subsumed into a collectivity convened around 'race' and nation. For the Fabians, state activity centres on the field of the social, including administration of the institutions governing the social, and the citizen is a member of this socialized collectivity. State activity for the new liberals focuses on the guaranteeing of the rights and duties of the individual.

Together the new liberal and Fabian visions of collectivism and state intervention provided the ground upon which the welfare state was founded and from which it crafted its practice. There is however, more embedded in these visions of collectivism and the increase in state intervention has a deeper bearing on our discussion of changing forms of citizenship. To elicit what these additional aspects might be we can turn to the writings of Antonio Gramsci: an Italian communist who was elected to parliament in 1924, arrested in 1926 and imprisoned for 20 years where he died in 1937. During his imprisonment, Gramsci produced a significant body of writing on the state, ideology and workers' struggle in capitalist societies.

What effect do you think the time, national context and specific circumstances in which Gramsci was writing had on his ideas?

the ethical state

hegemony

Gramsci is particularly well-known in the UK and other parts of Europe for his concept of hegemony, however, it is his conception of '**the ethical state**' that particularly interests us here. In order to grasp the idea of 'the ethical state' we need to begin from Gramsci's insistence on taking seriously the Marxist notion that human nature is historically determined rather than being abstract, fixed and immutable, and that human agency therefore has a powerful transformative capacity. Because of this adaptable quality of human nature, the relations of rule within capitalism involve attention to the ways in which individuals develop their dispositions, orientations, habits and daily practices. This is linked to the idea of '**hegemony**' – by which Gramsci meant the production of consent to ruling ideas and practices by the ruled so that dominant ideologies become naturalized as common sense. In this way, the ruled become inserted into the ideological apparatus and develop a 'will to conform' (Gramsci, 1971, p.260), including among other things to the state's version of appropriate daily living practices and collectivism. In this, then, we can see a connection to the points discussed by Hall and Schwarz in Extract 2.1.

In bourgeois societies the state assumes the role of producing citizens with this will to conform and thus the state is an ethical project, 'an "educator" in that it aims precisely to create a new type and level of civilization' (Gramsci, 1971, p.157) along with the citizen commensurate with such a civilization. The 'ethical state is also an "interventionist state"' in that it 'takes on the "protection" of the working classes against the excesses of capitalism' (Gramsci, 1971, p.262). This interventionist, enabling and educative role is what makes the state 'ethical' in that it is involved in the constitution of a certain kind of moral sensibility among the state's people. The ethical state brings out, or 'educes the citizen from the human being' (Lloyd and Thomas,

1998, p.7), and subjects this citizen to a mode of self-rule or regulation in which ambitions are channelled through the collectivism embodied in state institutions, including those of the welfare state. While the state monopolizes the instruments of force and coercion, the need for their use is tempered by the state's hegemonic success and its ethical dimensions. In this way, state and people are conceived as unified in one indivisible entity. Moreover, the ethical or educative principles and practices of the state inculcate within the people particular habits of mind, dispositions, normalized practices, ways of being, and identities in which homogenity and limited diversity are both imagined and assumed. Thus, the ethical state is tied to the formation of nation and nationalist sensibility as part of its evocation of citizens and citizenship. In sum, then, we can identify three interlinked dimensions to the ethical state and in later parts of the chapter you will see examples of these. The three dimensions are:

- a saturation of all aspects of society with the 'idea' of the state, so that rule is no longer simply equated with coercion and repressive apparatus, but also with the moral force of the state;
- a notion that the proper relation of the subject as citizen is one of subordination to the state and its moral and cultural economy (Lloyd and Thomas, 1998, p.115); and
- thus, the creation of 'the ethical subject' who is simultaneously informed and cultured and sacrifices self-interest to collective or national interest as represented in and by the state.

2.1 Imagining the welfare state: social security and the worker-citizen

Our discussion so far begins to show that the concept of the modern welfare state involved more than material social improvements (Pollard, 1969, p.404), since it was also invested in the constitution of a particular kind of citizen/subject. The successful achievement of this objective or imperative was (and is) not guaranteed since alternative understandings and visions of the state–citizen relation and collectivism make for counter-hegemonic struggles by various social groups. Chapter 1 pointed to some of these struggles in the discussion of new forms of citizenship claim made by new social movements from the 1970s. Similarly, we shall point to areas of contention in the post-war welfare state and show both how the meanings of the new citizenship was a deeply contested idea and social relation and how these struggles over meanings exposed the limits of the citizenship embedded in the Beveridgean welfare state.

First though let us spend a little time exploring the new citizenship. To facilitate this exploration we focus on the Beveridge Report, *Social Insurance and Allied Services* of 1942. In doing so we are using income maintenance as a prism through which to explore the shifting configuration of the state–citizen relation. As the Beveridge Report (1942, para 10) stated this was 'a plan of insurance – of giving in return for contributions benefits up to subsistence level, as of right and without means test'. But, while pivotal to the system of welfare initiated in this period, Beveridge himself was clear that this was only one element in a strategy aimed at attacking poverty and fostering new forms of state–citizen relation. This is why he spoke of the five giants: want because of lack of income; squalor because of bad housing; ignorance because of lack of access to education; disease because of lack of affordable health facilities; and idleness because of lack of employment opportunity. Each of these was to be addressed by the creation of an infrastructure of service provision and administrative criteria for accessing these services and benefits. Thus, we are not suggesting that citizenship can be reduced to a system of income maintenance. Rather, we are using it as a symbol of the shifting relations of state and citizen that was ushered in by the welfare state. In this we echo a Fabian pamphlet which noted that social security was 'becoming a symbol for ... society [and had] thus become a touchstone for the future' (Clarke, 1943, p.272).

Figure 2.2 Jarrow March, 1936

Let us begin by exploring the six principles that drove the Beveridge Report. We then invite you to consider four extracts taken from texts written in the 1940s and 1950s. Looking at contemporaneous texts such as these helps us to enter the discursive universe of this time, and also enables us to grasp something of the extent and tenor of debate about, and disputation over the newly created welfare state.

The Beveridge Report was controversial for its policy implications and for its *universalism*. The aim was to establish a system capable of providing for all the basic and predictable needs of the population (Jones, 1994, p.127), and the elimination of the reliance on voluntary or charitable organizations, or the hated means test of the national assistance scheme. Thus, alongside universalism the six principles were comprehensiveness; unification; classification (into categories of insured persons); adequacy of benefit; flat-rate contribution (with some exceptions); and flat-rate benefit (with variation depending on family size and effected by a system of family allowances, payable on the birth of the second and any subsequent children). Alongside these principles, the Beveridge Report also identified eight primary causes of need and recommended the ways these needs could be met and these are shown in Table 2.1.

Table 2.1 Beveridge's eight primary causes of need

Need	Provision
Unemployment	Unemployment benefit
Disability	Disability benefit or industrial pension
Loss of livelihood	Training benefit
Retirement	Retirement pension
Marriage needs of a woman	Marriage grant Maternity allowance Maternity benefit Widow's benefit Guardian benefit
Funeral expenses	Funeral grant
Childhood	Children's allowances
Illness, disability	Medical treatment and rehabilitation

Source: Jones, 1994, p.127

Equally important to the ethos and success of the Beveridge proposals for social insurance was a commitment by the government to full employment, defined as no more than 3 per cent of the economically active population being out of work. These levels of employment were to be maintained through what became known as Keynesian Demand Management, hence the designation of the welfare state as the Keynesian or Beveridgean welfare state (Hughes and Lewis, 1998). Such a commitment to full employment was forthcoming as the government White Paper on *Employment Policy* (1944) made clear when it stated 'as one of their primary aims and responsibilities (the government has) ... the maintenance of a high and stable level of employment after the war' (quoted in Pollard, 1969, p.351).

As we have already indicated, while the government was ready to accept responsibility for maintaining full employment and providing a national minimum of income in times of unemployment, this was not to lead to an abandonment of responsibility for self and family on the part of the worker-citizen. In subscribing to this combination of state guarantee alongside self-responsibility, the Beveridge Report remained squarely within the liberal tradition which privileged individualism and self-reliance.

In the light of your reading of Extract 2.1 from Hall and Schwarz (1985) are you able to see how we can make this claim?

ACTIVITY 2.2

Extracts 2.2 and 2.3 are taken respectively from Aneurin Bevan, who was Minister of Health (which also carried responsibility for housing at that time) in the Labour Government of 1945 to 1951, and John Saville, a leading economic and social historian working from a Marxist perspective and co-founder (with Ralph Milliband) and editor of *The Socialist Register*. Read carefully through these extracts and as you do so make a note of your responses to the following questions:

- In what ways do the two authors characterize the post Second World War social reforms?
- What conception of the individual citizen seems to underpin their views as represented in these extracts?
- What conception of the state seems to underpin their views as represented here?

Extract 2.2 Aneurin Bevan – Between democratic socialism and individual self-interest

In a society where the bulk of property is privately owned, public spending is always an invasion of private rights.

...

Many of the political tensions in individualist society came from this source. ... The strains so created are all the more intense because the objects of public spending commend themselves to the convenience of the majority of the nation. These include ... the various social services that enlightened opinion has caused the nation to adopt. The individual who is called on to alienate a painful part of his private income to the tax collector is not made any more willing because it is going to finance purposes it is not easy for him to condemn. ... As ... good citizen, he is pleased that his country should provide education, old age pensions, service pensions, widows' pensions, health services, an effective defence force and so on. But as ... the individual taxpayer, he resents paying the bill.

...

The conflict between the demands of public spending and the general class of taxpayer is further aggravated by the knowledge that many are able to escape their just share of taxes.

...

All this occasions the bitterest resentment among those citizens where social situation forces them to pay in full. The consequences from a socialist point of view of what really amounts to a penalization of the honest ... is exceedingly serious. The power and prosperity of tax evaders thwarts one of the main aims of socialism: the establishment of just, social relationships.

...

... as a device for financing expanding social services ... additional taxes ... will not resolve the deep antagonism between public and private spending that now holds the centre of the political stage.

... The individual finds his most selfish instincts mobilized against any reasonable order of social priorities, and politics degenerate into a squalid round of catch-penny propaganda.

... where property owning classes believe that the function of disposing of the economic surplus should lie with them, there is bound to be resentment when the State steps in and takes some of the surplus for its own purposes. ... The struggle is for the economic surplus ... a demand for more equality in the distribution of existing wealth ...

It is neither prudent, nor does it accord with our conception of the future, that all forms of private property should live under perpetual threat.

...

But it is a prerequisite of social stability that one type of property ownership should dominate. In the future it should be public property. Private property should yield to the point where social purposes and a decent order of priorities form an easily discussible pattern of life.

(Bevan, 1952, pp.106–18)

Extract 2.3 John Saville – The welfare state is bourgeois

In general this short period after the Second World War (i.e. 1945–50) may be compared with that of the Liberal Government after 1906, although in terms of social policy the Labour Government showed much less originality and initiative and were more in the stream of tradition than were the Liberals before 1914. Hence the relative care with which social legislation was passed after 1945, largely because the proposals represented a minimum which the Tories had already accepted in principle. The main contribution of these years was to make an extended range of social security benefits available to the whole population. Among these were the raising of the school leaving age, a comprehensive health service, retirement pensions and family allowances. It was a modest programme, and a couple of decades overdue by the standards of the previous half century and its achievement was followed by a partial retreat in 1950 with the imposition of charges for certain health services.

This growth in social security benefits in the twentieth century has involved an increase in expenditure per head of population of about twelve times between 1900 and 1950 (allowing for changes in the value of money). But the starting point was from a very low level, and for an economy as industrially advanced and as economically wealthy as that of Britain, the pace of change has been surprisingly slow. It is the success of the determined opposition to reform that merits attention – not the social legislation that has been achieved. The range and distribution of social security in Britain represents no more than elementary social justice for the mass of the people; and from the side of industry it can be reckoned as a sound economic investment. The struggle for any particular reform has always in this country aroused so much opposition that when it is achieved it is at least understandable that those who have spent half a life time on its behalf too easily believe that with its enactment a new period in social history is beginning.

...

A main reason why public opinion in general, and the Labour movement in particular, have become confused as to the essentially bourgeois nature of the welfare state is that both in the propaganda of the Labour Party and in the criticisms of its opponents, the legislation of the 1945 Labour Government was labelled 'socialist'.

...

[In contrast we need to note that] the increasing acceptance of the principle by successive governments in the twentieth century has meant that the social services have developed in such a way that the financial burden upon the rich has been very largely cushioned. Even more striking however – ... is the growth of direct and indirect taxation from working-class incomes to the point where much of the expenditure upon social services is no more than a transfer of income by taxation within the working class. Or, to put the matter more simply, to a very considerable extent the working class pay for their own social security benefits by compulsory contributions and a high level of indirect taxation.

...

The State now 'saves' for the working class and translates the services into social services'.

(Saville, 1957/8, reprinted in 1977 in Fitzgerald et al., pp.7–9)

COMMENT

For Aneurin Bevan the state has a number of roles to play in the context of the balance of social forces that the welfare state both expressed and helped to sustain. To some extent the state supplemented the activity of private enterprise, but through the administration of its taxation policy, the state acted as protector of those taxpayers who could not avoid paying, and punisher of those who could and did avoid such obligation. In this sense the state acted as a mediator of the tension that arose between the collective citizen and the individual taxpayer. Implicit in Bevan's suggestion of a tension between collective citizen and individual taxpayer is a conception of the individual as a split subject (though this is not a language that was prevalent in the discipline of social policy in the 1940s and 1950s). Split between an individualistic and self-serving sense of self and a collectivist sense of self. And in this, the state performs what for those like Bevan was its most important role – to promote social justice via redistribution. Thus, the social reforms embodied in the welfare state became an index of social priorities in which a collectivist sensibility was privileged. Such reforms were dependent however on the generation of an economic surplus even while they represented a vision of the future.

Saville on the other hand saw the social reforms as a mechanism for managing capital while maintaining the overall structure of class relations. Any redistribution was horizontal in character in so far as it was redistribution from one section of the working class to another, not from the rich to the poor(er). It is in this sense that the state compelled a certain kind of behaviour among the working classes – that is acceptance of savings (via national insurance) as a protection against any periods of unemployment or ill health. However, in Saville's approach little attention is paid to the individual since he (and it is the masculine subject that is called up here) was conceived only as a member of a class. The social reforms were conceived as modest, especially in light of the level of output as measured by gross domestic product.

2.2 The making of new citizens and discourses of citizenship

At the core of the difference of interpretation between Bevan and Saville is a conception not only of the role the state plays in organizing, controlling or mediating relations of property and economy, but also in terms of the relative influence or power different social groups and individuals should have in determining the shape or character of social relations. For Bevan, Beveridgean citizenship is the position from which state appropriation of a slice of the surplus is legitimated in the name of the public good. For Saville, citizenship is a position from which the working class is subordinated to the state, which in turn works in the interests of capital in the context of a given balance of social forces.

When translated into a question about who pays for welfare, an injunction that all citizens – who are equal before the law – assume equal responsibility for the collective good can mean that the costs of social welfare are to be shared by the major social classes in society despite the inequalities that result from capitalist social relations. This, in its turn, can also be thought of as being rooted in a conception of citizenship that goes beyond rights of democratic influence and participation, a certain minimum standard of living and the obligation to exercise a degree of self-sacrifice and social responsibility. It illustrates a central idea carried in the notion of 'the ethical state', this is that there is no real division between state and people (Gramsci, 1971, p.263).

Thus, the Beveridge proposals for social insurance conceived citizenship as involving much more than a contract between state and people about employment and minimum living standards. In the new world that was to follow the mass unemployment of the 1930s and the genocide and destruction of the Second World War, 'citizenship' was about both the promise for the future and the making of new men and women. The welfare state was about producing people whose subjectivities, identities and senses of belonging were founded on a judicious mix of individual, familial and national responsibility together with a sense of the collective good and their part in making it a reality.

To what extent can this be thought of as an example of 'the ethical state'?

In this, then, how people lived their lives – their everyday practices and moral codes – became a central element of the discourse of citizenship espoused by authoritative representatives of hegemonic thinking such as Beveridge and T. H. Marshall (1950/63, see Chapter 13). For Beveridge this revolved around an emphasis on the importance of individual enterprise, self-reliance and civic action. Here, we have testimony to the mutually constitutive relation between personal lives and social policy since in foregrounding practices of self-reliance and civic or voluntary action Beveridge – and by extension the discourse of citizenship in which his thought was embedded – was proposing a form of welfare and citizenship that assumed and constructed certain ways of being in areas considered the realm of 'the personal'. This is evident if we consider two other reports published by Beveridge in the 1940s, *Full Employment in a Free Society* (1944) and *Voluntary Action* (1948).

Figure 2.3 'Beveridge way'

ACTIVITY 2.3

Here we reproduce two extracts, one taken from *Full Employment in a Free Society* (1944) and the other from *Voluntary Action* (1948). Read through Extracts 2.4 and 2.5 carefully and make a note of the following:

- Which freedoms does Beveridge identify as key to a democratic society?
- How does he conceive the relation between these freedoms and a policy of full employment?
- What does he mean by voluntary action?
- What link does he see between voluntary action and citizenship?
- In what ways is 'the personal' of personal lives constructed in these extracts?

Extract 2.4 Full employment and freedom

The Report, as its title indicates, is not concerned simply with the problem of full employment. It is concerned with the necessity, possibility and methods of achieving full employment in a free society, that is to say, subject to the proviso that all essential citizen liberties are preserved. The precise effect of the proviso depends on the list of essential liberties. ... they are taken as freedom of worship, speech, writing, study and teaching; freedom of assembly and of association for political and other purposes, including the bringing about of a peaceful change of the governing authority; freedom in choice of occupation; and freedom in the management of a personal income.

...

Freedom in the management of a personal income complicates the problem of full employment. ... If men cannot be forced to buy just what has been produced, this means that demands for labour and its products cannot be fitted forcibly to the supply. There may be continual changes in the kinds of things on which consumers want to spend their money ... For freedom in the management of a personal income includes freedom to decide between spending now and saving so as to have the power of spending later. ... In a free society individuals must be allowed to plan their spending over their lives as a whole.

...

None of these freedoms can be exercised irresponsibly. Perpetual instability of economic or social policy would make full employment and any other social reforms futile or impossible. Bargaining for wages must be responsible, looking not to the snatching of short sectional advantages, but to the permanent good of the community. ... Work means doing what is wanted, not doing just what pleases one. All liberties carry their responsibilities. This does not mean that the liberties themselves must be surrendered. They must be retained.

...

The underlying principle of the Report is to propose for the State only those things which the State alone can do or which it can do better than any local authority or than private citizens either singly or in association, and to leave to these other agencies that which, if they will, they can do as well as or better than the State. The Policy for Full Employment is a policy to be carried through democratic action, of public authorities, central and local, responsible ultimately to the voters, and of voluntary associations and private citizens consciously co-operating for a common purpose which they understand and approve.

(Beveridge, 1944, paras 11, 15, 16, 44)

Extract 2.5 'Voluntary Action' and responsibility

The term 'Voluntary Action', as used here, means private action, that is to say action not under the directions of any authority wielding the power of the State. ... This study is confined to Voluntary Action for public purpose – for social advance. Its theme is Voluntary Action ... for improving the conditions of life for him and his fellows.

...

This Report is concerned specifically with action inspired by one or other of two main motives – Mutual Aid and Philanthropy. The first motive has its origin in a sense of one's own need for security against misfortune, and realisation that, since one's fellows have the same need, by undertaking to help one another all may help themselves. The second motive springs from ... the feeling which makes men who are materially comfortable, mentally uncomfortable so long as their neighbours are materially uncomfortable: to have social conscience is to be unwilling to make a separate peace with the giant social evils of Want, Disease, Squalor, Ignorance, Idleness, escaping into personal prosperity oneself, while leaving one's fellows in their clutches.

...

... vigour and abundance of Voluntary Action outside one's home ... [is among] the distinguishing marks of a free society. They have been outstanding features of British life.

The people of this small island have made several political inventions of value to the whole world ... To-day fresh political inventions are needed urgently ... in the domestic [i.e. national] sphere to reconcile the responsibilities of the State with the rights and responsibilities of individuals. It is clear that the State must in future do more things than it has attempted in the past. But it is equally clear ... That room, opportunity, and encouragement must be kept for Voluntary Action in seeking new ways of social advance.

...

[The Reports on *Social Insurance, Full Employment*, and this on *Voluntary Action*] have one thing in common. They are all assertions of *duty,* either of the community, that is to say, its leaders, or of the individual. *Emphasis on duty*

> *rather than assertion of rights* presents itself to-day as the condition on which alone humanity can resume the progress in civilisation which has been interrupted by two world wars ...
>
> (Beveridge, 1948, pp. 8–10 and 14, emphases added)

COMMENT

The freedoms Beveridge identifies are those of spoken and written expression, the freedom to gain knowledge, of political or religious assembly, of employment, and the deployment of personal income. These are key features of what he calls a free society, but they also impose constraints on a full-employment policy in the sense that they must not be sacrificed to the objectives of such a policy. In this context the freedom to dispose of personal income in whatever way the citizen chooses poses particular problems for the pursuit of full employment. This is because it limits the extent to which the state can compel people to save and therefore provide potential funds for future investment. Nor can the state compel spending in specified directions in support of particular industries or sectors.

Yet the direction of constraint flows the other way too, in that pursuit of the collective good imposes limits on these freedoms in so far as the citizenry are called upon to act responsibly. 'Responsibility' here is those actions that sustain the collective, but this is not a collective convened around interests of class, gender, ethnicity, sexuality or any other form of social difference. The call to avoid 'sectional advantages' implicitly therefore constructs the 'collective' as the national, and in this way the practice of citizenship assumed and promoted by Beveridge also constructs a form of belonging – that is national belonging. Or, to put it in terms suggested earlier, state and citizen are one and the ethical state produces the ethical citizen/subject. It is this belonging that underpins the definition of responsibility and restrains self-interest.

In moving to consider Voluntary Action, defined as all activity outside of the home that is not directed by the state but aimed at the promotion of the collective good, Beveridge begins to identify the domains where ethical citizenship might be practised. Voluntary Action provides a conduit for the expression and furtherance of citizenship because whatever the original motivation it is aimed at the collective and channels (in psychoanalytic terminology, one might say sublimates) self-interest in a positive way. Moreover, Voluntary Action is identified as a fundamental feature of the 'British character', and therefore its continued promotion is nothing more than an expression of the national.

To think about how 'the personal' is constructed in Extracts 2.4 and 2.5 we want to refer back to a point made in Chapter 1. There it was noted that the state assumes responsibility for structuring the shape of personal lives through notions of opportunity, constraint, legality, responsibility and morality. This is partly achieved by the social policy systems adopted and legitimated by the state. A second dimension of the mutually constitutive relation between personal lives and social policy is through the way social policy at national level determines the boundaries of 'the personal', in part by distinguishing between 'public' and 'private' domains.

We can see both these processes of constitution of 'the personal' in the two extracts here. Opportunity for free expression, for voluntary activity and association, for self-help and working toward the collective good must be protected and promoted. Similarly, there must be constraint on inappropriate state activity and on individual or sectional interest. These injunctions or principles of policy have the effect of beginning to demarcate the boundaries of 'the personal', especially as part of a practice of citizenship and to define what some of its content might be. Thus, the new welfare state was to foster habits and practices of responsibility and morality and these were conceived as corresponding to the national interest. In so doing the 'national interest' was folded into a discourse that equated long-standing traditions of the 'people of these islands', with the new social-democratic consensus that was institutionalized in the welfare state and which united state and citizen.

---

3 Expanding the horizon of citizenship: housing and the squatters' movement of 1946

structure of feeling

In many ways the four extracts reproduced above illustrate what Raymond Williams (1954, with Orram; 1961; 1977) called the '**structure of feeling**'. In devising this term Williams was attempting to provide a terminology capable of capturing a mood, sensibility or atmosphere associated with a specific historical period or generation.

> A structure of feeling describes the actual living sense of a culture in a particular historical period or in the experience of a particular generation. It is the area in which official consciousness of a period, as codified in legislation and doctrine, interacts with the lived experience of that period, and defines the set of perceptions and values common to a generation. The structure of feeling ... is not uniform throughout society, being most evident in the dominant social group. [But] it is a matter of feeling rather than thought ...
>
> (Macey, 2000, p.366)

Can you attempt to describe the structure of feeling that prevails in your social world?

Drawing on Williams' idea we can say that included in the structure of feeling of the post Second World War generation was a dominant conception of citizenship in which a state/people relation guaranteed a minimum standard of living, but did not sacrifice a moral economy in which self-reliance, responsibility and subordination of the sectional to the national prevailed. As the editorial in *The Times* stated on 1 July 1940:

> If [in Europe] we speak of democracy we do not mean a democracy which maintains the right to vote but forgets the right to work and the right to live. If we speak of freedom we do not mean a rugged individualism which excludes social organization and economic planning. If we speak of equality we do not mean a political equality nullified by social and economic privilege. If we speak of economic reconstruction we think less of a maximum (though this job too will be

> required) than of equitable distribution. ... The new order cannot be based on the preservation of privilege whether the privilege be that of country, of a class or of an individual.
>
> (quoted in Fraser, 1973, p.265)

Figure 2.4 Citizenship – only skin deep?

It was into this discursive frame that the citizens/subjects of the UK were invited and called upon to identify with, and make their own, a set of normalized subject positions and practices of everyday living. However, while among the effects of discourses is the creation of boundaries of intelligibility and the creation of specific identities (**Carabine, 2004**), whether, how and through what interpretive lens people will so identify can never be fully determined. There are always alternative subject positions or identities available, always a possibility that the same subject or idea is given different meanings. It is not that there is an *endless* range of possible identities or meanings available, but the indeterminacy of identity and meaning opens up fields of contestation. This is precisely what occurred in the 1940s and 1950s around the meanings and limits of the discourse of citizen. One way that we can illustrate this process of contestation over the meanings and limits of the new citizenship is by looking at the squatters' movement of 1946.

3.1 Between promise and provision

The question of housing presented the post-war government with one of its most acute problems, not least because it acted as a powerful material and symbolic index of the progress of the promised social transformation. As early as the 1940s housing had been identified as essential to any new system of national welfare as is evident from Beveridge's declaration that what was needed was an attack on the *five giants*, of which squalor was one. Similarly, Winston Churchill, the wartime Prime Minister, had remarked 'Most painful is the number of small houses inhabited by working folk which have been destroyed. We will rebuild them ... London, Liverpool, Manchester, Birmingham may have much more to suffer, but they will rise from their ruins ...' (cited in Addison, 1995, p.56). The provision of high-standard affordable housing was both a reward for the sacrifice made during the war years and a symbol of the move toward a system of greater equality. The 1949 Housing Act attempted to capture this more social, rather than economic, agenda by the development of a complex points system through which allocation was determined and which incorporated these social dimensions.

The promise was high. The government indicated that up to four million new houses would be built over the next decade or so, and 300,000 of these were to be forthcoming in the first two years after the war. Overall policy aims were the continuation of the slum clearance programme that had been interrupted by the war, a programme of rebuilding and renovation of war destroyed and damaged properties, and the rehabilitation and conversion of other existing stock. Demand for housing was huge, with returning troops, increased marriages, reunited couples and families, and an increase in the birth rate, all contributing. At the same time supply of building and other necessary resources was low and slow. As a result the building programme was below target and less than before the war, for example, 350,000 new houses were built in 1938, whereas in 1948 the number was 230,000. Moreover, it was estimated that in 1951 there were still three quarters of a million too few homes. Having said this, approximately 800,000 families were re-housed between 1945 and 1948, and the supply of the famous 'prefabs' (prefabricated homes designed as a temporary measure) did much to alleviate the pressure.

Nevertheless, it was not until the mid 1950s that a widespread improvement in the housing crisis was effected, and as a result the gap between the promise of housing provision and the reality that marked the five years after the end of war meant a high level of popular dissatisfaction. It was in this context that a wave of squatting developed across the country.

In the summer of 1946, between 40,000 and 46,000 people all across the UK took up the idea of responsible citizenship and attempted to resolve their own housing needs by occupying first, disused empty military camps, then, privately owned, but empty, flats and houses. It is unclear exactly when and

Figure 2.5 Bevan on a housing estate

where this movement began (some point to Edinburgh in December 1945), but many commentators agree that the occupation of a camp in Scunthorpe in June 1946 (when a cinema projectionist and his family moved in) was the beginning of mass action. From Scunthorpe occupations quickly spread to Sheffield, West Hartlepool, Doncaster, Durham, Glasgow, Brighton, Bristol, Taunton, Birmingham, Chalfont St Giles in Buckinghamshire, and elsewhere. Newspapers and cinema screenings by Movietone of current events quickly spread word of the occupations. For example, in September 1946 *The Daily Telegraph* recorded that:

> squatters poured into the ATS camp at Craigentinny, Edinburgh, over the weekend. ... About sixty families, comprising nearly 300 people, including children, are now living there. Army huts in the grounds of Coxhoe Hall, near Durham have been occupied by thirty-three families ... Squatters' representatives from camps in south-west Lancashire and Yorkshire formed an area committee in Liverpool last night to amalgamate to a 'national federation' being formed in London. ... A family which moved into Woodlands Sports Club, Gravesend, Kent, and took possession of the youth section club room, refused to be evicted. The club room was condemned for habitation.
>
> (quoted in Addison, 1995, p.65)

The reference here to an occupied building being condemned for human habitation indicates something of the physical condition of many of the military and other camps that were squatted. Often poorly built, suffering from bad layout, lack of private sanitation, sleeping or cooking facilities, extensive work was frequently required to make them suitable for civilian residence. In response to this, squatters quickly found collective ways of resolving the inadequacies, including the formation of committees charged with negotiating with local authorities for the provision of essential services and supply of much needed building materials (Gaster, 1989) and the adoption of communal living (Hinton, 1988). This encompassed everyday but essential tasks such as cleaning, where women often formed rotas, cooking utensils were pooled, and in some instances, child care was collectively organized. Such ordering of daily life often extended to the establishment of an agreed and standardized rent that was then paid into a special fund (Gaster, 1989). These ways of organizing everyday practices indicate the non-normative or different moral rationalities (Duncan and Edwards, 1999) prevalent among the squatters, suggesting that the project of 'the ethical state' can never completely close off the possibility of alternative identities or visions and ways of practising citizenship.

Yet these alternative moral rationalities sat alongside the concern seemingly felt by many of the squatters for traditional forms of respectability. Thus, while the practise of citizenship among the squatter communities had begun with an illegal act and often involved forms of collectivized living, normalized everyday habits and manners were not to fall by the wayside. For example, in Bristol one of the spokespeople for local squatters said, 'We are rather worried about the children's education and religious training' (quoted in Hinton, 1988, p.107). While a vicar working with other squatters in the area said, 'Their action was unusual, unconstitutional, but *let no-one think they are ruffians. They are ordinary people, they shave everyday, eat at tables, go off to earn their own living*' (quoted in Hinton, 1988, p.107, emphases added).

The initial government response to the military camps' occupations was one of opposition, often because of their poor condition and because they had been identified for alternative use. However, this response altered quickly either because such occupation 'brought a measure of relief from the housing shortage' (Addison, 1995, p.68), or because government departments 'had neither the capacity nor the inclination to ... prevent homeless civilians from entering empty property' (Hinton, 1988, p.108). Posed in this way the problem turned on the politics of denying homes to people whose citizenship claims were authorized by their wartime sacrifices, especially when the government had promised so much and rested its moral case for extended citizenship rights on such sacrifice. Moreover, the political case against opposing squatting of military camps was compounded when Polish troops having fought with (and often for) Britain in the Second World War and finding themselves homeless and stateless, also attempted to resolve their own housing need by squatting some of the disused camps. War Office and Cabinet officials felt that 'awkward political questions might arise if homeless British subjects were held up by Poles from entering the empty camps' (CAB 129/12, 13 August 1946, quoted in Hinton, 1988, p.108). In other words some politicians and senior civil servants were concerned that popular unrest might be exacerbated if it was felt that Polish people were not being prevented from occupying the camps but British people were. Such political questions are of course contingent, rather than natural, in that they are an effect of the normalized equation 'nationality = citizen = (privileged) rights', rather than a potential alternative equation of 'human need = citizen = rights'. A tension that continues to reverberate as Saraga shows in Chapter 4.

A second type of squatting at this time was that aimed at privately owned properties. As with the camps, examples of such squatting could be found all over the country, but it was particularly widespread in Birmingham and London. The London story attracted most media attention, in part because five people involved in the London actions were arrested for conspiracy, a charge indicating the determination of the government to come down very hard on those threatening private property.

Squatting of private property seems to have begun on 21 August 1946 in Dundee when 40 families occupied an empty mansion of 100 rooms. Not all the properties occupied were privately owned, many having been requisitioned by local authorities for conversion into municipally owned housing for the working classes. Indeed, it was this occupation of properties already earmarked as working-class housing that Labour Councillors used in arguments against those in the Communist Party who were involved in the squatting movement.

However, for the working-class people attempting to resolve their housing needs there was much more involved in this form of squatting than an internecine war between political parties on the left. In London the occupation of private property began on 8 September 1946 when a block of flats in Kensington called Duchess of Bedford House that comprised 100 self-contained flats, was squatted by about 400 people. Though owned by the Prudential Assurance Company the block had been requisitioned by the government and was now offered to the local authority for use as social housing. The local authority had refused this offer and the block was about to be handed back to the Prudential. After this incident, occupation of empty properties by squatters spread across London, especially its somewhat exclusive upper middle-class areas.

As already indicated, the squatting of private property was very fiercely opposed by central and local government, led in many ways by Aneurin Bevan's steadfast refusal to listen to, let alone negotiate with, the squatters. Essential services were cut-off from occupied premises; criminal and civil law were used against squatters; premises and streets were blockaded by police in an attempt to prevent further occupation and other people getting supplies into the squatters; and the MI5 and Special Branch were detailed to gather information on those identified as leaders.

All in all this kind of squatting lasted no more than a few weeks, but its impact was more extensive than the period of action might suggest. For example, people who had squatted the Duchess of Bedford were temporarily re-housed until well into 1947, while other squatters gained permanent re-housing. In addition, local authority requisitioning of private property was speeded up so that more housing in decent conditions was potentially available to working-class people at affordable rents. Moreover, those who were arrested for conspiracy were treated with relative leniency and bound over to keep the peace for two years, instead of facing the imprisonment they might have expected.

ACTIVITY 2.4

Extracts 2.6 and 2.7 are taken from recollections of people who were members of the Communist Party and active in the London squatting activities of 1946. They were recorded and published as part of a pamphlet of the proceedings of a conference organized by the Communist Party in 1984. You should read carefully through them and as you do consider what these accounts might tell us about the connections between personal life and claims of citizenship. When you have done this you should think about what kind of evidence is provided by *recollections* such as these.

Extract 2.6 Hilda and Barney Lewis

We had been on the Hammersmith housing list for over 12 months. When my husband came out of the forces we approached the council who said we had no chance of accommodation as we had no children. We were staying with friends in Shepherds Bush in a single room and sharing facilities.

On Sunday 8th September 1946, my brother-in-law ... came to say there was squatting taking place in Kensington that day. He warned us that there was a risk of being arrested and possibly imprisonment, but we were prepared to take the chance. ...

We set off at 1 p.m. with a small attaché case containing an alarm clock and a few necessities. ... We were some of the first people, but as we were approaching the flats, others began to pour in and lorries packed with men, women and children and their bits and pieces, were converging on the area. ...

There were a lot of visits to different departments of housing to try to get people accommodated. By this time we had had notice to leave the Duchess of Bedford. After about ten days ... it was arranged for us to be transferred to quarters at Bromley House, Bow.

... This was not satisfactory ...

We were finally promised a temporary home at Alexandra House, Hampstead, which up until now was an old ladies' home. ...

There were now 100 families at Alexandra House. This was an improvement on Bromley House. ... The drawback was the lack of privacy, as we all had to sleep together, wash together and eat together.

The dormitories were separated, one for mothers with babies, one for mothers with children over 3 years, one for women without children and one upstairs for men and boys over 8 years old. Meals were prepared by L.C.C. [London County Council] staff and served at large tables. Men who were at work were given meals in the evening and the women's committee noticed that these were bigger and of better quality than those served to the women and children. Consequently, we saw the supervisor and ... asked for the same treatment for everyone; ... and the matter was rectified.

Already a lot was happening, as two families had been rehoused, the Ministry of Health had launched a new housing drive and the L.C.C. had agreed to deal with all squatters' cases instead of the local town halls. By October 8th, five families had been found homes.

We stayed at Alexandra House for about another six months. ... We were able to get a few improvements where families could be together ... though this only meant separate curtained spaces ... Gradually people were being rehoused, those with children and particular problems being given priority.

Eventually, ... those that were left were moved to an L.C.C. halfway house at Queens Gardens, Lancaster Gate. Here we all had our own sparsely furnished room. Meals were supplied in a communal dining room. This proved to be much better. People continued to be rehoused. We were finally offered a very derelict pokey flat at Rotherhithe which we refused, so had to leave.

(Branson, 1989, p.18)

Extract 2.7 Joyce Alergant

Every effort was made [by the government] to alienate public sympathy, [for the squatters], and it was only a matter of time before five people, myself included, were arrested. The charge was no simple trespass charge, but one of conspiracy carrying with it the prospect of an unspecified term of imprisonment.

...

The formal appearance at Bow Street [magistrate's court] a couple of weeks later was a rather nerve-wracking business.

...

I think it was the narrowness of the dock that put me off as much as anything else, but certainly one of the worst moments I have ever lived through came to me while I was there. The proceedings were very formal. The name of each defendant was called in turn and the arresting officer gave formal evidence of arrest. The officer was then asked: 'And when arrested did he say anything?' and in each case the answer was 'No'. I was the last to be identified and the usual question came: 'And when she was arrested did she say anything?' and the answer came 'Yes'.

The next moments were quite traumatic. If only the floor would open and swallow me up. What could I possibly have said? How could I have let down my companions and my Part so?

The voice droned on: 'And what did she say?'

She said: 'How about getting in touch with my solicitors?'

After that I was in no fit state for anything, and ... we [were to] be tried at a date to be set at the Old Bailey.

...

> As the time of the trial grew nearer, one secret fear haunted me. It was one that I could discuss with no one, but try as I might, I could not rid myself of its presence. I was tormented by the possibility of being given bacon to eat whilst in prison! For all my atheism I had never been able to overcome my childhood conditioning. The energy I expended on this remote possibility was undoubtedly the height of absurdity, but this bogey presented itself as greater than any fear of being 'put away' even for a two year period. I could avoid the difficulty by declaring myself Jewish, but that would be a denial of my atheism ... There just didn't seem to be a way out.
>
> (Branson, 1989, p.26)

COMMENT

In section 2.3 we noted some of the ways that personal lives and social policy intersect in a process of mutual constitution. In the accounts reproduced here we can see some additional dimensions of this relationship. First, the accounts illustrate the way in which 'the personal' is in part constituted at a crossing point between that which is defined as 'public' – here access to social housing, the collective making of citizenship claims – and that which is defined as 'private'. In this instance the 'private' decisions to be involved in both the Communist Party and the squatters' movement. In so far as the 'private' of the squatters' personal lives explicitly included the organization of their daily living arrangements, we can see how what we do in our own homes is always, in part, shaped by forces operating outside it. We can also note that the individual circumstance of the Lewis' childlessness meant that they had no legitimate claim to social housing according to the entitlement criteria operating at the time.

Second, these accounts illustrate that 'the personal' is always in a state of being made and remade in the dynamic of social, emotional and psychic processes. Thus, Alergant's evocative description of her anxiety over the bacon captures well some of the ways in which 'that which belongs to me' is brought into being in the context of lived social relations, and provides some of the terrain on which wider social life is interpreted and engaged with.

Finally, in so far as these accounts speak of a *collective* action to press claims of citizenship in a context when a certain minimum standard of living had been promised as part of a new contract between state and citizen, they illustrate a third aspect of 'the personal' of personal lives. This is that 'the personal' encompasses, yet is not reducible to, the individual. Just as people are both individuals and are positioned as social subjects convened around (and indeed embodying) social divisions and inequalities, so too the content of their personal life is both individual and collective.

These accounts then offer a useful window into aspects of 'the personal' of personal lives, and especially how this is configured and deployed in the context of welfare claims and citizenship practices. But what sort of evidence are such recollections? This is an important question to consider in the context of social science analysis. First, we should acknowledge that the form and content of recollections are shaped by the audience and its questions since they are generally produced in dialogue with another or others. This can result in the recalling, revision or repression of memories about particular events and experiences to meet the audience's demands or expectations. In this context the fact that those remembering were or had been connected through their political beliefs, and that they were speaking at an event organized by those with similar beliefs, could have shaped what was recollected.

We need also to appreciate the significance of the present for our interpretation of recollections of the past. Such an approach helps us to reflect upon the ways in which Joyce Alergant's ability to remember so vividly her fear of 'being given bacon to eat whilst in prison' might have been aided by the wider context in which her account was produced. So, for example, the political climate of the 1980s could have redrawn her attention to issues of ethnicity and identity – raised by anti-racist discourses and practices – which, in turn, enabled her to articulate the extent to which such issues were embedded in her particular anxieties about imprisonment in the 1940s.

More generally, this widespread movement to resolve housing need illustrates well some of the ways in which citizenship claims were being made by people who felt that the gap between promise and actual provision was intolerable and unacceptable. In this the squatters' movement exemplifies some of the ways in which the mutual constitution of personal lives and social policy is an on-going and indeterminate *process*. The social reforms which began in the period of the Second World War represented an extension of social citizenship, at least at the level of entitlement and promise, and in terms of the formal settlement between state and citizen. In so doing, a reformulated identity or subject position of citizen had become available to people. However, establishing the boundaries limiting the meanings ascribed to the category 'citizenship' was (and is) more difficult since there is always an 'excess' of meaning. It is into this discursive 'excess' that the squatters moved, expanding the horizons of social citizenship by making claims to a citizenship that both demanded 'the rewards of heroism' (Woolton, 1940, quoted in Addison, 1995, p.55) and expressed itself as a political subjectivity willing to act outside the bounds of the law in the name of sectional interest.

4 Film and representations of citizenship

Our discussion of the squatters' movement has illustrated some of the contested meanings and limits of the new post-war citizenship, and considered the tensions between hegemonic prescriptions of citizenship and individual/group citizenship claims. To pursue the nature of these contestations and tensions further, we turn our attention now to the way in which meanings and experiences of citizenship were represented in the cinema, and how these representations can help us explore in greater detail what we identified in section 3 as 'the structure of feeling' that permeated this period.

In the immediate post-war years, cinema-going was one of the most widespread leisure activities with audiences reaching an all-time peak in 1946. Perhaps predictably going to the cinema was most popular among young people, but the composition of audiences was 'to a surprising degree ...in proportions not greatly different from their relation to each other in the nation as a whole ...' (Rowntree and Lavers, 1951, p.231). Although people went to the cinema for many different reasons, this extent of cinema attendance across the country and across the classes means that we can look to post-war films as a rich historical source for capturing 'the aspirations, obsessions and frustrations of those who spend time and money making or viewing them' (Andrew, 1998, p.181). This is not to suggest that films should be understood as transparently readable documents that 'reflect' the past, allowing us direct insights into the concerns and issues that dominated at the time of their production (Young, 1996). It is rather that we see film as a form of qualitative data that, although rarely used in the field of social policy, can be drawn upon to explore how a given set of sensibilities connect to ways in which knowledge about an issue is produced. However, like all research evidence it must be interpreted and evaluated through a consideration of its wider political and socio-cultural contexts, of the messages it promotes or silences, and of the multiple ways in which issues and experiences are represented and given meaning.

With such an approach to film as 'evidence', it is possible for us to interrogate how particular ideas about citizenship in the post-war years were articulated and validated while others were marginalized or elided through this immensely influential and widely consumed cultural product. There were, however, multiple representations of citizenship played out in different ways in different **film genres** – categories of film defined by their specific styles, thematic contents or structures. For this reason, we have selected four very popular films from genres that dominated particular years between 1944 and 1960 to illustrate some of the struggles over the meaning of citizenship and the portrayal of 'the citizen' at this time.

film genres

The first films we have chosen are *This Happy Breed* (1944) and *Passport to Pimlico* (1949). The former comes out of the genre which has been identified as 'the melodrama of everyday life' (Higson, 1995, p. 262), and the latter from the sub genre of **Ealing comedies**. Both these genres dealt with particular ideas about belongings and practices of the everyday that, as we emphasized at the beginning of this chapter, became increasingly embedded in meanings of citizenship in these years. They sought to re-imagine not only the nation following the enormous social and economic challenges of the Second World War, but also the relationship between the nation and its people (Higson, 1995; Richards, 1997; Street, 1997). A powerful argument about films in these genres is the extent to which they imagined the nation as a community that was stable, consensual and centred, and represented its people as 'one large happy family' (Higson, 1994, p.67). Analysis of *This Happy Breed* and *Passport to Pimlico* allows us some insight, therefore, into the hopes and aspirations of people at the end of the Second World War and, in turn, to the structure of feeling in this historical moment.

Ealing comedies

However, as we have emphasized, neither meanings of citizenship nor structures of feeling were uniform in the post-war years. This is well illustrated by the very different representations of nation, citizenship and identity that were played out in the extremely popular cycle of Gainsborough **costume**

costume dramas

dramas. Films in this cycle were produced in England at the Gainsborough studios during and just after the Second World War, and can be loosely categorized as 'escapist bodice-rippers' which 'provided their audiences with subversive pleasures to be found in ... their shockability; their attractive rebels and their sumptuous costumes' (Street, 1997, p.57–8). Although these films 'received unparalleled critical opprobrium since they did not conform to the criterion of "good taste" ... they are crucial in any mapping of the field of popular taste in the 1940s and should be given major currency in any debates about the cultural resources ... in that period' (Harper, 2001, p.99). We have, therefore, selected *Madonna of the Seven Moons* (1944) from these Gainsborough costume dramas to explore how ideas of belongings – and especially the gendered meanings embedded within them – were also being used to question and subvert dominant approaches to citizenship that were circulating at the end of the Second World War, and to imagine alternative identities and subject positions.

New Wave

We then move to the end of our period when another very influential genre – British '**New Wave**' – was emerging. Here we consider the ways in which citizenship and 'the citizen' were represented by a genre which 'embraced the death of Empire, the rise of working-class affluence, the emergence of a distinctive youth culture and the revival of the intellectual left' (Richards, 1997, p.148). Using a key New Wave film, *Saturday Night and Sunday Morning* which was the third biggest box-office success of 1961 (Hill, 1986, p.45), we explore the significant shift in the portrayal of belongings and everyday practices, which now sees them associated with the constraint and limitation of personal lives. This film, like others in the same genre, is thus a useful source for tracing the many struggles over citizenship, especially in relation to normative constructions of everyday life in the later post-war years. In this it captures something of the ways in which the cinema was a central force in the construction, reproduction and validation of the structures of feeling that might be understood to mark late 1950s and early 1960s Britain.

4.1 Consensus, national identity and citizenship

We begin with *This Happy Breed* which was released in 1944 – the moment when the Second World War was coming to an end and aspirations for a more egalitarian future were being articulated, as we have emphasized, through the Beveridge Report and other government action that extended the British welfare state. The film follows the life of the Gibbons family – a lower middle-class family living in Clapham, South London – in the years between 1919 and 1939 while, at the same time, setting this 'private' sphere in the 'public' context of significant political and social events of the period. Home and family are, however, always dominant in this film at both the level of the national and the individual. The film opens with an aerial shot of London and a narrator declaring that with the return of men after the end of the First World War 'hundreds and hundreds of houses are becoming homes once more' and then shifts to the Gibbons family moving into their new home together. The conclusion to the film uses this same narrative strategy in reverse so that the audience watches the family leave their home before the camera pans out to the wider horizons of the city. As Higson (1994, p.71) argues, 'The shots that open and close the film are ... crucial in establishing the family/knowable community/nation relationship in as fluid and seamless a way as possible'. The construction of this relationship means that the Gibbons family home has also been interpreted as a metaphor for the nation – a space of security, stability and humanity where desire and responsibility are carefully balanced and where restraint is consistently admired (Higson, 1994). It should not be surprising then that the intersection of such powerful symbolism with the physical absence of a home motivated individuals like Hilda and Barney Lewis to challenge the new contract between state and citizen by joining the squatters' movement despite 'a risk of being arrested and possibly imprisonment' (see Extract 2.6).

The characteristics displayed by the Gibbons family can also be understood as representing a way of being, sense of self and community belonging that were so central to the new regime of citizenship that was under construction in the final years of the Second World War. The film's focus upon the Gibbons' extended family rather than the experiences of one family member emphasizes 'the social', and the responsibilities that individuals have for and to each other. The patterns of daily living in a regime of worker-citizenship – embedded in the Gibbons home through patriarchal authority, women's dependency and parental control – are portrayed as 'natural' and indicative of family life across the nation. The personal life of each member of the Gibbons family is represented through their relationship to other family members and their position within the family. This is captured cinematically by a repetitive return to the family gathered together in ordinary moments of daily life (Higson, 1994, p.71).

What emerges in the film is an absolute insistence on the Gibbons family – as a metaphor for the nation's people – maintaining its sense of self and belonging through the family home and its everyday practices and rituals. No opportunities are offered for broadening conceptions of 'the people' to those living outside the boundaries of the 'traditional' family or those whose personal lives were not constructed around for example, the culturally specific rituals of tea-drinking. In this film and other productions of the same period (see, for example, *Tawny Pipit*, 1944; *Millions Like Us*, 1943; *Brief Encounter*, 1945) the people are firmly represented as 'white Anglo' and there is little or no acknowledgement of the rapidly expanding 'racial' and ethnic diversity of Britain's population. As a result, for example, the significant role played by black and Asian British soldiers in the Second World War, the numbers of racialized minority communities across the country, and the presence of black American GIs in both rural and urban parts of Britain are absent. This is despite the extensive anxieties articulated in the press about a perceived growing black 'presence' throughout the first half of the twentieth century. The assumption in this film is, therefore, that 'white people are just people' (Dyer, 1997, p.2) whose personal lives can be understood as reflecting a human norm. Yet, as all the chapters in this volume illustrate, the complex intersections of nation, 'race'/ethnicity and citizenship define the parameters of 'the personal' and, in the context of social policy, shape its content through the regulation of access to welfare services and benefits.

Can you think of a British film you have seen recently in which there were similar absences in representations of 'the people'?

The scale of control by the state over personal lives was regarded as beneficial for society during the Second World War. However, as the post-war period continued to be marked by rationing and regulation, there was an increasing sense of resentment about, and resistance to, the bureaucratic control of everyday life indicating a fragility, if not faultline between state and people that gives testimony to the limits of 'the ethical state'. *Passport to Pimlico* has come to represent these struggles and throws some light on how the new regime of citizenship was perceived at a popular level during the second half of the 1940s.

Ealing films 'have been most persistent in the popular conception of late 1940s and early 1950s Britishness, particularly in America' (Street, 1997, p.69) and this comedy film, one of Ealing Studios's most successful, has a long history in shaping perceptions of post-war Britain and the meanings of citizenship. It is about the discovery of a treasure trove in a Pimlico bomb site, which held an ancient document proving that Pimlico belonged to the Duchy of Burgundy. The residents of Pimlico are thus offered an opportunity to free themselves from post-war restrictions and rationing, and the petty bureaucracy that appears to constrain their personal lives as British citizens. This is realized in a confrontation with local police when the film's central characters reject the licensing laws and tear up their identity cards, thereby formally refusing their citizenship status and declaring themselves 'Burgundian'. As one of the characters paradoxically insists later in the film: 'It's just because we are English that we're sticking up for our rights to be Burgundian'.

The archetypal language of citizenship is used to suggest the effects of this new territorial relationship between Pimlico and Britain. For example, when a bus pulls up in Pimlico, the conductor calls to the passengers: 'Step lively all you aliens' and one of the characters in the film, Miss Reid, is identified as a 'displaced person'. At the same time, Pimlico's 'foreignness' is evoked through the practices of boundary construction that define Pimlico as 'other' within the nation and through the notions of belonging that Pimlico's residents reject and challenge. As a result Customs posts are established on Pimlico's boundaries, and Immigration Officers check the status of all those leaving and entering the borough.

By allying themselves to Burgundy, the residents of Pimlico are able to reject the frustrating constraints of post-war Britain and its effects upon their personal lives and, to reinforce this point, the film is dedicated to the memory of ration books. One reading of the film might suggest, therefore, that the rights and duties of citizenship conferred upon the British people by the Beveridge Report that we discussed earlier were held in little regard. At the same time we might want to consider the extent to which audiences were being encouraged to question how arbitrary boundaries construct the nation, identify people as 'alien' and thereby regulate their presence and withhold their claims to citizenship. However, the scenes of unregulated profiteering that are shown to consume the streets of Pimlico as the community is besieged by gamblers and contraband racketeers mean that audiences are primarily

Figure 2.6 *Passport to Pimlico* (1949)

offered a very bleak picture of the effects upon a community of separation from the nation. Pimlico's stability is undermined by the chaotic waves of criminality which, in turn, unsettle the patterns of daily living and sense of belonging among its residents. It is only when a compromise is reached and Pimlico 'returns' to Britain – signified by a thunderstorm and the end of a heat wave that had marked its alliance with Burgundy – that those practices of the everyday linked to citizenship can be resumed. The dominant message of the film is, therefore, that 'rationing and restriction are better than the unrestrained growth of free enterprise. Co-operation is better than competition, community than individualism' (Richards, 1997, p. 136). The modes of regulation that shaped personal lives under the post-war welfare state's new regime of citizenship are thus shown to be a preferable option, despite the frustrations portrayed in the film, to the uncontrolled and uncontrollable alternatives.

4.2 The Gainsborough costume drama: hybrid identities and citizenship

The emphasis on stability and conformity that shaped so many post-war films and so much work by film critics does not, however, run across all films produced in the same period. Here, the work of feminist critics and historians (Cook, 1996; Harper, 1994) have been very influential for they have demonstrated the popularity of other film genres, particularly the Gainsborough costume dramas, and the ways in which these offer insights into more ambivalent attitudes towards dominant meanings of citizenship and national identity. By looking at films like *Caravan* (1946), *Madonna of the Seven Moons* (1944) and *The Wicked Lady* (1945), which were particularly successful with working-class women, but have seldom been integrated into studies of 'national cinema', feminist critics have questioned the extent to which notions of a consensual nation and a quintessential Britishness were portrayed and accepted in popular films. In particular, they have highlighted women's uncertain relationship to national identity and citizenship since, at the start of the Second World War in 1939, women had only been fully enfranchised citizens since 1928. This meant that their connection to citizenship and national identity was still being constructed at the point when their subject positions had to be redefined to take account of their wartime roles. These were then redefined again in the post-war years in light of Beveridge's vision of welfare. How individuals experienced and negotiated their shifting subject positions in the past can be difficult to ascertain (**Doolittle, 2004**; **Holden, 2004**). But, if we take the hugely popular Gainsborough costume dramas as a channel through which to open up the values, experiences and feelings of their predominantly working-class audiences, it is possible to point not only to some of the ambivalences around the gains and limitations of this 'new' citizenship, but also to the instability of national and gendered identities.

Why might such an approach to these films be important for understanding more about the structure of feeling at the end of the Second World War?

In this context Pam Cook (1996, p.90) has argued that these costume dramas suggest how 'identity is fluid and unstable ... and that national identity is not pure, but mixed'. Such a concern with questions of identity is particularly evident in *Madonna of the Seven Moons*. This film, set in the late 1930s, features the central character, Maddalena who has a 'dual personality' as a result, the film suggests, of being raped as a young girl. As Maddalena, she is a devout, modest woman who leads a quietly affluent life in Rome with her wealthy husband. She is portrayed as being conservative both in her style of dress and in her values. However, following an incident at her daughter's birthday party, Maddalena secretly dresses in 'gypsy' clothes, takes her jewellery and travels to Florence. The character's arrival in Florence and her passionate reunion there with her lover, Nino Berucci, demonstrate that Maddalena (now Rosanna) has lived with Nino previously during her marriage, on one occasion for a whole year, and that she is unaware of her 'other life' as dutiful wife and mother. Now, as Rosanna, she is confident and assertive, both sexually in her relationship with Nino, and in her dealings with his gang of thieves and pickpockets.

The character of Maddalena/Rosanna thus represents the tensions and contradictions in the construction of women's identities during this period, particularly through their relationship to home and family. Maddalena is constituted through a restrained, diffident and family-oriented femininity,

Figure 2.7 *Madonna of the Seven Moons* (1944)

which is in stark contrast to Rosanna who embodies an exciting, erotic and uninhibited female sexuality (Cook, 1996). These polar opposites can be understood to represent equally the traits of Britishness (personified in Maddalena) and a Europeanized 'other' (depicted by Rosanna). Using these oppositional differences we can begin to unpick the threats that the 'other' might be understood to pose to a nation determined to reinvent itself and the notion of citizenship by shaping personal lives, through the inculcation of the notions of constraint, legality, responsibility and morality. So, for example, Rosanna challenges not only what were seen to be the appropriate boundaries of women's personal lives in the 1940s, but also their construction and regulation for she has no 'home' other than the bedroom she shares with her lover above his tavern and no family ties. She celebrates such freedom in her own everyday life and in the world around her. In a visit with Nino to a large overgrown garden, Rosanna declares her preference for it over other more cultivated spaces: 'because it's so wild. It's broken the shackles that made it so neat and tidy'. We can see, therefore, that Rosanna's very individual power and freedom – experienced *outside* the home and family that belonged to her as Maddalena – unsettles the collective practices of responsibility, respectability and morality deemed central to the new regime of citizenship and, in turn, offers an alternative way of being and sense of self for women.

The dominant paradigm of national citizenship with its expression in the daily patterns of living can thus be seen as deeply unsettled by the Gainsborough cycle of films, which made visible and explored cultural diversity, mobility and transgression. Their emphasis on sexual relationships that cut across the boundaries of nation and class, and their location in the past, foregrounds a time and place when notions of individual responsibility for self and family, and the state's unity with its people, had little influence.

Yet, the final scene of *Madonna of the Seven Moons* can also be understood as representing the tensions between, on the one hand, constraint, duty, and responsibility and, on the other, freedom, choice, desire and passion: tensions which discourses of citizenship were also struggling to mediate in this period. As Maddalena/Rosanna lies on her deathbed, her husband places a crucifix on her breast while her lover, standing outside, throws a rose also onto her breast and the film concludes with a final shot of these two powerful signifiers of the tensions that shaped her personal life. Symbolically, therefore, the film fails to resolve or repress the conflicted aspects of its central character because of the excess of meaning that surrounded the gendered norms of women's personal lives – despite the reformulated subject position of women as citizens in the post-war welfare state.

4.3 The 'New Wave' genre: class, masculinity and citizenship

We can see then the different ways that the struggles over meanings of citizenship were played out in many films of the 1940s. However, by the late 1950s another genre, the British New Wave, was emerging that explicitly challenged the system of citizenship brought into being by the post-war welfare state. Between 1959 and 1963 the New Wave films emphasized the vitality of the present rather than the past, and foregrounded the 'realities' of working-class life in post-war Britain, particularly the frustrations of young white, urban working-class men with their everyday lives. We should note though that the New Wave genre had little direct comment to make on the nature of women's lives, although analysis of many of its films throws up 'a pervasive misogyny: the idea of marriage as a trap and the end of freedom for the male, the maltreatment of women by violence or exploitation, abuse or neglect' (Richards, 1997, p.153).

In what ways might such representations of gender relations throw light on the intersections of personal lives and social policy in this period?

The enormous success of this genre coincided with the exact moment when the long-term decline in cinema-going as a mass leisure pursuit was acknowledged (Laing, 1986). This trend alongside other social and economic changes to UK society has implications for our understanding of citizenship and the 'worker-citizen' in the later years of our period. The immediate post-war period of austerity that had been portrayed in *Passport to Pimlico* was gradually being transformed into a period of affluence, because of low levels of unemployment, rising wage rates and the growing availability of consumer goods (**Mooney, 2004**). The levels of affluence, independence and security enjoyed by young adults, however, were to become of growing concern in the 1950s and was represented in the media by a breakdown in moral values, an erosion of respect for the older generation and an excessive interest in money and material possessions. This is typified in a remark made by Noel Coward in 1957: 'I ... cannot understand why the younger generation, instead of knocking at the door, should bash the fuck out of it' (quoted in Weight, 2002, p.271). However, it was working-class life that was seen to be at risk from the UK's new found affluence with writers on the intellectual left, like Richard Hoggart in his influential *Uses of Literacy* (1957), arguing that the values of traditional working-class communities were being lost in the materialism and consumerism that increasingly marked popular culture.

ACTIVITY 2.5

Take a moment to read Extract 2.8 from Hoggart's *Uses of Literacy*. How is 'the personal' understood in this passage? In what ways are leisure practices described as constructing a sense of belonging and how are they critiqued?

Extract 2.8 Public space, private bewilderment

I have suggested earlier that working-class people cannot fail to be aware today, to a degree hardly known before, of the larger and public aspects of social life. They are aware of an area of life in which they undoubtedly have a part but which they often find difficult to comprehend. They naturally try to understand that outside life better by relating it to the personal and local life in which they know and act and suffer and admire. In such circumstances the desire for an assurance that the values of the local and the personal do count, that some sentiments which all can understand and appreciate as 'decent' are common to all, grows stronger. They are glad when a voice from that huge outer world uses their accents. Many politicians know this; most of the journalists who write features about the Royal Family know this. The proprietors of some holiday camps know this; their camps are vast and garishly splendid, but the cheer leaders set out to link everyone in 'pally' groups, and the WCs are marked 'lads' and 'lasses'. The promoters of football pools know this; they issue invitations to join their 'gang', 'circle', or 'group'. The wireless-variety and TV-cabaret stars of programmes specializing in false intimacy know this. The radio 'disc-jockeys' and the producers of radio programmes with 'resident teams' know this. Advertising broadcasters know this; they announce themselves as speaking from 'Your neighbourly radio' – and run programmes with such titles as 'Neighbour's Choice' and 'Friendly Fun' ... What a phoney sense of belonging all this is, this which is offered by the public pals of this publicly gregarious age; it would be better to feel anonymous; one might then be moved to some useful action to improve matters.

(Hoggart, 1957, pp.198–9)

COMMENT

We can see from Extract 2.8 that Hoggart understands 'the personal' as belonging to the individual and, thus, relating to individual experiences, attitudes and feelings. In this 'the personal' is held to intersect with 'the local', that is class-based neighbourhoods and communities, but not with 'public aspects of social life'. Hoggart thus identifies 'the personal' of the working classes as a clearly bounded and distinguishable 'private' context – lived out in the local domestic arena – and under threat because of its increasing infiltration by such media as radio, television and film. As a result, Hoggart's critique of the different forms of working-class leisure and their effects assumes a passively uncritical consumption of their values and aims. The sense of belonging that he argues is produced through popular culture is held, therefore, to be both superficial and without substance. Yet such an interpretation does not recognize the extent to which 'the personal' offers opportunities to negotiate and refuse dominant norms and attitudes not only in policy terms, but also in the context of Hoggart's discussion of the 'challenges' being experienced by working-class communities because of social change.

The concerns raised by Hoggart about the erosion of working-class values, attitudes and ways of being offer insights into how the personal lives of working-class women and men were conceptualized in this period. Similarly, research in the emerging discipline of sociology (for example, Young and Wilmott, 1957) looked at how the clearance of slum housing and changing patterns of education and employment were impacting upon working-class people and shaping their relationships, sense of self and belonging. There was, in addition, a growing interest in the extent to which the newly affluent working class might be undergoing a process of 'embourgeoisement'; that is coming to support and accept middle-class values and opinions in the context of full employment. Although the embourgeoisement thesis was ultimately refuted by the end of the 1960s (Goldthorpe et al., 1968), it was explored in a number of different arenas including the New Wave film *A Kind of Loving* (1962).

However, *Saturday Night and Sunday Morning* (1961), another film in the New Wave genre, overtly rejects the embourgeoisement thesis and also the much repeated claim that 1950s' Britain offered greater social mobility for working-class men. It vividly portrays the ways in which physical, emotional, material and psychological constraints continued to shape the personal lives of working-class people despite their British nationality status and their concomitant access to welfare services and benefits. Moreover, the film's central character, Arthur Seaton, can only be described as an 'anti-hero' who rejects any relationship he might have to those aspects of the citizenship regime – a way of being, a sense of self and community belonging – that were so well represented in *This Happy Breed* and *Passport to Pimlico.*

Saturday Night and Sunday Morning offers an uncompromising portrayal of working-class life in which Arthur Seaton exists only through the two worlds of paid work and leisure. In both these worlds, Arthur powerfully articulates his awareness of the state's intervention in his personal life and questions the benefits that he – as 'worker-citizen' - has been afforded by the state. In an early conversation with a friend, he complains: 'I work for the factory, the income tax and the insurance already. That's enough for a bit. They do you right, left and centre. After they've skinned you dry, you get called up in the army and you get shot to death'. Arthur emphasizes the demands and responsibilities imposed on him by the state – to work, pay income tax and insurance contributions and do his national service. There is little reflection on the gains afforded by the state to the 'worker-citizen' in this period, or acknowledgement that Arthur might be located in a wider regime of citizenship that could be traced through everyday practices of family and working life, and related notions of responsibility, moral standards and duty. Marriage and parenthood are represented as something to be avoided, while work relations are shown to be both superficial and competitive. Arthur has little respect for his parents, whom he defines as 'dead from the neck up', or neighbours whom he believes to be meddlesome and mean-minded, or work colleagues who are exploited and humiliated by him.

The result is a film that questions the meanings and effects of citizenship for young working-class men for whom paid work is neither fulfilling nor rewarding (except financially). Their way of being and sense of self is shown to be shaped not by their relationships to family and community or their class identifications, but by an individualistic search for freedom, pleasure and short-term gratification.

Figure 2.8 *Saturday Night and Sunday Morning* (1961)

Anything and anyone that stands in the way of that search is brutally dispatched as demonstrated by Arthur's rejection of working-class respectability and his pregnant married lover. Yet, at the same time, the film treats the character and his frustration at the constraints of his personal life with some sympathy. His employment in the Raleigh bicycle factory is noisy, dirty and repetitive, and life outside work amounts to little more than drinking binges and fishing from desolate urban river banks. Work is shown to be both degraded and degrading, offering little of substance or value to young men whose rights and claims have been so tightly entwined with its pursuit by the post-war welfare state.

Saturday Night and Sunday Morning concludes with a scene in which Arthur and his girlfriend, sitting on a hillside, look down at a new housing estate and reflect that after they marry one of the houses may belong to them. Arthur, however, also comments that the estate is being built on countryside where he had roamed as a child with friends. The conflict between the freedom and escape that this land had offered the young Arthur, and the demands and needs for adequate homes that were being addressed by 1950s' and 1960s' slum clearance and house building programmes is an interesting one and points, again, to an excess of meaning around citizenship that the film is unable to resolve. It reveals a core tension in the relation between the citizen and the state which we stressed earlier; namely the subordination of individual freedom (Arthur's right to roam) to ensure that the collective interests of 'the people' (for housing) can be met while, at the same time, insisting on the importance of that freedom in discourses of citizenship. What the character of Arthur Seaton exposes is the extent to which the ideological project of the post-war welfare state to create 'the ethical subject' who could successfully negotiate and manage this tension was far from successful. There were undoubtedly material and physical gains for individual working-class women and men as a result of the collective provision of welfare services and benefits. But, if we take the New Wave genre as some indication of the structure of feeling in this period, we can see that the resulting limitations upon personal lives – in terms of sense of self, identity and opportunities for alternative ways of being – were clearly understood and deeply resented.

5 Conclusion

In this chapter we have explored the development of a widened and deepened social citizenship that was instituted in the period following the Second World War. We have argued that the foundations of this expanded citizenship were provided by the recognition of the enormous social, economic and political costs of the mass unemployment of the interwar years, the sacrifices made by people in the war years themselves and an ideology of constrained collectivism in which an 'ethical state' attempted to suture state and people into a single unity. Drawing on the theoretical perspectives of Gramscian Marxism and feminist cultural analysis we have shown that this expanded citizenship gave rise to a number of tensions. There was the tension resulting from the perceived need to balance a degree of collectivism with the interests and workings of the capitalist economy and the promotion of a sense of individual and national responsibility. There was the tension resulting from the gap between promise and provision and the actions of groups of people seeking to promote sectional interest and the satisfaction of their needs. And there was the tension, expressed in cinematic representations of these decades, that resulted from the ambivalences of this new citizenship in terms of uncertainties as to the gains and losses it entailed. In exploring these aspects of the 'high moment' of social citizenship that the welfare state expressed and institutionalized we have suggested that citizenship is a profoundly relational, negotiated and indeed contested set of relations. We have drawn on recollections, contemporaneous policy documents and films as different forms of qualitative data and these have helped us to illustrate the mutually constitutive relation between personal lives and social policy as expressed in engagements with and struggles for forms of citizenship.

Further resources

Ruth Lister's *Citizenship: Feminist Perspectives* (2003) provides a comprehensive and complex discussion of feminist engagements with and claims to citizenship; Maurice Roche's *Rethinking Citizenship* (1992) is also valuable, providing an exploration of a number of differing approaches to citizenship. If you would like to know more about the political, social and cultural contexts of this chapter, the following may be helpful: Steven Fielding et al.'s *'England Arise!': The Labour Party and Popular Politics in 1940s Britain* (1995); James Obelkvitch et al.'s *Understanding Post-War British Society* (1994); and Becky Conekin et al.'s *Moments of Modernity: Reconstructing Britain, 1945–1964* (1999). Nicholas Timmins offers a very comprehensive history of the development of welfare in the post-war period in *The Five Giants: A Biography of the Welfare State* (1996). For an in-depth picture of British cinema in the 1940s, 1950s and 1960s see Christine Gledhill and Gillian Swanson's *Nationalizing Femininity: Culture, Sexuality and British Cinema in the Second World War* (1996); Ian MacKillop and Neil Sinyard's *British Cinema of the 1950s: A Celebration* (2003) and Wendy Hewing's *British Cinema in the 1960s* (2003).

References

Addison, P. (1995) *Now the War is Over: A Social History of Britain, 1945–1951,* London, Pimlico Press.

Andrew, D. (1998) 'History and film' in Hill, J. and Gibson, P.C. (eds) *The Oxford Guide to Film Studies*, Oxford, Oxford University Press.

Bevan, A. (1952) *In Place of Fear*, London, Heinemann.

Beveridge, W. (1942) *Social Insurance and Allied Services* (The Beveridge Report), Cmnd 6404, London, HMSO.

Beveridge, W. (1944) *Full Employment in a Free Society,* London, HMSO.

Beveridge, W. (1948) *Voluntary Action,* London, HMSO.

Branson, N. (ed.) (1989) *The London Squatters 1946* (Pamphlet 80), London, Communist Party History Group.

Carabine, J. (ed.) (2004) *Sexualities: Personal Lives and Social Policy*, Bristol, The Policy Press in association with The Open University.

Clarke, R.W.B. (1943) *The Beveridge Report and After,* London, Fabian Society.

Conekin, B., Mort, F. and Waters, C. (eds) (1999) *Moments of Modernity: Reconstructing Britain, 1945–1964,* London, Rivers Oram Press.

Cook, P. (1996) *Fashioning the Nation: Costume and Identity in British Cinema,* London, British Film Institute.

Doolittle, M. (2004) 'Sexuality, parenthood and population: explaining fertility decline in Britain from the 1860s to 1920s' in Carabine (ed.) (2004).

Duncan, S. and Edwards, R. (1999) *Lone Mothers, Paid Work and Gendered Moral Rationalities,* Basingstoke, Macmillan.

Dyer, R. (1997) *White,* London, Routledge.

Fielding, S., Thompson, P. and Tiratsoo, N. (1995) *'England Arise!': The Labour Party and Popular Politics in 1940s Britain,* Manchester, Manchester University Press.

Foucault, M. (1992) *The Archaeology of Knowledge,* London, Tavistock.

Fraser, D. (1973) *The Evolution of the British Welfare State,* London, Macmillan.

Gaster, J. (1989) 'The army camps squat' in Branson, N. (ed.) *The London Squatters 1946* (Pamphlet 80), London, Communist Party History Group.

Gledhill, C. and Swanson, G. (eds) (1996) *Nationalizing Femininity: Culture, Sexuality and British Cinema in the Second World War,* Manchester, Manchester University Press.

Goldthorpe, J.H., Lockwood, D., Bechhoffer, F. and Platt, J. (1968) *The Affluent Worker: Industrial Attitudes and Behaviour,* Cambridge, Cambridge University Press.

Gramsci, A. (1971) *The Prison Notebooks* (trans. Q. Hoare), London, Lawrence and Wishart.

Hall, S. and Schwarz, B. (1985) 'State and society, 1880–1930' in Langan, M. and Schwarz, B. (eds) *Crisis in the British State, 1880–1930,* London, Hutchinson.

Harper, S. (1994) *Picturing the Past: The Rise and Fall of the British Costume Film,* London, British Film Institute.

Harper, S. (2001) 'Historical pleasures: Gainsborough costume melodrama' in Landy, M. (ed.) *The Historical Film: History and Memory in Media,* London, The Athlone Press.

Hewing, W. (2003) *British Cinema in the 1960s,* London, British Film Institute.

Higson, A. (1994) 'Reconstructing the nation: this happy breed' in Dixon, W.W. (ed.) *Re-Viewing British Cinema 1900–1992: Essays and Interviews,* Albany, State University of New York Press.

Higson, A. (1995) *Waving the Flag: Constructing a National Cinema in Britain,* Oxford, Oxford University Press.

Hill, J. (1986) *Sex, Class and Realism: British Cinema 1956–63*, London, British Film Institute.

Hinton, J. (1988) 'Self-help and socialism: the squatters' movement of 1946', *History Workshop Journal*, vol.25, pp.100–26.

HMSO (1944) *Employment Policy*, Cmnd 6527, London, HMSO.

Hoggart, R. (1957) *The Uses of Literacy*, Harmondsworth, Penguin.

Holden, K. (2004) 'Personal costs and personal pleasures: care and the unmarried woman in inter-war Britain' in Fink (ed.) (2004) *Care: Personal Lives and Social Policy,* The Policy Press in association with The Open University.

Hughes, G. and Lewis, G. (eds) (1998) *Unsettling Welfare: The Reconstruction of Social Policy*, London, Routledge in Association with The Open University.

Jones, K. (1994) *The Making of Social Policy in Britain, 1830–1990* (2nd edn), London, Athlone Press.

Laing, S. (1986) *Representations of Working-Class Life, 1957–1964*, Basingstoke, Macmillan.

Leeson, S. (1938) *The Ethical Basis of Citizenship*, London, Association for Education in Citizenship.

Lister, R. (2003) *Citizenship: Feminist Perspectives,* Basingstoke, Palgrave Macmillan.

Lloyd, D. and Thomas, P. (1998) *Culture and the State*, London, Routledge.

MacKillop, I. and Sinyard, N. (eds) (2003) *British Cinema of the 1950s: A Celebration,* Manchester, Manchester University Press.

Macey, D. (2000) *Dictionary of Critical Theory*, Harmondsworth, Penguin.

Marshall, T.H. (1950/63) 'Citizenship and social class' in *Sociology at the Crossroads and Other Essays,* London, Heinemann.

Mooney, G. (ed.) (2004) *Work: Personal Lives and Social Policy*, The Policy Press in association with The Open University.

Obelkevich, J. and Catterall, P. (eds) (1994) *Understanding Post-War British Society,* London, Routledge.

Pollard, S. (1969) *The Development of the British Economy 1914–1967* (2nd edn), London, Edward Arnold Limited.

Richards, J. (1997) *Films and British National Identity: From Dickens to Dad's Army*, Manchester, Manchester University Press.

Roche, M. (1992) *Rethinking Citizenship: Welfare, Ideology and Change in Modern Society,* Cambridge, Polity Press.

Rowntree, B.S. and Lavers, G.R. (1951) *English Life and Leisure: A Social Study,* London, Longmans, Green and Co.

Saville, J. (1957/8) 'The welfare state: an historical approach' reprinted in Fitzgerald, M., Halmos, P., Muncie, J. and Zeldin, D. (eds) (1977) *Welfare in Action*, London, RKP in association with The Open University. (First published in 1957/8 in *New Reasoner 3*. Reprinted in 1975 in Butterworth, E. and Holman, R. (eds) *Social Welfare in Modern Britain*, Fontana.)

Street, S. (1997) *British National Cinema*, London, Routledge.

Timmins, N. (1996) *The Five Giants: A Biography of the Welfare State,* London, Fontana Press.

Weight, R. (2002) *Patriots: National Identity in Britain, 1940–2000*, London, Macmillan.

Williams, R. (1961) *The Long Revolution,* London, Chatto and Windus.

Williams, R. (1977) *Marxism and Literature*, Oxford, Oxford University Press.

Williams, R. and Oram, M. (1954) *Preface to Film*, London, Film Drama.

Young, L. (1996) *Fear of the Dark: 'Race', Gender and Sexuality in the Cinema*, London, Routledge.

Young, M. and Wilmott, P. (1957) *Family and Kinship in East London,* London, Routledge and Kegan Paul.

CHAPTER 3

Differentiated Citizenship: Psychic Defence, Social Division and the Construction of Local Secondary School Markets

by Helen Lucey

Contents

1 Introduction

This chapter sets out to illustrate the interconnectedness of personal lives and social policy by looking at one particular process that has come to hold enormous meaning and influence at the most private and public levels: transfer from primary to secondary school. This move takes place in the UK at the end of Year 6 when most children are aged 11 and is a 'critical moment' in the biographies of individuals (Thomson *et al.*, 2002). Going to 'big school' will usually mean losses of some kind: of friends, teachers and familiar surroundings. It will mean getting used to a new timetable, curriculum and different teaching and learning styles. There are potential gains too, in the making of new friends, and of beginning to gain independence from the family – as such, it can be eagerly anticipated. Hopes and fears for the future are brought into sharp focus and come to rest on this biographical moment, and it is increasingly seen as vital that children get a place at the 'right' secondary school.

Transfer from primary to secondary school has been the site of intense policy intervention and regulation since the 1940s, and from that time structural, professional and curricular reforms transformed the educational landscape. From the 1990s the process of primary–secondary transfer began to take place in a policy context which stressed choice, diversity, performance and productivity, with parents/carers constructed as 'citizen-consumers' in competitive 'secondary school markets'.

However, these and other official accounts of educational policy and discourses of citizenship tend to gloss over the ways in which both policy and discourse impact upon and are 'lived' by actual people. They privilege rationality and agency, and emphasize sameness and equality. Such accounts are riddled with gaps and silences because they deny that people and governments may be subject to fears and desires, emanating from *within*, that are profoundly irrational, and that there are forces from *without* over which people have little or no control. As a potentially defining stage in the lives of children, secondary school transfer can be extremely anxiety-provoking. Despite this, the policies that govern and regulate school choice are presented as allowing choice and rational decision-making in an equal landscape, ignoring the disparities and differences that exist between local secondary school markets in different parts of England and Wales – between urban, suburban and rural areas. Moreover, they also deny that there are significant and enduring inequalities along social axes such as gender, social class, disability, 'race'/ethnicity and region.

Aims

This chapter aims to:

choice

- Address some of the gaps in official accounts of school **choice** by exploring how personal lives and social policy are mutually constituted both psychically and socially.
- Examine the 'states of mind' that can arise for children and parents/carers who are conceived of as citizens (or 'citizen-consumers') and become the recipients of changing school-choice policy.

- Explore the ways in which educational policy itself holds certain anxieties about the very citizens at which it is aimed.
- Illustrate how these anxieties, carried through social policy, become active in the social world where they fuse with individuals' anxieties and shape the personal lives of children and parents, carers, teachers and schools to produce everyday practices that have real effects – some positive, some negative.

Part of the challenge is how to think about and articulate the non-rational in the analysis of the relationship between personal lives, social policy and public institutions. We argue that, for this, a theoretical framework is needed that can work with both the social and psychic elements of human experience. It is for this reason that we use a psychosocial perspective, an approach that seeks to highlight the connections between spheres of experience that are more usually considered as separate and unconnected.

Section 2 looks at changing conceptions of citizens and citizenship since the 1980s and the application of market principles in education. In section 3, we sketch out the principal elements of a psychosocial approach and in section 4 the theoretical details of this framework are explored. Here, key concepts from the Kleinian and object relations schools of psychoanalysis are laid out. Section 5 considers the application of psychoanalytic concepts to social analysis. In section 6, we use a psychosocial framework to explore data taken from an empirical study of children's perspectives and experiences of 'choosing' a secondary school in order to demonstrate how this process, and the policies surrounding it, are mutually constituted through a dense matrix of private and public, individual and group, psychic and social processes.

All the empirical data referred to in this chapter comes from a qualitative study of children's transitions from primary to secondary school, which I conducted with Diane Reay (Lucey and Reay, 2002a, 2002b; Reay and Lucey, 2003) entitled 'Secondary school transfer: children as consumers of education'. It was funded by the Economic and Social Research Council. The study was located in two London boroughs, Ashbury and Eastcote, and eight primary schools took part. In Year 6 (aged 10–11 years) we conducted group interviews with 454 children and individual interviews with 45 children. We also interviewed 58 parents, teachers and headteachers. Any material quoted within the chapter but not attributed comes from unpublished material from this study.

2 The active citizen-consumer

All social policies contain implicit or explicit ideas about the value systems, moral codes and everyday lives of the subjects to which a policy relates. Although presented as altogether rational, it would seem that rather less rational notions and judgements about certain populations – in particular the poor, the working classes and racialized groups – inform the social policies to which these groups are subject. It could be said that anxieties about certain groups of people lie at the heart of much social policy formulation. We can see this if we look at the history of mass education in the UK. From its earliest beginnings in the late nineteenth century, educational reform was concerned not only with the improvement of the everyday lives and life chances of the working classes, but also with their regulation. Education was seen as the way to eradicate what were said to be the bad habits of mind and body that were seen as the cause of their impoverished lives. It was also a way for the governing upper class and the expanding ranks of professional middle classes to guard against their fears that 'the masses' might turn to riot and revolution if deep social inequalities were not addressed. Education was seen as the key means through which to curb the crude, unreasonable and aggressive nature of the working classes and promote in them the reason and rationality purportedly characteristic of the liberal, democratic 'subject' or citizen. In this sense education was a key site for the operation of 'the ethical state' referred to in the previous chapter.

Although important ideas about the subject of social policy have come to be articulated through the notion of the 'citizen', it is not a stable category and has undergone much contestation and reconceptualization over the last century. In the late 1980s, under the auspices of the New Right, there was a decisive shift from the idea of citizens as passive recipients of welfare towards a far more 'active' notion of citizenship that emphasized competitive self-interest, individual rights and personal responsibilities and obligations. This view was heavily influenced by rational choice theory, originating in the economics of consumption and constructed around the idea that people rationally calculate the likely costs and benefits of any action before deciding what to do. These ideals of citizenship are ones that the Labour governments of the late 1990s and early 2000s incorporated into the 'Third Way'. Through a commitment to market principles in public service provision, Labour further developed the idea of the '**citizen-consumer**' that was enshrined in Conservative policy documents such as *The Parent's Charter* (DES, 1991) and *The Citizen's Charter* (1991), both published in the same year. These represented citizenship both as a status and as a form of rights to information and to choice. Here, the citizen was conceptualized as an autonomous, self-conscious chooser who has real power as an active consumer (as opposed to a passive recipient) of services.

citizen-consumer

This model of the citizen emerged alongside other ideas about how rapid local, national and global changes have impacted on the social world to produce a 'risk society' (Beck, 1992). In contrast to an earlier, idealized world, characterized by certainty, there were now seen to exist unavoidable risks beyond government control and for which the new citizen-consumer must take individual *responsibility*. As David Miliband MP, Minister of State for School Standards, said in 2002: 'When creativity is at the heart of the learning process it contributes to the soft skills that are central to active citizenship; group work, communication, improvisation, problem-solving and the management of risk and uncertainty' (Miliband, 2002).

The active citizens summoned up in this quotation were charged with the responsibility of managing their own welfare through a process of continuous assessment that enabled them to make choices about how best and from what source to meet their welfare needs. This entailed a new balance between individual and collective rights and between rights and responsibilities. While

Figure 3.1 'Hailing the young as citizens'

the forces that influence peoples' personal lives remained highly structured, at the same time the ideology of the 'active citizen' encouraged citizens to seek solutions on an individual rather than a collective basis. This had the effect of 'individualizing' experiences: viewing setbacks and crises as personal failure, even though these were often connected to processes and structures far beyond personal control.

2.1 The citizen-consumer and quasi-markets in education

ACTIVITY 3.1

We can set the scene by looking at a piece of official policy on school choice. Extract 3.1 below is a short extract from *The Parent's Charter*, a pamphlet that was delivered to every household in Britain in 1991 under the Conservative government of John Major. As you read the extract, think about and make notes on:

- the conception of the 'citizen' that is embedded in the Charter;
- the key characteristics of this citizen;
- whether the citizen being addressed is the parent or the child.

Extract 3.1 *The Parent's Charter*

This charter will help you become a more effective partner in your child's education. As a parent you have important responsibilities. Good schools work better if they have your active support. Your child's education is your concern – and you will want to play your full part at every stage. ...

You have a **right to a free school place for your child** from age 5 to age 16, and a school or college place from 16 to 18.

You have a duty to ensure that your child gets an education – and you can choose the school that you would like your child to go to. ...

When the time comes to choose a school, most parents find it helpful to talk to other parents and visit some schools, as well as reading prospectuses. When you have made up your mind, you have the **right to say which school you prefer**.

(DES, 1991, pp.1, 8, 9, original emphases)

COMMENT

This extract contains an elaboration of ideas about the citizen as consumer conceptualized as an individual making rational choices. Parents were to be given greater freedom of choice about which school they sent their child to. Autonomy is a core characteristic of the modern 'citizen-consumer' for whom being able to exercise the right to choose from a range of options in a diverse market is an important aspect. Alongside the 'right to choose', the Charter stressed the 'right to know' and promised that schools would provide certain kinds of information about each child's progress and performance and that of the school. This represented one of the ways in which the citizen/parent was reconceptualized – no longer a passive recipient of a state service for their children, but rather an active agent who kept an eye on the providing agency – that is, the school – and did something about it if the agency failed or did not deliver what was wanted by the citizen/parent. You will note that this document does not address children: it is parents who are viewed as the key actors in school choice. The dominant view of children as passive is reflected in their marginalization and their subsequent invisibility in policy and research. Note too that the 'right' accorded the active citizen (the parent) is to say which school they prefer. This is not the same as successfully getting a place in that school.

Sharon Gewirtz (2002) traces the shift in education policy and provision from what is termed 'welfarism' through to 'post-welfarism'. The welfarist settlement, developed from the mid 1940s to the mid 1980s, was based upon a pledge to tackle social inequality by redistributing social goods on a fairer basis. This ideal was reflected through educational policy which created the post-war expansion of secondary schooling, the introduction of comprehensive schooling and the raising of the school leaving age. However, in the post-welfarist phase of the 1980s and 1990s, 'the formal commitments to Keynesian economics and distributive justice were dropped and replaced by formal commitments to market "democracy" and competitive individualism' (Gewirtz, 2002, p.2).

A key piece of legislation in the structuring of education markets in England and Wales was the 1988 Education Reform Act. This allowed schools to opt out of local education authority (LEA) control and become grant-maintained – funded directly by central government. Such schools received higher levels of funding than LEA schools and were granted greater autonomy and control over their pupil admissions. This move went hand in hand with the construction of parents/carers as consumers in that they could vote on whether or not a school opted out. Removing restrictions on enrolment meant that parents/carers were no longer limited by catchment area and were able to look for places in schools further away. This led to increased competition between schools, which were compelled to give much more information to parents/carers and, thus, self-consciously to market themselves. (We have used the term 'parents/carers' here in recognition that parental figures are not always linked biologically to their children. In the rest of the chapter we use the term 'parent' but this should be taken as referring to all parental figures, whether or not biologically related to the child.)

Interwoven with these developments was a stress on quality and the raising of standards in education, where standards became narrowly understood as academic achievement. The Education Reform Act introduced a national curriculum which had regular testing of pupils built into it through Standardised Attainment Tests (SATs) administered at the end of four 'Key Stages': in Year 2 (age 7), Year 6 (age 11), Year 9 (age 14) and at GCSE (age 16). It is these results that are published in national league tables. The 1992 Education Act set up the Office for Standards in Education (Ofsted) and a new schools inspection regime. Moves towards a model which stressed efficiency, effectiveness, choice, diversity, performance and productivity may have been initiated by Conservative governments in the 1980s and 1990s, but they were subsequently enhanced and extended by the Labour governments that first entered power in 1997. The 1997 Education Act pushed the focus on efficiency and achievement further by requiring each school's governing body to set performance targets for its pupils in all public examinations and Key-Stage assessments and to make them public. The constant auditing of schools became a routine feature of pupils', parents' and teachers' lives.

"Congratulations! It's a pass."

Figure 3.2

ACTIVITY 3.2

Keeping in mind the points raised from *The Parent's Charter* and from the policy developments outlined above, read Extract 3.2, in which some Year 6 children aged between 10 and 11 years, who attended an inner-city primary school, talk about the local secondary schools and about their experiences of choosing a secondary school. All the children are white British. Ngaio, Alex and Annie are from professional middle-class families; Kimberley and Victoria are from working-class families. As you read, make a note of:

- the key concerns of the children;
- how these concerns compare with the main issues in Extract 3.1 from *The Parent's Charter*;
- what the children's talk tells us about the lived experience of quasi-markets in education.

Extract 3.2 Competition, choice and the management of limited opportunity

Victoria: Westbury is very good, but I wouldn't be able to get in, because –

Kimberley: – it is quite short, where they restrict the area. Yeah, it's only 0.6 of a mile.

Helen: Why is that do you think?

Alex: Because loads of people want to get in.

Annie: Because Westbury, there are only a couple of mixed [co-educational] secondary schools left, except for Chiltern is mixed, but Chiltern's not a very good school. Westbury's quite a good school.

Ngaio: I think with Danemouth Girls you have to put it down as your first choice or you've got no chance of getting in.

Victoria: I wanted to go [to] Westbury. But in the end I just had to go to Danemouth Girls because it's nearer, and if I would have put Westbury as my first choice, and then if I didn't get in Danemouth Girls wouldn't want me then.

COMMENT

The children's narratives highlight how the principles and aims of a particular social policy can be contradicted by personal experience. Although it is children who are the recipients of schooling, they are rarely considered as active players in educational decision-making. This extract reveals that, far from being passive and/or naïve, they have considerable knowledge of the local education 'market' in which they are trying to make choices. *The Parent's Charter* emphasizes that parents have the right to choose which school their child goes to (see again Extract 3.1). However, the children's comments reveal that exercising this 'right' is not straightforward when quasi-market principles are governing schools and that choosing and 'getting' are not the same thing (Reay and Lucey, 2003). They are clear about which schools they have 'no chance' of getting a place at. We learn that popular schools like Westbury operate active mechanisms of exclusion which militate against choice because, as Alex says, 'loads of people want to get in'. Victoria's comments reveal how children and parents must develop strategies of risk management and compromise in order to get even their second choice.

If families do not live in the right place for the 'right' school (and this in itself is a highly contingent equation, complexly connected to social class, gender, ethnicity, religion and culture), then negotiating the difficulties posed by an unequal secondary school market requires knowledge of the system, cultural capital and financial capital – as Figure 3.3 suggests, parents who are able to are prepared to pay inflated house prices in order to move into the catchment area of a desirable school. It also requires the management of the anxieties provoked by a confrontation with the inequities of the education system at a **biographical moment** that is deeply implicated in the construction of subjectivity. After all, going to the 'right' school is all about the person we are and the person we want to become. Jack, a 10-year-old, white British working-class boy at the same school as the children in the group, makes this

biographical moment

How much will it cost you to live near the best schools?

A survey reveals a strong link between good schools and soaring house prices, writes Robert Winnett

THE average home near a top state school costs almost ... ing poor schools cost an average of £81,242.

Bruno Rost of Experian says: ... very easy to identify

Yolande Barnes, head of research at Savills, an estate estate agent, says: "Compared with private school fees, buying a home close to a good state ...

CAN YOU AFFORD TO LIVE NEAR A GOOD SCHOOL?

City/School	House price[1]	City/School	House price[1]	City/School	House price
Birmingham	**£74,112**	**Derby**	**£69,626**	**Manchester**	**£58,490**
Heart of England School	£162,252	Highfields School	£95,094	Urmston Grammar	£72,347
Bishop Vesey's Grammar	£109,429	John Port School	£94,329	Parrenthorn High	£52,041
Sutton Coldfield	£87,096	Thomas Alleyne's	£78,084	The King David High	£51,421
Bishop Walsh	£86,102	The Ecclesbourne	£77,714	St Monica's	£48,290
Selly Park for Girls	£78,244	Landau Forte College	£60,521	Audenshaw School	£44,742
King Edward VI Five Ways	£72,753	Chellaston School	£55,395	Fairfield Girls	£39,758
			£81,567	**Middlesborough**	**£61,835**
				Stokesley School	£114,238
					£78,221

House prices up to 20% higher in areas with good state schools, study shows

Will Woodward
Education editor

Parents are prepared to pay almost 20% more for their homes ... house prices in Coventry to test statistically anecdotal evidence that house prices were higher because of the schools ... – more than £20,000 higher. Inside Finham Park's catchment area in Earlsdon ... "It doesn't surprise me, but it saddens me ..."

Figure 3.3 Some school catchment areas affect house prices

connection succinctly: 'Most people that's been to Sutton Boys, they have very bad exams and have been like a pizza boy. Which I don't mind, because I like pizza, but I don't want to sell it' (quoted in Lucey and Reay, 2002a)

The children's narratives graphically reveal the gaps and contradictions between official accounts of school choice and the lived experiences of a moment in which the individual's 'personal' clashes with the 'public' world of social policy.

3 A psychosocial approach

> ... the most persuasive and rounded stories are psychosocial. They move between the intimate, local and particular and the wider culture and institutions. We need more than sociology to develop these accounts ...
>
> (Froggett, 2002, p.32)

Shifts in the conception of the citizen, the ways in which these influence an important moment in the life of children and parents, and the institutional responses generated by the competitive atmosphere of 'name and shame' league tables, coalesce to produce a set of dynamics that are both social and psychic. Given this complex relation between internal and external forces, analysis of this phase of transition requires a **psychosocial approach**. The main features of such an approach are:

psychosocial approach

- A psychosocial perspective emphasizes the dynamic, relational nature of psychic and social life. It assumes that there are clear, though complex, connections between states of mind and individual, social, institutional and political life.
- In order to map those connections, a psychosocial approach brings concepts together that can take account of the *interior* processes of the human mind (to look at individual and group emotions) with those that

relate to the *exterior*, public arenas of the social world (to examine structure and power).

- This approach assumes that *unconscious* as well as conscious processes come to bear on the everyday practices that make up personal lives and shape social policy.
- A psychosocial approach maintains that anxiety, and the strategies developed to defend against the difficult feelings that anxiety provokes, plays an important part in the construction of private, social and institutional lives.
- A psychosocial approach assumes that there are levels of our perception and experience that are deeply irrational. The privileging of rationality and reason in educational policy and discourses of citizenship denies important aspects of human experience.
- A psychosocial perspective on welfare policy maintains that public institutions embody contradictions that are inherent in the lives of citizens (Hoggett, 2003).

3.1 Research evidence

The study 'Secondary school transfer: children as consumers of education', on which this chapter draws, was concerned to make links between the larger, 'macro', political picture in which children were located and the everyday, 'micro' landscapes of their personal lives. A psychosocial approach provided a valuable framework through which to do this. A psychosocial approach means paying attention not only to the 'objective facts' of a narrative, but also to the patterns underlying accounts of experience: to the organization of stories; the occurrence of words and images; to contradictions; and to absences and silences (Lucey et al., 2003). Only fragments of the children's narratives are presented here, although the extracts exemplify themes that were consistently present across this large data set. However, while I know this as one of the researchers, it can be difficult for readers who are not privy to the knowledge and information that informs and shapes my analysis – information relating to the children, schools, the history and character of local areas and the development of education markets in that particular locale. This indicates that the relationship between research data and the theoretical arguments and claims made by those working with such data are always mediated by a process of interpretation.

What problems can you envisage that may lead to misinterpretation when selecting data for an argument in this way?

ACTIVITY 3.3

Table 3.1 is an extract from the performance tables for secondary schools for 2002, showing GCSE and GNVQ (General National Vocational Qualification) information for a few of the schools in the London Borough of Haringey. Study this table and consider the issues it can and cannot address about secondary schools.

Table 3.1 Performance tables, secondary schools, 2002: GCSE/GNVQ results

	Pupils aged 15			GCSE/GNVQ results			
	Total	SEN	% SEN	5+ A*–C	5+ A*–G	No passes	Average capped point score
England: average	—	—	—	51.6%	88.9%	5.4%	34.7
Gladesmore Community School	229	131	57.2%	30.0%	77.0%	14.0%	25.2
Our Lady's Convent Roman Catholic Girls' School	82	12	14.6%	54.0%	94.0%	1.0%	38.4
Beis Rochel d'Satmar Girls' School	49	—	—	8.0%	20.0%	10.0%	18.8
Yesodey Hatorah School	50	—	—	84.0%	100.0%	0.0%	55.9
Park View Academy	126	23	18.3%	16.0%	74.0%	6.0%	21.4
The Skinners' Company's School for Girls	105	42	40.0%	34.0%	83.0%	3.0%	28.6
The John Loughborough School	59	16	27.1%	24.0%	68.0%	5.0%	23.2

Note: SEN = Special Educational Needs.

Source: based on information available from Department for Education and Skills (DfES) website: http://www.dfes.gov.uk/performancetables

COMMENT

Performance tables can tell us about the examination results of pupils in individual schools. They facilitate comparison between schools elsewhere in the local education authority and across the country as a whole and allow them to be ranked, based on numerical data. This is just the sort of information that the rational, responsible citizen-consumer needs in order to make the best choice of school. However, psychoanalytic theory, and perhaps your own recollections of transition to secondary school, would suggest that the human experience hidden by these tables is far more complex.

In order to move between inner experiences of the self, to those of the family and group and out into the wider culture and institutions, we need a theoretical 'tool-box' that can accommodate all rather than treat them as separate fields of experience and therefore of enquiry. In the next section we outline a theoretical perspective that provides just such a 'tool-box' which underpins a psychosocial approach. This is psychoanalysis.

4 Psychoanalysis

The strength of psychoanalytic theory is its capacity to cast an alternative light on the personal and policy moment embedded in the transition to secondary school. Sigmund Freud (1856–1939) laid down the core conceptual foundations of psychoanalytic thought and is often considered to be the 'founding father' of psychoanalysis. But psychoanalytic theory did not stop with Freud. During the last 90 or so years his work has been variously developed and disagreed with by numerous post-Freudian theorists including Melanie Klein, those who developed the object relations school of psychoanalysis such as Donald Winnicott, John Bowlby and Wilfred Bion, the French psychoanalyst Jacques Lacan and, more recently, feminist post-structuralists such as Julia Kristeva and Juliet Mitchell. The perspective used in this chapter derives from the work of Klein and the object relations school, who have in common the idea that individual identity is formed through relationships, beginning with the mother–child relationship. Internal worlds are created very early in life by relating to and introjecting – that is, taking into the self – 'objects', beginning with part objects such as the mother's breast, but coming to include whole people, groups, things, places and institutions. Thus intrapsychic, interpersonal and group experiences are the foundation for the development of identity, and both conscious and unconscious interpretation of these relationships becomes the basis for relationships with others in later life. Although psychoanalytic theory and practice are divided into a number of schools, and while there has been and still is much contestation in the discipline, there are nevertheless a number of concepts central to all schools of psychoanalytic thought.

4.1 The unconscious

unconscious

All psychoanalytic theory is underpinned by the concept of the **unconscious**. This has remained one of the key features that differentiates it from academic psychology and most other disciplines within the social sciences. The existence of an unconscious was proposed by Freud in the late nineteenth century when he observed that patients under hypnosis related memories, stories and wishes, of which they had no memory when awake. Although excluded from consciousness, these thoughts nevertheless had powerful effects on the individual. They affected moods, behaviour and even brought about changes in physical functioning. Such findings led Freud to arrive at some of his most fundamental conclusions regarding unconscious processes, repression and symbolism. He proposed that part of the personality sets up a resistance against certain memories, impulses or wishes. They are inadmissible into conscious thought because they are felt by the conscious part of the personality to be bad or forbidden, or because they simply do not make sense to the person. However, although they are repressed, they are not passive, but remain dynamic in the person's unconscious and continually strive for expression. This material finds symbolic expression through symptoms – the symptom is a compromise between the repressed ideas and feelings, and the repressing forces. Therefore symptoms have meanings. It is important to stress

Figure 3.4 Clockwise from top left: Sigmund Freud (1856–1939), Melanie Klein (1882–1960), John Bowlby (1907–1990) and Donald W. Winnicott (1896–1971)

that in Freud's model such intra-psychic conflict and compromise solutions do not only lie in the domain of mental illness, but are an essential part of human development.

The idea that our behaviours and interactions are partly the product of irrational and unconscious processes has profound implications for much contemporary social science and policy discourse. For example, the idea of the unconscious seriously disrupts current conceptions of the citizen-consumer as one who makes choices only based on a rational, conscious process (as discussed in section 2). It challenges the notion that we always know what we are doing and why we are doing it and instead acknowledges that the unconscious can contain many obstacles to the exercise of rational choice and to the fulfilment of consciously held goals.

A further aspect of the relation between the conscious and unconscious is the idea that there is continuity and coherence between apparently unconnected conscious thoughts (that is, thoughts of which we are immediately aware and which we can recall to consciousness at will). Here, we can think of there being gaps in and between conscious thoughts, which are filled by unconscious ideas: sometimes it is only by bringing such unconscious ideas into consciousness that we can make full sense of the thoughts. The idea of making central that which is usually excluded, marginalized or understood as separate and unconnected is a useful one for social science analysis. Psychoanalytically inflected social analysis follows Freud who used phenomena such as parapraxes (slips of the tongue) and dreams as evidence of the existence of the unconscious. For example, in Extract 3.2 (section 2.1), on children's conversation about choosing secondary schools, Victoria's comment 'if I didn't get in Danemouth Girls wouldn't want me', highlights how exclusionary practices of popular and over-subscribed schools are understood on two levels. The conscious part of Victoria's mind rationally accepts this as simply how the market works. But the words she used about not being 'wanted' by the school may also give a clue to unconsciously held fears of rejection.

4.2 Anxiety

anxiety

The concept of **anxiety** is central to psychoanalysis – especially in its Kleinian and object relations versions – and is closely connected to the unconscious. It is important to be clear about how this understanding of anxiety differs from traditional sociological and psychological conceptions. There is a wide range of research and literature which is concerned with anxiety, fear and stress, from examination anxiety (Eady, 1999) to fear of crime (Hales et al., 2001). This work tends to operate on the premise that anxiety relates to a conscious process or state and therefore can be quantified. Implicit too is the idea that, once identified and measured, anxiety is open to intervention that speaks to a person's rational side and rests on the idea that a fear or concern can simply be treated or resolved by pointing to the facts – for example, the idea that concerns about academic standards at GCSE or A level can be abated by an appeal to the 'facts' of academic rigour in both teaching and examining processes. This is quite different to the way in which anxiety is understood in psychoanalytic theory – as inevitable, 'normal' and absolutely central to the development of the personality (Freud, 1936; Klein, 1952). It is important to stress that, in this framework, it is anxiety that circulates at the level of the unconscious that is the focus of attention.

4.3 Klein, anxiety and the earliest moments of life

Let us turn now to the influential work of Melanie Klein who was concerned with the development of the mental structure and psychic activity in the human infant from birth. It is worth evoking those earliest days, weeks and months of life. Remember that, as small babies, we are physically powerless and completely dependent on the care of others: we cannot feed or keep ourselves warm; we cannot even move if we are in danger; our vision is poor; we have no words to communicate our needs; we have no sense of time;

objects (we don't know yet that they are people) come and go, some bringing pleasure such as milk and warmth and some discomfort or pain, such as a nappy change. It is not difficult to imagine that this developing awareness, that is both conscious and unconscious, of unpredictable experiences of warmth and care, threat and danger, and satisfaction and frustration, is, then, a source of great anxiety.

In this new world of sensation, where there is no language to help process and rationalize this new and strange world, the baby's processing of experience is at a primary level: that is, at the level of the unconscious and therefore of **phantasy**. Rather than stories which we make up to amuse ourselves – that is, 'fantasies' – 'phantasies' may be described as 'stories' we are deeply involved in and convinced by and which go on independently of our conscious awareness or intention (Segal, 1985). At first the main focuses of these phantasies are the mother and the source of milk, the breast – both understood as the primary carer. In dynamic relation to changing external circumstances, the infant experiences and builds an *internal* reality, made up of shifting emotional states and unconscious phantasies; love of the breast that appears when she or he is hungry as well as rage and hatred of the breast that keeps her or him waiting. Melanie Klein developed this idea further and suggested that this internal reality may also provoke anxiety about the destructive power of one's own feelings towards the mother.

phantasy

All of this means that our phantasies are active well before words are. Julia Segal cites the example from the psychoanalyst Susan Isaac of a 20-month-old girl who was terrified of her mother's shoe which had a flapping sole. Because she could not speak the little girl screamed and backed away. It was 15 months later that she suddenly pointed to where the shoes were and said to her mother in a frightened voice: 'They might have eaten me right up.' As Segal (1985, p.34) has said: 'The words articulate the phantasy, but what is lost in this verbal version is the screaming terror which accompanied the original phantasy experience.' Words are used to take away fears, to modify anxieties that arose before words could be used. Anxieties which we can name, talk about, perhaps attach to an experience such as 'I'm worried that I'll be bullied at secondary school' are in our conscious minds as thoughts and feelings. They may come and go as circumstances change. But within a psychoanalytic framework, these consciously articulated fears and worries are the outward representations of anxiety that is held at the level of the unconscious. Fears of bullying may be a way of representing unconscious fears of threats to the ego that could not be survived – fears of annihilation that are literally unthinkable, that are unnameable in the conscious mind. Such threats resonate with the fears of survival and dependence experienced as a helpless infant.

In psychoanalytic terms, then, anxiety is a fairly constant feature of life from infancy. However, it is not an entirely negative force, but is, rather, an integral, necessary and 'normal' force in the construction of 'self'. It provides one way in which we learn to cope with and adapt to the tensions between the satisfaction and frustration of our wishes and desires. It is one of the influences stimulating an internal rearrangement in the light of external factors and relationships. The experience of unconscious anxiety continues throughout life and is often provoked when we encounter wider social factors

Figure 3.5 This picture represents anxiety through the image of a lost and lone child, thereby evoking the feelings of vulnerability and fear that are at the core of unconscious anxiety

that have the capacity to destabilize or threaten our sense of self and/or our needs. Among these wider social factors may be institutional rules and practices such as those determining the transitions from primary to secondary school and the opportunities or constraints on our choices at this time.

Theoretical understanding of this dynamic between the inner world of anxiety and fear and the external world of social interaction and institutional process highlights the limitations of a conception of the citizen and citizenship as only premised upon rationality.

Are you clear about the meanings of these key concepts?

ACTIVITY 3.4

Now think about your own transfer from primary to secondary school. Through your memories of that time, try to re-enter the emotional space of that phase in your life and move beyond the objective 'facts' of which school you went to, with whom and where, to the subjective meanings and feelings embedded in and surrounding the transfer, not only for you, but also for your siblings and parents, perhaps even for your classmates and teachers.

- How did you understand this move as a 10-, 11- or 12-year-old child?
- What fears and excitements did you have about going to secondary school?
- How did you feel when you found out which secondary school you were going to?
- What was the reaction of the people in your life to the school?

COMMENT

As a time of great change, primary–secondary transfer is bound to stimulate a lot of feelings – positive and negative. Some of the negative feelings might include fears of bullying by older, bigger children; of humiliating rituals of initiation visited upon newcomers; of not making friends; of getting lost in the 'big' school; of school work being too hard; and of fearsome, unsympathetic or lax teachers. You may also have experienced feelings of excitement about growing up, gaining more independence, meeting new people and learning new things. For some children, going to a new school is an opportunity to leave behind difficult or constraining relationships and a chance to try out and forge different identities. Parents may also invest heavily – in terms of their ambition for their child and in terms of time, money and energy – in which school their child goes to and this can impact greatly on the child's experience of the move. For my parents, who had left school in rural Ireland when they were fourteen, my passing the eleven-plus examination was a cause for celebration. Unlike my siblings, who went to the mostly working-class local Catholic secondary modern school, I would be going to a prestigious convent grammar school where there would be opportunities to 'do well'. 'Doing well' meant not having to work long hours in heavy, dirty, often boring and low-paid jobs like my mum and dad did. But as an 11-year-old who just wanted to be the same as everyone else, their aspirations and excitement could not lift the internal gloom that settled over me that summer as I realized that, from now on, I was 'different' to everyone else in my family.

Whether positive or negative, a psychosocial perspective holds that all aspects of the transition can provoke anxieties which, although articulated in the present, may also refer to and reawaken old anxieties. Many children worry that they will not be able to go to the secondary school that their friends are going to, an anxiety that may be spoken about as a concrete fear. At the same time, anxieties can circulate at unconscious levels of the psyche, where they are far less accessible to the rationalizing effects of language. At this level, the worrying idea of being separated from friends and of not knowing anyone in a new school environment may spring from deep-seated fears of abandonment, of being alone and of not coping. A child's excitement about leaving 'baby school' may be undermined not only by the unconscious knowledge that she or he is still very vulnerable and dependent, but also by the fear that growing up may mean having to forfeit the care and protection of others. Many secondary schools respond to these anxieties through a range of policies and practices such as allocating Year 7 children to 'friendship groups' and 'buddy' schemes with older children. Children and parents are very concerned about getting a place in a school that is 'right' for them and has a good local reputation. These concerns may be a way of representing unconscious and pre-existing anxieties about difference, belonging and failure, and are harder to respond to within competitive school markets.

Children and parents respond to the uncertainties and changes contained in the move to secondary school in different ways. How those anxieties are managed internally is, in psychoanalytic terms, related to the ways in which our anxieties, both threats to the ego and our own feelings of rage and aggression, were responded to in early childhood.

4.4 Psychic defences against anxiety

From her observations of infants Klein (1952) argued that the process of

splitting

splitting was the most basic and earliest of psychic defences. From the perspective of the newborn infant she paints a world that is polarized: full of delicious sensations, as well as unpleasant ones. For the baby who has no sense of boundaries between self and other, some of these sensations are felt to emanate from inside the self and can feel persecutory – we can see how a distressed, crying baby seems literally to be wracked by its own tears and cries. Klein stated that splitting is a necessary and normal part of emotional development, enabling the baby to bring order into this chaotic environment. Splitting is a way of organizing and keeping separate good and bad experiences and feelings. It allows the baby to keep all those parts of her- or himself (and those of the mother – remember that the baby has no sense of separateness from the mother) which promote life and growth, safe from those sources inside and outside that threaten to destroy life. This is necessary to enable the small infant to sustain hope and trust that good experiences will return and thus make intolerable anxiety bearable.

projection

Projection is a defensive process closely connected to splitting. The mechanism of projection is used to expel feelings, positive and negative, out of ourselves and on to another person or object. 'Objects' may be people, places or other items from the external world that become invested with instinctual energies, emotions or ideas. As such, they come to 'stand for' parts of our inner self, albeit at an unconscious level. Destructive feelings such as hate, envy and anger, which belong to us but which we cannot acknowledge as our own, are then felt to be inside someone else: at first the mother, father and siblings. This defensive organization has implications for adult and social relations too: aggressive and harmful feelings can be attributed to particular political, social or racial groups, as well as things, spaces and places (Aitken, 1998). These 'bad' objects are then **demonized**.

demonized

We have already mentioned that in Kleinian psychoanalytic theory the infant is capable of angry or hateful feelings towards the mother that keeps her or him waiting (see section 4.3). Another way of protecting ourselves from the full knowledge of our *own* capacity for aggression is to project out good aspects of the self in order for them to be kept safe from our own destructive aggression. This 'good' object then becomes '**idealized**' and psychically separated off so that the goodness is preserved and kept from danger. Of course we all have a tendency to idealize and it is important to be able to. This will be mobilized, for instance, when we fall in love. Idealization also helps us in adversity to maintain hope for a brighter future. On the other hand, a need to continue to idealize a partner at all costs would bar the way to a more realistic love relationship based on being able to acknowledge and accept at least some of the faults of the other person.

idealized

Splitting and projection make it possible to maintain one kind of attitude and feeling at a time, leaving whatever contradicts it out of one's conscious mind and projecting it on to someone else (see, for example, **Holden, 2004**). Kleinians would understand this tendency to keep opposing emotions separated, whether in different people and groups, or from one another in one's own mind as coming from the wish to avoid inner conflict. Psychic defences can operate to construct and maintain boundaries, to keep apart the 'good' from the 'bad', 'us' from 'them', 'self' from 'other'. Ideas about whom we resemble and from whom we differ take shape within parameters about who can and cannot 'belong', based on an infinite range of 'credentials' including skin colour, gender, religion, language, clothes, where one was born, what kind of house one lives in, what kind of school one goes to. This provides a useful way of thinking about how identities of individuals and of groups are formed along axes of social divisions.

4.5 Love, ambivalence and reparation

At this point it is important to stress that, although a Kleinian model of human development does not shy away from negative emotions, it is balanced with powerful positive emotions such as love and reparation. Within the relational framework of Klein – that is, that our identities are formed in dynamic relation with others – anxieties and fears are closely connected to the difficulties of being simultaneously an individual and a social animal (Bion, 1961) and the struggle between good and bad feelings that lie at the centre of psychic life. Conflicts and tensions are set up between opposing desires and needs: the desire for individual freedom versus the desire to belong to a 'good' community, desire for connection versus fear and contempt of dependency, and so on. However, in recognizing this struggle, a Kleinian perspective privileges the possibility of making good the damage we are capable of, thereby offering an optimistic view of humankind (Rustin, 2001).

In attempting to make sense of and cope with a less than 'perfect' environment, the growing infant will gradually learn that the good and the bad 'breast' (that is, the one that gives and nourishes and the one that withholds and frustrates) are, in fact, the same object and the tendency towards splitting will diminish. Under the patience and nurturance of the primary caregiver, the child will be able to achieve a more integrated and realistic position: 'This responsive holding and graduated failure is the prototype of all future forms of containment that we find in families, communities and institutions. It allows us to tolerate the uncertainty and frustration of an imperfect world' (Froggett, 2002, p.42).

This integration involves recognizing and learning to relate to 'others' who are not 'me', who are independent of me. Importantly, it involves the tolerance and acceptance of the basic fact that good and bad co-exist in individuals, groups, the self. This is no mean feat for children or adults as it involves much conflict and struggle and we cannot realistically expect to achieve it fully and/ or all of the time. Thus **ambivalence**, whereby opposing feelings such as love and hate coexist in the same object or context, is a more realistic position.

ambivalence

5 Psychoanalysis and social analysis

So far we have outlined some core psychoanalytic concepts as applied to the individual, or more accurately, the individual in her or his relations with the primary caregiver. Hopefully, you are beginning to see that these ideas can be applied to social analysis. Paul Hoggett brings together ideas from social theory with a psychoanalytic perspective on anxiety to develop the notion of 'social anxiety' and applies it to the experience of citizenship in contemporary Britain:

> The concept of 'social anxiety' refers to the anxiety that the western citizen has about a range of intimate fates which could befall him ... fear of death, fear of physical and mental degeneration, fear of pain and sudden incapacity, fear of madness, fear of enduring and chronic mental turmoil, fear of indigence, fear of violation of bodily integrity as a consequence of violent attack or rape, fear of helplessness and loneliness, fear of failure. ... Clearly we can see how the intensity, if not the initial basis, of many such fears is influenced by our culture, a culture in flight from dependency and the acceptance of human limits. As a consequence we prefer not to think about such fates, and find it difficult to talk about them openly even to trusted intimates. And for this reason such fears take on the form of anxiety, that is, fears that cannot be easily named ... 'I fear' becomes 'I am frightened of', the danger within becomes the danger without – the mad, the bad, the sad, the old, the sick, the vulnerable, the failures, and so on, receive not just our compassion but also our fear, contempt and hatred.
>
> (Hoggett, 2003, p.11)

Individually and collectively, then, our anxieties can influence not only how we see others but also the mechanisms we mobilize in the face of institutionalized or wider social forces. Approaching the human subject in this way has profound implications for how the citizen is conceptualized.

Different conceptualizations of the citizen-consumer embedded in policy on school choice and that of the psychosocial subject are compared in Table 3.2.

Table 3.2 Key characteristics of the citizen-consumer and the psychosocial subject

Citizen-consumer	Psychosocial subject
Rational	Rational and irrational
Consciously motivated	Consciously and unconsciously motivated
Individual	Individually, family, socially orientated
Active and confident	Anxious and defended
Competitive and self-interested	Aggressive and reparative, loving and hating
Powerful choosers	Constrained in the face of social and psychic structures
Equal in terms of opportunity	Unequal in terms of gender, social class, 'race', disability and location
Future orientated	Psychically and socially rooted in the past
Risk-avoiding	Risk-taking, contradictory

5.1 Anxiety and social policy

There is a body of work that uses Kleinian ideas to focus on the ways in which public organizations and institutions deal with social anxieties (Menzies Lyth, 1988; Obholzer and Zagier Roberts, 1994). This work explores how unconscious states of mind operate in dynamic conjunction with the way in which organizations and/or work processes are structured. In this light, authoritarian regimes and depersonalized modes of relating to people, whether employees, patients or clients, are seen as defensive formations, whose core purpose is to hold at bay the mental conflict and pain aroused in the performance of the tasks of the organization, whether these be tasks of teaching, nursing or industrial production. This conflict stems in part from being confronted with aspects of subjectivity that we find difficult to accept in ourselves, such as vulnerability and dependency (**Fink, 2004a**). These projected and disowned aspects of the self are then viewed in others with, in the words of Hoggett above, 'fear, contempt and hatred'.

We discussed earlier the idea that difficult and contradictory aspects of experience may be reflected and supported in welfare policy. Hoggett (2003, p.11) suggests that the welfare state is 'founded upon ambivalence' because it denies dependence and vulnerability and instead puts this on to the 'other'. Discourses of citizen-consumers, who are conceptualized as powerful, autonomous choosers who can quite literally make anything happen and do not need anyone else, contain such denials on a grand scale. School-choice policies and the construction of quasi-markets in education also reveal the kinds of defensive formations to which psychoanalysis refers. Examples of this might be splitting between 'good' and 'bad' schools, pupils and communities; the provocation of anxiety at both individual and collective level; splitting between 'us' and 'them' – whether this be between groups convened around social divisions, or between teachers and other education professionals, on the one hand, and parents and children, on the other. This is not an entirely 'top-down' process: governments and their policies also have to 'hold' those aspects inherent in the lives of citizens that the citizens themselves do not want to face and, in doing so, state administrations can set themselves up to do tasks that are impossible, such as eradicate educational failure. We can then have a situation in which 'failure is inevitable' (Hoggett, 2003, p.14).

ACTIVITY 3.5

Read Extract 3.3 which is taken from a speech entitled 'Transforming secondary education', by the then Minister for Education, David Blunkett.

- Do you think that all schools would want to work together?
- What is David Blunkett's approach to failure?

Extract 3.3 New Labour magic: the eradication of failure

We need all schools to achieve high standards for all pupils if we are to build a successful and inclusive economy and society in the 21st Century. So our vision goes beyond simply building individually excellent schools. We need to establish an excellent and diverse education system where schools work together; where schools learn from each other; where good practice and ideas are shared rapidly; where pupils are a part of a wider learning community – with the school at its heart but where learning doesn't stop at the school gate. This means no excuses for low standards. It does mean targeted support to tackle disadvantage and barriers to learning. It means failure is tackled quickly and decisively wherever it occurs. It also means that parents should feel confident to send their children to any secondary school wherever they live. ...

We must be relentless in our drive to raise standards and eliminate failure in secondary schools.

(Blunkett, 2000)

COMMENT

'Excellence' was one of the guiding concepts for Labour's proposed transformation of secondary education (DfEE, 1997). However, an educational vision in which failure cannot be tolerated involves denying that success and failure are irrevocably tied together. Certainly, the limited criteria set for educational success (that is, examination results) means that such success is dependent upon the continued presence of, rather than the eradication of, failure (Shostak, 2000). As MacDonald (2000, p.24) points out: 'There is no independent standard. The first thing that a competent technologist of attainment tests asks of the customer is, "What percentage of the testees do you want to fail?".'

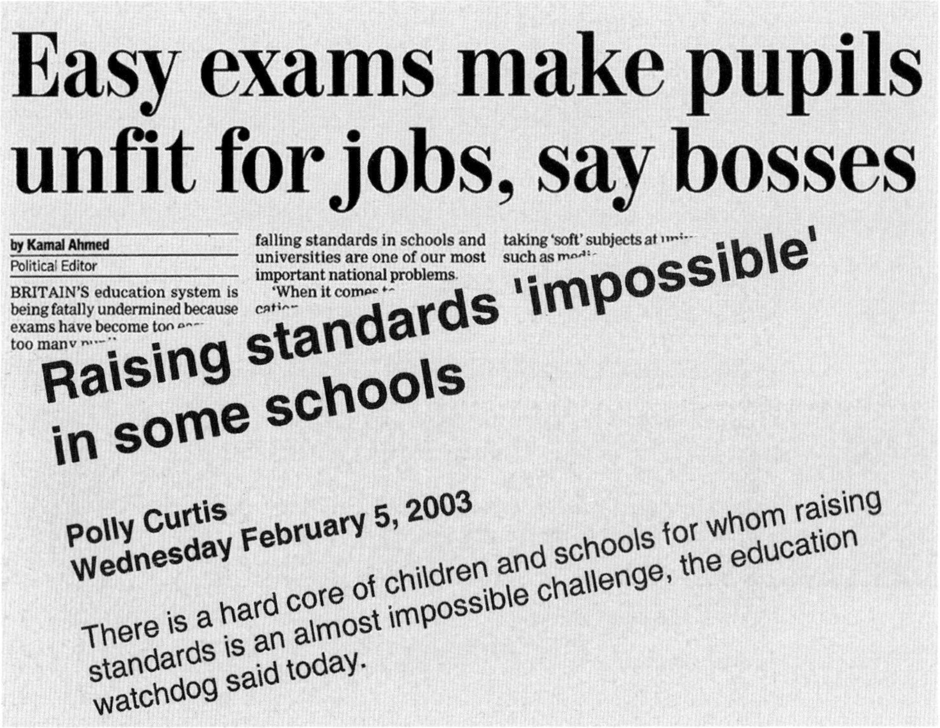

Easy exams make pupils unfit for jobs, say bosses

by Kamal Ahmed
Political Editor

BRITAIN'S education system is being fatally undermined because exams have become too ea... too many pu...

falling standards in schools and universities are one of our most important national problems.
'When it comes to catio...

taking 'soft' subjects at uni... such as medi...

Raising standards 'impossible' in some schools

Polly Curtis
Wednesday February 5, 2003

There is a hard core of children and schools for whom raising standards is an almost impossible challenge, the education watchdog said today.

Figure 3.6 Standards of schools and pupils come under attack

Government policy which aims to raise the educational standards of the working classes (the children of the professional middle classes are already succeeding educationally) certainly contains a desire for social equality. This needs to be acknowledged. However, there is a tension between these benign, reparative elements that wish to 'make good' enduring educational inequalities based on social divisions and the unconscious fears and phantasies on the part of the professional and governing classes about the loss of status and privilege that social equality might mean for them. This ambivalence reveals itself in a number of ways. Rising passes at A level provoke annual debates about whether or not the A level exam is getting easier. It would seem that excellence on a mass scale is a contradiction in terms – for it is the masses who are seen to dilute and contaminate the quality and 'purity' of the very excellence they are exhorted to achieve.

6 Personal lives and secondary school choice

In section 4.4, we discussed the Kleinian concept of splitting whereby bad or good attributes are disowned in the self and instead are felt to reside in the other through the process of projection. Splitting of the good parts of the self in order to protect them from the more destructive aspects of the self may lead to the idealization of objects, whereas demonized objects are those that must

Figure 3.7

'hold' those dispelled destructive elements. We now want to explore this idea of splitting and projection further in relation to secondary school markets. In doing this we will also point to some of the ways in which our personal lives are shaped within the dynamic relation between internal worlds and institutional or social forces.

ACTIVITY 3.6

Extract 3.4 is taken from unpublished material from the 'Secondary school transfer' study and comprises some comments from Year 6 children (aged 10–11) expressing their views about local secondary schools. None of the children had yet received decisions on their secondary school applications. Hassan and Samira are from Somalia and their families are working class; Mohaimin is Bengali and his family is working class; Sophie and Michael are white British and from middle-class families; Melissa is white British and working class. As you read the extract:

- identify the main reasons that schools are deemed to be 'good' or 'bad' schools;
- think about the emotions that the different schools evoke in the children's minds – for example, pride, fear, excitement. What implications might their comments have for how they see themselves?
- consider how psychic boundaries are reflected in actual policy.

Extract 3.4 Children constructing 'good' and 'bad' schools

HL: Right, so tell me about the secondary schools that you think are good and the ones that you think are not so good.

Sophie: There's not many good schools in Tonworth (local area). Most of the good schools are in like Eastcote Town. There's High Hill, there's Hamlyn Girls and places like that. So there is not a very big variety of good schools in Tonworth.

Samira: I want to go to Franklin, but it's too far from us.

HL: What's good about Franklin then that makes people want to go there?

Michael: There's no bullying or anything. There's nothing bad about it. One of my mum's friends have a kid and they live really close to Franklin so they could get in, but they still didn't get in. And they spent loads of money and then they still couldn't get in.

HL: What do other people think?

Mohaimin: I think Laurel school is the best.

Samira: I heard that not everyone gets a chance to go there because they have to do a test first.

Michael: You've got to be a genius to get into Laurel, and if you do the tiniest bit wrong then you just get expelled. And you get a really good education. And in Franklin you used to have to do a test, to see if you were good enough.

Mohaimin: It's like a private school.

Hassan: I think the teachers are strict at Laurel because everyone is so nice.

Mohaimin: But in Deerpark yeah, Deerpark is not very good –

Hassan: – Because there's loads of racists and lots of bullying.

Melissa: My mum said it's really not a good school and they say that the teaching is very very poor and you don't get a good education and you won't get a good job, you won't get a job.

Samira: All the people that haven't been accepted in the other schools, that smoke and stuff, they got expelled and then they always go to Deerpark. So that makes it even worse.

Michael: But they say it might be better now that it's changed.

Melissa: No way. When my mum saw that piece of paper that said 'new improved Deerpark', she just started laughing and said 'oh yeah, right'.

HL: What are the pupils in good schools like?

Mohaimin: Like in High Hill and Franklin, the children are kind, and they don't mess about and they're interested in learning.

HL: Have you visited those schools?

Mohaimin: No –

Michael: – I know that school.

Mohaimin: – But when we went to Deerpark, yeah, the kids after school they were all running around and stuff. We do that, but in the classrooms, and they were getting paint and throwing paint at each other and the teacher was in the classroom.

Hassan: She didn't really care. She didn't do anything.

Melissa: Teachers can't be soft and just say 'OK so I'll give you another chance', they can't do that because then they're going to keep on doing it and take advantage of that teacher, so they should really stand up to the child.

Michael: I know, my brother goes there y'know and I've been there for open evenings.

HL: And what about you?

Michael: I'm going there I think. I don't mind because my brother says it's alright and he can look after me. Some of the teachers were funny.

Sophie: If I don't get into Hamlyn Girls then it's my second choice, and that's the same as Jasmina and Sarah in my class.

Melissa: I think there's bullying in every school.

HL: How do you find out about schools?

Michael: Before we go to secondary school they bring us these kind of magazines to show our parents ... Most of them, yeah, shows all the schools, and all their grades and if they've got swimming pools and all the other stuff, and you can see that in their grades how high or low they go each year.

Sophie: Yeah. My dad looked at that and he saw that Hamlyn Girls was a really good school, ninety three per cent, or something like that.

Samira: Because last year High Hill was the highest school, the best school.

Sophie: And Deerpark and Saxon Road, they were the last, I think about thirty schools or something in the borough.

COMMENT

In this extract we can see how phantasy and the everyday practices of personal lives become woven together with social policy. The children's narratives reveal how conscious fears and unconscious phantasies about bullying; racism; 'poor', 'soft' and uncaring teachers; the bad behaviour of pupils; and future job prospects, merge with and are shaped by educational policy and the practices of schools. This connects with the points made by Hoggett (2003) about 'social anxiety', in the quotation at the beginning of section 5 above, and is most evident in tendencies to 'demonize' or 'idealize' certain secondary schools and the people who attend them. These schools become 'containers' in which bad (demonized) and good (idealized) aspects of the self and others are placed (Lucey and Reay, 2002a).

In the 'Secondary school transfer' study demonized schools were characterized by children as schools that 'nobody wants to go to', although in fact 22 per cent of the sample, almost all from working-class backgrounds, did go to them. Deerpark, which features so negatively in the children's comments, was put under special measures as a 'failing' school – a 'get tough' strategy that was used extensively by the Labour governments of the late 1990s and early 2000s in order to 'eradicate failure'. As a result, the school received a new name, school uniform, headteacher and several senior teachers, as well as the ethos and physical environment being given a 'makeover'.

The construction of some schools as demonized was highly dependent upon the production of an idealized opposite. Franklin, the highest performing comprehensive in Eastcote borough, is out of the catchment of all of the primary schools that took part in the 'Secondary school transfer' study, from which Extract 3.3 is taken. Nevertheless, to children like Michael, it fulfilled all the criteria of a 'perfect' school. This perfection relied heavily on distance, which meant that it could be a much 'emptier' symbolic space, into which their own wishes and desires could be projected. Franklin school also became an idealized object, kept safe from their own destructive feelings. The exclusionary practices of schools, whether through catchment or selection tests, merged with the children's psychic projections and served to make them more attractive.

Note also how Michael and Sophie, both from middle-class backgrounds, try to resist the dominant negative discourse about Deerpark; Michael's brother was already there and it was Michael's first choice and Sophie's second choice. In actuality, the working-class children who were most likely to go to demonized schools had positive and negative experience and knowledge of them, often with relatives, friends and neighbours attending them. Children often emotionally worked towards repairing the image of a demonized school and their sense of themselves in relation to it. This helped them to move towards a more 'integrated' and ambivalent view of such schools. However, this was a difficult position to maintain under the weight of splitting that was supported not only individually and within the peer group, but also in government-produced 'league tables' and dominating discourses about successful and failing schools. Children's knowledge of a school's position in the local hierarchy of schools, whether through being put under special measures or scoring the 'highest' on league tables, influenced how they came to view themselves.

The children and their parents may be acting like active citizen-consumers in that they have gathered information about the range of options offered to them in a competitive market. However, the children not only face the obstacles and limitations imposed by the market, but also their own and their parents' deeply held feelings about difference and failure. The extract highlights, too, how measures designed to 'raise standards', based on a separation of schools into successful or failing, support and were in turn supported by tendencies to defend against anxiety by splitting.

6.1 Pupils, divisions and hierarchies

Although Labour administrations in the 1990s and early 2000s identified school failure as primarily the result of poor teaching and weak management (Ofsted, 2004), in the minds of these Year 6 children, it is the pupils who are deficient. Deviancy, criminality and aggression were routinely ascribed to the pupils of demonized schools, as was stupidity and failure. John Shostak has noted that

"First thing in the morning I'm ringing the school about the amount of homework he's getting."

Figure 3.8

regimes of school effectiveness were highly directed towards producing a standardized ideal, of both schools and children. This involves a 'purifying process', in the course of which aspects of subjectivity which have no legitimate place in an 'ideal' inevitably emerge as 'waste products' (Shostak, 2000, p.42). The idea that demonized schools contained expelled 'waste products' – with pupils, teachers and buildings referred to as 'rubbish', 'shit' and 'crap' – were prevalent in children's narratives. Similarly, rubbish was often a feature of the physical environment in which the children in these urban boroughs lived and which also partly shaped their personal lives.

Through metaphors of waste and rejection, demonized schools also became repositories for 'stupid' and 'thick' pupils, whilst idealized schools only took 'geniuses'. However, these divisions could be confusing and contradictory, when the children were so heavily implicated in their own unequal categories. After all, the majority of working-class children knew that they would be going to local, average or under-achieving comprehensives. In competitive markets, children are constructed as 'objects of the education system, to be attracted, excluded, displayed and processed, according to their commercial worth, rather than subjects with needs, desires, potentials' (Gewirtz, 2000, p.13). That they are differentially valued was not lost on these 10- and 11-year-olds. They were aware of a hierarchy of selection in terms of 'cleverness' and had an accurate idea of where they themselves were positioned in this system. While both working-class and middle-class children talked about the 'intelligence' of certain schools' pupil populations, it was only working-class children who related this in some ways to themselves, thereby revealing fears of being thought 'stupid':

> [I want to go to] a school where the kids don't treat you like you're stupid and the teachers actually help you properly and they don't just forget about what you've said and stuff like that.
> (Seline, 10 years old, Turkish/Italian working class girl)
>
> I'd like to get a good education because I don't want to be known as a 'thick' person or a 'stupid' person, so I'd really like a good education. I like to see what the GCSE marks were.
> (Sheena, 10 years old, African-Caribbean working class girl)
>
> (quoted in Lucey and Reay, 2002a)

Their internal fears and defences are supported in the external world through social discourses which themselves contain enduring phantasies about the inferior intellectual capacities of the working classes compared to the innate 'intelligence' of the middle classes (Carey, 1992). This in turn has influenced the opportunities open to such children in their adult lives. For the majority of working-class children, the fear and shame of being thought of as 'stupid' resonates through generations of family and peer group educational failure and underachievement. This is not to deny that middle-class children too may suffer from powerful unconscious fears around the demonstration of their intellectual capacity, as we will see in section 6.2 below (Walkerdine et al., 2001). But it has been well documented since the 1970s that children from different class backgrounds are treated differentially throughout the education system (Willis, 1977). Middle-class children may hold unconscious fears of not being clever *enough*, especially in a social milieu where outstanding educational achievement is the norm, but they need not be afraid of being treated as stupid. Meanwhile, working-class children, who are often thought of and treated as stupid, are acutely aware of the long-reaching and powerful effects of such labelling. For both groups, then, the content of their personal lives will be influenced by the wider educational structure.

Can you see why a combination of psychic and social analysis enables a more complex understanding of the process of transition between schools?

6.2 In the fullness of citizenship: the middle classes and fears of failure

We have considered how fears and phantasies of aggression, failure and poverty, held at the level of social policy as well as in the imaginations of children and parents, come to impact on the development of secondary school markets. We now want to consider the experiences of those who are normally considered to be the 'winners' in the education system – the professional middle classes. Bringing a psychosocial perspective to bear in this analysis allows an engagement with aspects of our subjects' narratives which are hard to make sense of within current educational and political discourses.

ACTIVITY 3.7

Read the case in Extract 3.5 below of Sally and her mother and their experiences of primary–secondary transfer. As you do so, identify the strategies used to maximize Sally's position in the transfer process.

- What does this story tell us about discourses of 'cleverness' and the middle classes?

Extract 3.5 Managing anxieties in a competitive school market

Sally, a white British girl living in the borough of Eastcote, came from a professional middle class family where both parents were in full-time paid employment. She attended Drayton primary school where the pupil population was ethnically mixed but predominantly working class. Sally had been privately coached in Mathematics and English since year 5 (aged 9–10) to make up for her parents' perceived shortfall in her primary school curriculum. They lived in the catchment area for Hamlyn Girls, a comprehensive school popular amongst her peer group and the school on which Sally herself was keen. Despite being educated in a comprehensive herself and having taught in inner city state schools for over twenty years, Sally's mother felt that none of the local comprehensive schools would be able to provide a stimulating enough environment for an 'academic child' like Sally. Therefore Hamlyn Girls was to be a last resort. Instead, Sally was entered for four selective schools.

The entrance procedure for these schools was difficult for Sally, not least because she failed the examinations for three of them. However, one of the schools for which she was entered was Longford House, a voluntary aided, selective, co-educational school whose pupils consistently performed highly. [Voluntary aided schools are maintained by the local education authority and have a foundation which is usually religious. This foundation appoints a governing body which then acts as the admissions authority and can make decisions about selection procedures to the school.] Sally achieved a low pass on this test and was put on their long waiting list. By the end of the summer term, Sally still did not know to which school she would be going. She expressed a number of worries about going to Longford House such as not knowing anyone, a long journey by bus and train and doubts as to whether she would fit into a school where 'so many clever people go'. She did not know how to explain her concerns to her mum and dad.

Her mother could see that this was a difficult time for Sally and even worried that Sally was expressing her anxieties physically: 'she's never had too many colds and whatnot as this year. I think she's somatizing actually'. Her mother also found the uncertainty a strain, but felt that she needed to take 'a longer view' on Sally's education and so was 'prepared to sit with the anxiety of not knowing'. Four weeks before the beginning of the Autumn term, Sally was offered a place at Longford House.

In her first term at Longford House Sally felt that she struggled to 'fit in' academically and socially. The institutional ethos of the school cohered around high achievement and Sally was not keeping up. The pupil intake was largely white, suburban and middle class and although this was how Sally herself could be described, she had come from a primary school that was ethnically mixed, urban and largely working class and she did not identify with her new peer group. Furthermore, she had to get up at 6.30 to be in school by 8.35.

> I've just got so much going on and I go so early and I get back so late, it's really stressful and tiring.

While her mother rationalized this:

> I think it's an enormous waste of their time and energy and it's an enormous shame, but I was prepared to contemplate enormous journeys for her, if it meant that she got into a school with a good offer academically and creatively and all the rest. I felt that the trade off was so much better, that she'd get so much more out of it.

(Lucey and Reay, 2002b, p.327)

COMMENT

Sally's story illustrates very clearly one of the strategies that some middle-class parents increasingly used in order to get their children into the 'right' schools. For those parents rich in cultural and social capital but poorer in financial capital, employing private tutors with a view to entering children into selective schools' examinations could be a cheaper strategy than buying a house in the catchment area of a preferred school. This would seem to be entirely appropriate behaviour for the modern, rational citizen-consumer, who considers a range of options, weighs up the risks and actively works to 'manage' their lives in a rational way. But what anxieties might lie behind this story?

We have already seen how this particular moment in children's present personal lives is intimately tied up with their *future* personal lives. Children and parents made strong links between the kind of secondary school they got into, the qualifications they were likely to gain, the jobs they would do, the sort of person they would become. For the professional middle classes, however, the main objective at this decisive moment was less to ensure social *mobility* as to guarantee social *reproduction*. This depends upon gaining the right kinds and number of educational credentials at the right grades – from GCSEs to postgraduate professional qualifications – to ensure entrance into one of the professions, new or old. Longford House was exactly the kind of school that appeared to guard against the possibility of failure: with 98 per cent of pupils achieving five A–C passes at GCSE and high scores for AS and A levels, the fears of failure that middle-class parents (at least in the Greater London Area) potently projected on to the state comprehensive system could be allayed.

We have discussed how the psychoanalytic concept of 'splitting' describes the process whereby we unconsciously defend against anxiety-provoking feelings or knowledge, about ourselves or others. Sally's mother was aware that taking the tests and waiting for a decision was difficult for her daughter. Estimates that students could expect to take more than 75 tests and examinations during their school careers and that examination stress is a significant contributory factor in insomnia, bulimia and anorexia has led to mounting parental and teacher concern that pupils are being 'tested to destruction' (Smithers, 2000). Knowledge of her daughter's distress caused Sally's mother upset, but her investment in the 'longer view' meant that the full implications of this knowledge and her own anxieties in relation to her daughter's feelings had to be defended against in order for the process to continue. Gains in the imagined future are threatened by losses in the visceral present: these are contradictory knowledges that must be kept apart. Investing in the future by putting aside present desires could also be understood as the capacity for 'deferred gratification' – Sally's exhausting journey would bring valuable future returns in the form of boosted educational performance.

For Sally, this investment was producing considerable anxiety. She worried about going to a school so far away, where she would not know anyone. Although her parents may have been convinced of her cleverness and potential, she feared that she might not be able to keep up because 'so many clever people go there'. Other research has found that middle-class girls who do very well at school are beset by feelings of not being 'good enough' (Walkerdine et al., 2001). As indicated in the extract, Sally said, 'I don't really know how to explain it to my mum and dad' and indeed, explaining that she did not want to go to one of the top performing schools in the UK, would have been difficult after her parents had invested a lot of time, energy and money in trying to ensure that this was exactly where she went. How could they 'hear' such difficult information without it threatening to expose and undermine the very foundations of their classed subjectivities?

Sally's parents would seem to embody the model of the autonomous, knowing, risk-assessing citizen-consumer. They were informed choosers who took stock of the local secondary school market long before Sally was to transfer from primary school. They perceived the weaknesses of that market and sought to find solutions to these themselves – by employing tutors and entering Sally into examinations for selective schools and by sending her to a school far away. Yet their story reveals the anxiety that may lie beneath their actions as well as the very real costs involved in living that ideal, even for those who are socially and economically advantaged.

7 Conclusion

This chapter has taken primary–secondary transfer as a critical moment in the lives of children and parents to illustrate how ideas held and carried in the notion of the 'citizen-consumer' and operationalized in the development of 'quasi-markets' in education, have shaped the thoughts, practices and personal lives of children and parents as they choose a secondary school. It has considered how their thoughts and actions have, in turn, impacted on local education markets. We have argued that all human experience is both psychic and social and that this pertains not only to individuals and groups, but also institutions, governments and social policy. In order to cast more analytical light on this dynamic, we have applied psychoanalytic concepts to the social analysis of children's and parents' experiences of primary–secondary transfer. We have shown how this psychosocial approach helps us to reinflect conceptions of citizenship and therefore to grasp the interweaving of personal lives and social policy.

Further resources

If you want to follow up some of the issues or topics discussed in this chapter here are some useful readings: Stephen Frosh provides an accessible overview and guide to the theoretical foundations of various schools of psychoanalysis in *Key Concepts in Psychoanalysis* (2003). For an example of how a psychosocial understanding of identity can be applied to research practice see Wendy Hollway's and Tony Jefferson's *Doing Qualitative Research Differently: Free Associations, Narrative and the Interview Method* (2000) in which they bring together concepts from Kleinian psychoanalysis and discourse analysis in their study of gender difference, anxiety and the fear of crime. This chapter has referred to the work of Isabel Menzies Lyth in relation to the study of social systems as defences, but it is well worth reading the original paper: 'The functioning of social systems as a defence against anxiety' in *The Dynamics of the Social: Selected Essays, Vol.2* (1988). Paul Hoggett is among those who have built considerably on Menzies Lyth's work: for a detailed analysis of the impact of emotions on social and political processes in the context of welfare see his *Emotional Life and the Politics of Welfare* (2000).

References

Aitken, S.C. (1998) *Family Fantasies and Community Space*, New Brunswick, NJ, Rutgers University Press.

Altrichter, H. and Elliott, J. (eds) (2000) *Images of Educational Change*, Buckingham, Open University Press.

Beck, U. (1992) *The Risk Society: Towards a New Modernity*, London, Sage.

Bion, W. (1961) *Experiences in Groups*, London, Tavistock.

Blunkett, D. (2000) 'Transforming secondary education', speech to Social Market Foundation, 15 March, http://www.dfes.gov.uk/speeches (accessed on 2 December 2002).

Carey, J. (1992) *The Intellectuals and the Masses*, London, Faber and Faber.

DES (Department for Education and Science) (1991) *The Parent's Charter: You and Your Child's Education*, London, HMSO.

DfEE (Department for Education and Employment) (1997) *Excellence in Schools,* London, The Stationery Office.

Eady, S. (1999) 'An investigation of possible correlation of general anxiety with performance in eleven-plus scores in Year 6 primary school pupils', *Educational Psychology*, vol.19, no.3, pp.347–59.

Fink, J. (2004a) 'Questions of care' in Fink (ed.) (2004b).

Fink J. (ed.) (2004b) *Care: Personal Lives and Social Policy*, Bristol, The Policy Press in association with The Open University.

Freud, S. (1936) *Inhibitions, Symptoms and Anxiety*, London, Hogarth Press.

Froggett, L. (2002) *Love, Hate and Welfare: Psychosocial Approaches to Policy and Practice*, Bristol, The Policy Press.

Frosh, S. (2003) *Key Concepts in Psychoanalysis*, New York, New York University Press.

Gewirtz, S. (2000) 'Bringing the politics back in: a critical analysis of quality discourses in education', *British Journal of Educational Studies*, vol.48, no.4, pp.352–70.

Gewirtz, S. (2002) *The Managerial School: Post-Welfarism and Social Justice in Education*, London, Routledge.

Hales, J., Henderson, L., Collins, D. and Becher, H. (2001) *2000 British Crime Survey (England and Wales): Technical Report*, London, National Centre for Social Research.

Hoggett, P. (2000) *Emotional Life and the Politics of Welfare*, Basingstoke, Macmillan.

Hoggett, P. (2003) 'A service to the public: the containment of ethical and moral conflicts by public bureaucracies', paper to the *Defending Bureaucracy Workshop*, St Hugh's College, Oxford, March.

Holden, K. (2004) 'Personal costs and personal pleasures: care and the unmarried woman in inter-war Britain' in Fink (ed.) (2004b).

Hollway, W. and Jefferson, T. (2000) *Doing Qualitative Research Differently: Free Associations, Narrative and the Interview Method*, London, Sage.

Klein, M. (1952) *Developments in Psycho-Analysis*, London, Hogarth Press and Institute of Psychoanalysis.

Lucey, H. and Reay, D. (2002a) 'A market in waste: psychic and structural dimensions of school-choice policy in the UK and children's narratives on "demonized" schools', *Discourse: Studies in the Cultural Politics of Education*, vol.23, no.3, pp.23–40.

Lucey, H. and Reay, D. (2002b) 'Carrying the beacon of excellence: social class differentiation and anxiety at a time of transition', *Journal of Educational Policy*, vol.17, no.3, pp.321–36.

Lucey, H., Melody, J. and Walkerdine, V. (2003) 'Developing a psycho-social method in one longitudinal study', *International Journal of Social Research Methodology*, vol.6, no.3, pp.279–84.

MacDonald, B. (2000) 'How education became nobody's business' in Altrichter and Elliott (eds) (2000).

Menzies Lyth, E. (1988) 'The functioning of social systems as a defence against anxiety' in Menzies Lyth, E. *The Dynamics of the Social: Selected Essays, Vol.2*, London, Free Association Press.

Miliband, D. (2002) 'A new vision for citizenship', speech given at the US–UK Conference, Washington, DC, 21 November, http://www.dfes.gov.uk/speeches (accessed on 1 July 2003).

Obholzer, A. and Zagier Roberts, V. (eds) (1994) *The Unconscious at Work*, London, Tavistock.

Ofsted (2004) *Annual Report of Her Majesty's Chief Inspector of Schools: Standards and Quality in Education 2002/03*, http://www.ofsted.gov.uk/publications (accessed on 7 March 2004).

Reay, D. and Lucey, H. (2003) 'The limits of choice: children and inner city schooling', *Sociology*, vol.37, no.1, pp.121–43.

Rustin, M. (2001) *Reason and Unreason: Psychoanalysis, Science and Politics*, London, Continuum.

Segal, J. (1985) *Phantasy in Everyday Life*, Harmondsworth, Penguin.

Shostak, J. (2000) 'Developing under developing circumstances: the personal and social development of students and the process of schooling' in Altrichter and Elliott (eds) (2000).

Smithers, R. (2000) 'Exam regime harms pupils', *The Guardian*, 4 August.

The Citizen's Charter. Raising the Standard (1991), Cm 1599, London, HMSO.

Thomson, R., Bell, R., Henderson, S., Holland, J., McGrellis, S. and Sharpe, S. (2002) 'Critical moments: choice, chance and opportunity in young people's narratives of transition to adulthood', *Sociology*, vol,6, no.2, pp.335–54.

Walkerdine, V., Lucey, H. and Melody, J. (2001) *Growing up Girl: Psychosocial Explorations of Gender and Class*, London, Palgrave.

Willis, P. (1977) *Learning to Labour: How Working-Class Kids Get Working-Class Jobs*, Farnborough, Saxon House.

CHAPTER 4

Who Counts as a Refugee? Personal Lives and the Shifting Boundaries of Citizenship

by Esther Saraga

Contents

1 Introduction

This chapter explores the dynamic interrelationships between citizenship, personal lives and social policy for people who have fled their country of origin seeking asylum in the UK.

Aims

More specifically, the aims of this chapter are to explore:

refugees
asylum seekers
citizenship
personal lives
social policy

- Changing constructions of '**refugees**' and '**asylum seekers**' over the last century.
- Ways in which the study of refugees and asylum seekers raises profound questions about the basis and legitimacy of claims for '**citizenship**'.
- How the **personal lives** of refugees and asylum seekers have been shaped by **social policy** that constructs them as 'other'.
- How refugees and asylum seekers have negotiated and resisted these effects and themselves shaped social policy.
- How 'knowledge' about refugees and asylum seekers is produced and reproduced through research.
- How poststructuralist, feminist and postcolonial theoretical perspectives address some of the issues listed above.

rights
belonging
practices of the everyday

These issues are considered in relation to the different aspects and meanings of citizenship that were introduced in Chapter 1: people's legal and political status, their **rights**, opportunities to work, access to welfare, sense of identity and **belonging**, and **practices of the everyday**.

economic migrant

Throughout human history people have migrated from their place of birth for different reasons – for example, to seek new ways of surviving, to colonize new lands, to establish new markets for trade, or because they feared for their lives in their country of origin. Large movements of refugees around the world, as in the late twentieth century, are often linked to wider regional or global struggles, as illustrated in Figure 4.1. People flee mainly because of war, repression and human rights abuses rather than poverty (Crawley and Loughna, 2003). However, the distinction between being a 'refugee' or an '**economic migrant**' is neither simple nor straightforward.

aliens
national identity

To explore some of the reasons why people have sought refuge in the UK in particular, we are using the personal stories of four individuals, placing the interpretation of these accounts in the social policy context of two particular historical moments – the decade following 1933 and the period between 1991 and 2003. During this latter period 'asylum' was constructed by successive UK governments as a 'political crisis' in the context of a 'crisis' of the UK welfare state, a drive towards a common European asylum policy (Bloch and Schuster, 2002) and a claim that the forces of globalization are irresistible. Dominant official and media discourses assumed that increasing numbers of people were seeking asylum in the UK because of the generous welfare benefits available, that the 'welfare state' could not afford this, that the UK was already overcrowded, that there were not enough jobs and that the presence of so many '**aliens**' or foreigners was a threat to 'community', '**national identity**' and 'our' way of life. Figure 4.2 shows some typical headlines from UK

Figure 4.1 Crossing the River Gillo – by Mac Anyat, aged 17. From *One Day We Had To Run* – written by Sybella Wilkes and published by Evans Brothers Limited. Copyright © Sybella Wilkes 1994. All rights reserved. This image may not be reproduced, stored or transmitted in any form or by any means without prior permission of Evans Brothers Limited

newspapers in the early 2000s, in which 'asylum seekers' are clearly constituted as one of the most demonized groups of people in the UK media.

The sets of interconnections between citizenship, personal lives and social policy can be thought about in the following way.

First, refugee and asylum policy and practice raise important questions about the nature of citizenship in relation to the rights and sense of belonging that citizenship as a status conveys. For example:

- Should citizenship be based upon place of birth, parental nationality, place of residence, or simply human value and dignity, regardless of these issues?
- Should globalization mean that rights of citizenship can no longer simply be tied to birth in a specific nation-state?

Second, the mutual constitution of personal lives and social policy comes into stark focus for the person who flees one country and has to negotiate entry to a life in a new country (each of the countries having its own particular social, economic, political and cultural forms). The personal accounts that follow in section 2 illustrate these connections well.

Third, exploring these interconnections illuminates the relationship between citizenship as a set of rights and claims, on the one hand, and as cultural or national identity on the other.

Figure 4.2 Newspaper headlines from the early 2000s

The primary theoretical perspective through which these issues are explored in this chapter is post-structuralism, because of its emphasis on the production of social meaning and the effects of such meaning or 'knowledges' on the experiences of different social constituencies. Post-structuralism is also used because this emphasis on meaning systems – or discourses – allows us to think about alternative or counter discourses through which opposition to dominant policy discourses may be presented. Forms of feminist and postcolonial theory will also be drawn on. Feminism alerts us to the impact of gender on the experiences of refugees and asylum seekers and how discourses of gender run through relevant policy. Postcolonial theory draws attention to questions of 'nation', its peopling, and national identity in colonial and neo-colonial configurations of power. It helps us to consider links between contemporary government approaches to refugees and asylum seekers and the generalized anxieties over multiculturalism and cultural identity prevailing in the UK in the early twenty-first century. The nature of the evidence used in our explorations is also a theme running through the rest of the chapter, as indeed it has throughout this book.

2 Personal lives

We start our exploration of the interrelationship of personal lives and social policy with the personal stories.

ACTIVITY 4.1

Read Extracts 4.1, 4.2 and 4.3 below, and make notes on areas of similarity and difference. What questions are raised about the relationship between personal lives and social policy?

Extract 4.1 Lotte and Wolja, 1938

On September 1st 1938, Lotte arrived at Harwich in England to join Wolja, the man she was going to marry. They had known each other for two years in Germany, and wanted to make their lives together, knowing that, as Jews, this would have to be outside Germany, the land of their birth and their identity. They both came from non-observant Jewish families, but since 1933, when Hitler came to power in Germany, they had gradually, but systematically, lost rights and opportunities to work.

In 1932, aged 19, Lotte had entered Berlin University to study medicine, but she was expelled in 1934. Wolja had completed his education, including in 1935 his PhD in Mathematics and Physics, but as a Jew he was unable to obtain work; he lived with his parents on their savings. Although born in Berlin, his father came from Romania and his mother from Poland. He grew up with Romanian citizenship, was naturalized as a German citizen in 1932, but lost this citizenship again in 1935, under new laws designed to preserve the 'purity' of the German 'race'.

Lotte and Wolja knew that their lives could also be threatened in the future. Making a decision to leave was one thing; finding a way of doing it was another. At the time that they met, Lotte was living with her widowed mother in Berlin, planning to join her older sister and husband in Palestine. Meeting and falling in love with Wolja changed these plans. As a stateless person, with little money and poor eyesight, he had difficulty finding a place of refuge. For Switzerland he needed to fit a quota based on 'nationality'; the USA refused him a visa because of his poor eyesight, despite his finding affluent relatives to 'vouch' for him. Eventually in May 1938 Wolja was granted permission to enter the UK 'to seek work', following the decision of the British government to grant visas to 'desirable' immigrants such as qualified scientists.

For four months Lotte made arrangements for her own departure to England, organizing her mother's journey to Palestine, and packing and shipping as much of their joint possessions as she could. As a woman, she could seek to enter the UK on a 'domestic permit', her only option as she lacked professional qualifications. So she had to wait for Wolja to find a family in England who would take her. The letters between them during this time reveal many of their feelings. He was extremely anxious and lonely in England. Although he had some friends (other German Jewish refugees), they tended to be in couples, already married. He relied on these friends and on Jewish refugee organizations for financial support. Despite his scientific qualifications, and his feeling of how much he could offer to the UK professionally, it was difficult to find work. He was registered in the UK as an 'alien', with temporary permission to stay. He did not know whether he would still be here when Lotte arrived, or more generally what would become of them both. Her letters express anxiety about having to do domestic work. She writes: 'I have never enjoyed housework, it is not in my nature; please try to find me somewhere to work with children'. Both had learned English in school; they thought they would be safe in England, and could probably find work; if not they would try America again. They married in July 1939, just before the outbreak of World War II. He fought a 5 year battle with the Home Office to be recognized as stateless, rather than German, and was naturalized as a British citizen in 1947.

(E. Saraga, 2003, unpublished biography: reproduced with kind permission of the author)

Extract 4.2 Victor, 1987

The following [paragraphs] recount my seven-year battle with the British government to obtain political asylum, the destructive force this process has on human dignity and human rights, and the ultimate journey into exile. ...

... In September 1984, the Air New Zealand jumbo jet on which I was travelling landed at Gatwick Airport. Shortly afterwards, I stepped out of the business-class seat (courtesy of Reuters News Agency) into a cold and wintery England, leaving behind the warmth of my native Fiji. The cold of England was, however, warmed with English hospitality. ...

... As I got into the car for Oxford University, it finally dawned on me that I was now in England, a country which had not only existed in my history and geography school books but had dominated every aspect of my life in Fiji. ... Now, I felt as if the Empire's stepchild had come 'home', even though I had only arrived to study on a Reuter's fellowship at Oxford.

Although Fiji had shrugged off British colonial rule in 1970, ... The Queen remained the constitutional head of Fiji ... and Her Majesty continued to stare in our faces from the coins and notes in circulation in post-independent Fiji. ...

[But] ... democracy died in Fiji on 14 May 1987 and with it, my hopes of returning home.

It was also the beginning of a long and seemingly endless struggle to secure refuge in my 'imagined home' in England, and to join a long line of political dissidents in exile. ...

But who would provide refuge to me? The most obvious and immediate host was Her Majesty's Government in Great Britain. From my childhood ... I was taught to sing 'God Save Our Gracious Queen'. Now I was singing to Her Majesty's British Government, 'Save Me From the Dictators in Fiji'. Were they going to respond to my call? Was there protection under the Union Jack (also fluttering in the left-hand corner of the Fiji flag) from the winds of Fijian racism? Was I going to be reluctantly transformed from Reporter to Refugee?

...

The ordeal of waiting for a decision for asylum is a long, arduous, and painfully frustrating experience. Indeed, the British Home Office took three long years to relay its initial decision. On 8 August 1990, it notified me that the application for refugee status had been carefully considered but refused. No reasons were furnished. However, I was granted exceptional leave to remain (ELR) in the United Kingdom until 8 August 1991 ... because of 'the particular circumstances of the case' . ...

... The advantages of full refugee status, as opposed to exceptional leave, are not very great, but I wished to appeal nonetheless. ...

Seven years after I made my original claim, I was finally granted Refugee Status under the United Nations Convention Relating to the Status of Refugees ...

(Lal, 1997, pp.3, 4, 6, 7, 9, 10, 49–50)

Extract 4.3 Françoise, 2001

Françoise, a 21-year-old from Cameroon, arrived in the UK in June 2001. She spent most of her pregnancy in detention. When we met, she and her baby had been locked up for five of his six months. Françoise was either sold or given away when she was four years old, and brought up in a Muslim farming family. When she was 17, she was told that she would become one of her foster father's wives. When she refused, she was locked up and beaten. She ran away.

On arrival in Britain, she was held at Oakington detention centre, where asylum seekers are fast-tracked through the process by in-house lawyers. Her asylum plea was rejected and she was dispersed to Leeds, pending an appeal. Soon after arriving, she discovered that she was pregnant. When Françoise got to the Leeds address given to her by the Home Office National Asylum Support Service (Nass), she was told that there was no room and so was sent on elsewhere. Her lawyer at the time told her that she didn't need to inform Nass because he had her details and would keep in touch.

Her baby was born prematurely, at 34 weeks. She spent three weeks in hospital in Leeds, then went back to the flat she'd been allocated. A week later,

'They came for me at 7am. They said, "Your case is over, you are going into detention." They started to put my things into bags. I could not even tell the health visitor that we were going.'

Unfortunately, her asylum paperwork had not kept up with her and notification of her appeal hearing had been sent to the wrong address. It was rejected without her having a chance to speak for herself. 'She fell into the gap that many dispersed and bewildered asylum seekers experience,' says her current lawyer, Eileen Bye.

In Françoise's absence, her case was turned down and she was detained pending removal. It doesn't seem to have mattered that she knew nothing of the hearing, let alone that she had a month-old premature baby. 'How can they remove me when they have not heard my case?' she asks. 'What will happen to him if I go back? I have no money, no family.'

(McFadyean, 2002)

COMMENT

Although we have only had glimpses of Lotte's and Wolja's, Victor's and Françoise's stories, we can imagine the deep emotional pain of the series of losses they experienced in either being forced to leave, or being unable to return to, their home, family, friends and the familiarity of everyday life. Undoubtedly their pain was exacerbated by the uncertainty of their status in the UK.

We can pick out some similarities and differences in their stories:

- Lotte, Wolja and Françoise were all young, in their twenties;
- All four people fled, or in Victor's case did not return to, their country of origin because they feared for their lives.
- For Lotte, Wolja and Victor it was not easy to find a place of refuge; they came to, or stayed in, the UK because it offered safety, rather than choosing it specifically as a destination. Even Victor, for whom the UK was already his 'imagined home', did not envisage staying permanently.
- These four people fled at different historical times, came from very different parts of the world and experienced very different kinds of persecution. Lotte and Wolja, persecuted as 'Jews', came from Europe; Victor could not return home to Fiji because of his political activities; and Françoise fled from Cameroon because of persecution within her family.
- Lotte, Wolja and Victor were all well educated. Wolja had a PhD, and Victor was a reporter who had gained a Reuter's fellowship to study at Oxford University; Lotte's education had been interrupted.
- Gender played a key part in these stories. Whereas Wolja could come to the UK to 'seek work', Lotte could only come on a 'domestic permit', although this was not her choice of work. Françoise's experiences, the reasons for her flight and her time in detention were structured through her gender and the domestic practices of gender in her place of origin.

- The language and terminology have changed. Lotte and Wolja were subject to controls as 'aliens'. In the 1990s, policies referred to 'asylum seekers' and 'refugees', with a crucial distinction being made between these two categories of people.

Flight

He was carrying only

His papers,

His caution,

A friend's farewell,

A suitcase too small to be seen,

And his misgivings of what the road might conceal.

Mahdi Muhammed Ali

Figure 4.3 'Flight': a poem written in 1979 by Mahdi Muhammed Ali, an Iraqi poet living in exile in Damascus since the late 1970s; translated by Salaam Yousif (Source: Weissbort, 2003, p.13)

These four personal stories come from very different sources. The story of Lotte and Wolja is constructed from their children's memories of stories they had told, together with information in letters and documents found after their deaths. Victor wrote his own story in order 'to sketch in the human dimension of the ordeal (and the peril) in applying for political asylum in Great Britain' (Lal, 1997, p.62). Françoise's story is taken from an article in *The Guardian* newspaper in 2002. Although their lives were shaped by social policy, they did not simply accept its effects. They all experienced themselves as people with needs and rights that they would pursue. We return to these stories many times, both to explore further this relationship between personal lives and social policy, and to consider what kind of 'knowledge' or evidence such stories constitute.

3 Social policy and citizenship

Immigration law and policy do not traditionally appear under the heading of 'social policy'. We argue here for a broader definition that includes these, since the laws, policies and procedures concerned with the rights of people to enter the UK and to claim refuge can have a profound effect on personal lives, as our personal stories have already shown.

Immigration and asylum is a rapidly changing area of social policy. Four major pieces of legislation were enacted between 1993 and 2002. Asylum seekers have been controlled and monitored as much through the guidance and rules issued to relevant agencies and bureaucrats who implement the legislation as through primary legislation. Table 4.1 lists some of the important developments since the beginning of the twentieth century. We shall not explore these in detail – this is a resource to refer to throughout the chapter.

Table 4.1 Some developments in immigration and asylum legislation, 1905–2003

1905	**Aliens Act** Targeted 'undesirable aliens'; asylum seekers exempted
1914 and 1919	**Aliens Restriction Act and Aliens Act** Controlled the activities of aliens
1920 and 1925	**Aliens Orders** Included removal and restriction of entry of black seamen
1948	**Universal Declaration of Human Rights** Includes the right to seek and enjoy asylum in other countries
1951	**United Nations Convention Relating to the Status of Refugees** A refugee is someone who: – has a well-founded fear of persecution for reasons of race, religion, nationality, membership of a particular social group or political opinion – is outside the country they belong to or normally reside in – is unable or unwilling to return home for fear of persecution Limited to those who became refugees as a result of events occurring before 1951, and, by many states, to events in Europe
1962	**Commonwealth Immigration Act** Introduced work voucher scheme for Commonwealth immigrants
1967	**UN Protocol** Extended the 1951 UN Refugee Convention to cover any person, anywhere in the world at any time
1971	**Immigration Act** Gave immigration officers powers to detain asylum applicants
1987	**Carriers' Liability Act** Introduced fines on airlines and shipping companies for carrying undocumented passengers

1990	**Dublin Convention** European Union (EU) countries given the option to remove applicants who have travelled via another 'safe' EU country back to that country
1993	**Immigration and Asylum Appeals Act** First piece of legislation introduced into British law targeted at asylum seekers: – fingerprinting introduced – practice of returning asylum seekers to 'safe' third country – rights to social housing reduced – 48-hour limit on appeal after a negative decision – carrier's liability extended
1996	**Asylum and Immigration Act** – benefit entitlement withdrawn from 'in-country' asylum applicants (successfully challenged in the courts) – internal 'policing' – fines for employers taking on anyone without appropriate documentation – complete differentiation between 'asylum seekers', refugees and those with 'exceptional leave to remain' in relation to housing and housing benefits – local authorities had statutory duty to provide for destitute single asylum seekers under 1948 National Assistance Act; families supported under 1989 Children Act
1999	**Immigration and Asylum Act** – asylum seekers removed from mainstream welfare benefits system; entitled to £10 cash and vouchers redeemable at specific supermarkets – worth in total 70 per cent of basic income support – if they can prove they have no other means of support – National Asylum Support Service (NASS) now responsible for their welfare – introduction of pre-entry controls – Airline Liaison Officers at airports in 'asylum producing countries' [sic] introduced or reinforced – carrier's liability extended to include trucking companies – NASS provides accommodation for anyone recognized as destitute – dispersal policy: accommodation only offered outside London and the south-east; no choice over destination – no welfare provision for those granted refugee status

2002	**Nationality, Immigration and Asylum Act** – replacement of vouchers by a cash voucher system – end to the presumption that all destitute asylum seekers should receive support from NASS; eligibility restricted to those who have applied for asylum 'as soon as reasonably practicable' after arrival in the UK – power to remove subsistence-only support option – applications from 'white list' of 'safe countries' assumed to be 'clearly unfounded', with no right of appeal; Home Secretary can add more countries as he or she sees fit – asylum seekers no longer able to work or undertake vocational training, until given a positive decision, however long that takes – greater powers to tackle illegal working – development of accommodation centres with full board and education for children *Citizenship and nationality:* – requirement to pass English language test (older people and disabled people exempt) – citizenship ceremony involving an oath of allegiance – power to remove British nationality if a British citizen has done anything 'seriously prejudicial to the vital interests of the UK' – the right for children to be registered as British citizens
2003	**Asylum and Immigration (Treatment of Claimants etc.) Bill** Seen by the Home Secretary as the third phase of reforms to the asylum and immigration system, following the 1999 and 2002 Acts. Received its Second Reading in the House of Lords on 15 March 2004. Proposals include: – penalties for arriving in the UK without documentation – withdrawal of support from families who have unsuccessfully reached the end of the asylum process – restricting asylum seekers' access to asylum appeals – increasing the Home Secretary's powers to remove asylum seekers to a 'safe third country' without fully considering their asylum application

Source: based on Teichmann, 2002; Lewis, 2003; Immigration and Nationality Directorate website: www.ind.homeoffice.gov.uk (accessed on 4 April 2004); Refugee Council website: www.refugeecouncil.org.uk (accessed on 4 April 2004); Chapter 1 of this volume

4 Refugees, asylum seekers and citizenship

The two historical moments we are considering were not chosen arbitrarily; they are both significant times in the overall history of people seeking asylum in the UK. Some important relationships between them give us a starting-point for looking at continuities and discontinuities in both policy and experience.

Firstly, Lotte and Wolja were admitted to the UK under the 1905 Aliens Act. This was the first fully implemented legal attempt to control the entry of 'foreigners' into the UK. It aimed to keep out all 'undesirable aliens', while exempting those seeking asylum or refuge. After the First World War came increasing possibilities for states to control their borders, including the introduction of passports. However, refugees were still seen as unwilling migrants, rather than people seeking a better life in a rich country.

During the late 1980s and 1990s, as issues around 'asylum seekers' came to prominence in the public agenda, the dominant historical 'memory' was that Jewish refugees were welcomed to the UK in the 1930s as 'genuine' refugees and model immigrants, who made no demands upon the welfare system, were willing to 'assimilate', and made great contributions to the social and cultural life of the UK. Historical research shows, however, that the reality of their experience was very different. The UK government was very reluctant to admit refugees from Nazism in the 1930s and many were deported (see Figure 4.4). It did not want permanent settlers in a country considered to be overcrowded and which had mass unemployment. Jewish refugees were admitted temporarily only when the English Jewish community assumed all the costs of receiving and supporting them (London, 2000). We will consider later the implications of this deal for understanding 'citizenship'.

These two historical moments are connected in a second way. The United Nations (UN), formed out of the aftermath of the Second World War and in the context of the beginning of the Cold War, published the Universal Declaration of Human Rights in 1948 and the Convention Relating to the Status of Refugees in 1951. The Convention developed out of the very specific experiences of the Holocaust and the 60 million people displaced from their homes by the Second World War. The UK was one of the first signatories to the Convention, but no clear procedures were put in place for guaranteeing refugees' rights. Rather, as Bloch and Schuster (2002, p.397) argue, 'refugees and asylum seekers alike were "looked after" ... because it was politically expedient to respond humanely to those fleeing, mostly from the Soviet Bloc or its allies. They "deserved" compassion and, by extension, access to welfare because of what they had "endured"'. Indeed, the term 'asylum seeker' was first used to refer to political dissidents from the Soviet Union.

Crucially, the Convention created a formal definition of a 'refugee', although, until 1967, this applied only to people fleeing from European countries (see Table 4.1). In the early 1990s, the break-up of the Soviet Union and the increase in political turmoil worldwide resulted in the closing of doors for

Figure 4.4 Czech Jewish refugees being deported from Croydon airport, 31 March 1939

migrants into Western Europe at a time when the EU was allowing its citizens free movement within member states. Since the rights of refugees were governed by international rather than national laws, 'asylum' became the only legal route for entering most Western European countries. Concern about the 'crisis' of numbers and the costs to the welfare state resulted in moves to tighten up the interpretation of who qualifies as a 'refugee'. However, it is important to put the European and UK 'crises' into context. In 2002, 'developing countries' provided asylum to 72 per cent of the world's refugees. Within the EU: 'The UK received the highest number of asylum applications ... but ranked fifth when population size was taken into account' (Shaw and Durkin, 2003, p.7). In the early twenty-first century, paradoxically, both those campaigning for the rights of refugees and asylum seekers and those wishing to limit them (including the UK Government) agree that the Convention no longer speaks to the current global situation.

The plethora of legislation and social policy since the early 1990s is widely understood as successive attempts to 'stem the flow' of refugees. They include:

- the development of ever tighter controls on ways of entering the country;
- the creation of disincentives for people to come to the UK, through restricting their access to welfare;
- increasingly, in the early twenty-first century, detention and 'criminalization' of those seeking asylum or refugee status who are in the UK;
- deportation of those seeking asylum whose claims are 'unsuccessful'.

Despite these dominant views in the 1930s and today, a series of tensions and contradictions within government policies can be identified. A continuity of approach can be seen as successive UK governments, both pre- and post-1951 and continuing into the twenty-first century, have wished to be seen to be carrying out their international obligations to refugees, and to maintain the picture of the UK as a 'safe haven', which welcomes refugees and recognizes their contribution to economic, social and cultural life. The 1951 UN Convention provided a clearer definition of who counts as a refugee. A significant change in the approach took place from the 1990s with a splitting of the category 'refugee' into two distinct groups – 'asylum seekers' and 'refugees' – as a result of the belief that the majority of people seeking asylum were not 'genuine refugees' in the terms of the 1951 Convention. Since the early 1990s, therefore, everyone seeking asylum on the basis of their claim to be a refugee, is called an 'asylum seeker' within law and social policy. 'Refugees' are those whose claims have been recognized; they are entitled to the same social and economic rights as UK citizens. Although not legally citizens, they have full access to medical treatment, education, housing and employment. We can see how the state organizes a connection between personal lives and social policy through identification of the categories that link people to welfare, in this instance through the different statuses accorded people within the procedures of the asylum process.

In developing tight controls and regulations, governments have claimed to recognize the fears of many of their citizens about spiralling costs of welfare services and benefits, and the threat to the 'British way of life' that asylum seekers are assumed to pose. Indeed, being able to welcome 'genuine refugees' is said to be dependent upon controlling and penalizing the majority of asylum seekers who are in fact 'bogus'. In this way, a long-standing tenet of UK policy – that 'good race relations' depend upon strong and fair immigration controls – is reinforced (Lewis, 1998).

Counter voices have also helped to shape social policy and personal lives. These have included asylum seekers and refugees themselves, historians of the 1930s and a range of UK community and voluntary organizations. These latter organizations have often been called upon to provide material and psychological support to asylum seekers and refugees. They have been in the forefront of campaigns first to challenge the regulations and legislation, and their administration, and second to 'nail the myths' about refugees and asylum seekers presented in much of the media.

4.1 Feminist perspectives: who counts as a refugee?

The UN Convention has a very narrow definition of a 'refugee', which does not 'accommodate those people who are forced to leave their country of origin because of economic and/or social disruption caused by environmental, political or economic turmoil or war. These are precisely the reasons that propel most refugees from the underdeveloped South' (Lewis, 2003, p.327). If we examine this definition further through a feminist theoretical perspective, we can see how social policy operating at a national or international level makes assumptions that create the boundaries of a gendered personal.

ACTIVITY 4.2

Look again at Extracts 4.1 to 4.3 in section 2.

- In what ways were the experiences of the four people structured through gender?
- To what extent did class also play a role?

COMMENT

Both gender and class helped to construct the experiences of the people concerned. Wolja was allowed to enter the UK to seek work, but only because he was professionally qualified and had 'cultural capital' to bring with him. Lotte was persecuted as a 'Jew', not as a woman; but, as a woman, a 'domestic permit' offered her the (only) way out of Nazi Germany. By contrast, Françoise was persecuted within her family because she was a woman.

It is easier to recognize the ways in which Lotte's and Françoise's experiences were constructed in part through gender, because Wolja's and Victor's experiences are normalized. That is, their experiences as male refugees are taken as the norm for all refugees. The ways in which women and men live their lives in relation to one another are so taken for granted in everyday practices, that it is harder to see that male experiences are gendered. Similarly, we find implicit gender assumptions within social policies and practices which have contradictory implications for both women and men. On the one hand, in both historical moments men have been viewed as the principal asylum applicant in applications from couples and/or families. In addition, in the late twentieth century 'permission to work', when granted, was usually only given to the (male) principal applicant. This dependence on their husbands is problematic for women, who may lose all their rights if the marriage ends. Women on the receiving end of domestic violence are particularly vulnerable. On the other hand, there is evidence that men have more to lose than women in terms of status, and are less able to adjust emotionally to a changed status, particularly if they are unable to work and act as a 'breadwinner'. Indeed, for some women, becoming a refugee may be the first time they experience an independent status and an opportunity of new roles within the community (Sales, 2002).

The concept of domestic service, which offered Lotte her escape route, is itself one constructed through both class and gender. The UK was the only country offering a 'specific scheme of rescue for the Jews through domestic service' (Kushner, 1994, p.112). Many of the women refugees were recognized not to be of 'the domestic class' by the Home Office, which accepted that such women would probably want to take up another occupation. However, by keeping them in domestic service for a few years the '"large unsatisfied demand" for servants in Britain' could be satisfied (Kushner, 1994, p.97; **Holden, 2004**). Kushner suggests that:

> the predomination of class factors in Britain worked to the overall advantage of those trying to escape from Nazism. The desire to maintain the lifestyle associated with the employment of servants, as well as a genuine determination to help the Jews, enabled a

scheme of rescue without parallel to be implemented at that time. The 20,000 Jewish women were treated in a variety of ways, including the extremes of sympathy and naked exploitation.

(Kushner, 1994, p.114)

More generally, it has been argued that: 'The 1951 UN Convention ... and the 1967 Protocol ... [have been] interpreted through a framework of male experiences during the process of asylum determination in the UK' (Refugee Women's Legal Group, 1998, p.1), thus denying women effective protection under international law. Women and children constitute the majority of the world's refugees, albeit as a minority of the asylum seekers in Europe (Kofman and Sales, 2001). However, the original Convention does not include the kind of 'gender-specific' persecution that Françoise experienced. Women have to claim that their persecution as women resulted from their membership of a recognized social group. Canada, the USA and Australia have all produced gender guidelines which recognize these difficulties, but no agreed gender guidelines exist within the EU, even though the European Parliament called in 1985 for women to be recognized as a 'social group' in the terms of the Convention (Kofman and Sales, 2001).

The Refugee Women's Legal Group argues that:

> women suffer the same deprivation and harm that is common to all refugees ... [but] The experiences of women in their country of origin often differ significantly from those of men because women's political protest, activism and resistance may manifest itself in different ways. For example:
>
> - Women may hide people, pass messages or provide community services, food, clothing and medical care;
> - ...
> - Women who do not conform to the moral or ethical standards imposed on them may suffer cruel or inhuman treatment;
> - Women may be targeted because they are particularly vulnerable ...
> - ... [or] persecuted by members of their family and/or community.
>
> (Refugee Women's Legal Group, 1998, p.1)

Similar difficulties in having their claims for asylum recognized under international law face women and men who are persecuted on the ground of their sexuality as lesbians or gay men, and transgender people (Saiz, 2002).

5 Citizenship, identity and belonging

With the onset of the Second World War, because they came from Germany, Wolja and Lotte became 'enemy aliens' overnight, an identification they resisted. By contrast, both Victor and Françoise were viewed as 'asylum seekers'. In all cases, their status derived from their country of origin. The discussion of gender and sexuality in section 4 reveals a tension around the idea of citizenship as a status reflecting 'human rights' rather than rights that flow from membership of a nation. In this section, we will explore further such contested ideas about citizenship by considering how post-structuralist and postcolonial theoretical perspectives help us to think about the relationships between citizenship, identity and belonging.

5.1 Post-structuralist perspectives: the production of social meaning

A post-structuralist theoretical perspective focuses our attention on ways in which social meanings are produced, and the consequences of those meanings in this instance for refugees and asylum seekers. It also alerts us to look for alternative or counter discourses.

ACTIVITY 4.3

Table 4.2 includes a list of terms used in discussions of migration.

- Do the definitions provided reflect the social meanings that are produced when these terms are used in the media and social policy?
- How might people identified through these terms resist such meanings?

COMMENT

- Although some of these words signify particular legal statuses and rights, they are also discursive categories; that is, they carry meanings that help to locate people in a symbolic chain of associations in which they are categorized as more or less deserving. They may also help to construct people's sense of identity and belonging.
- In public, media and political discussion, the very words 'refugee' and 'asylum seeker' carry silent adjectives with them – 'genuine' and 'bogus'.
- Most asylum seekers are assumed to be 'economic migrants', used in the media as a term of abuse for people who have tried to use the asylum procedures to seek a better life, even though many of them have left places ravaged by war or famine.
- Categorizing very diverse peoples as 'asylum seekers' or 'refugees' focuses on their common experiences of suffering and exile, while ignoring the impact of other social divisions in their lives. This can homogenize them and reinforce stereotypes.

We saw from our personal stories that there are huge differences in people's experiences, and in the meanings of those experiences. Moreover, although personal lives reflect the bigger societal picture of power, inequality and difference, there is always an 'excess'. That is, individuals can also resist these identifications and see themselves, for example, as people with basic human rights.

Table 4.2 Migration terminology

Alien	Used in earliest legislation (1828, 1838 and 1905) to describe those 'outside' the nation
Refugee	Someone forced to flee their country of origin because of war, famine or persecution
Convention refugee	Someone whose circumstances meet the criteria of the 1951 UN Refugee Convention
Asylum seeker	Used since the 1990s for people seeking refugee status, whose claim has not yet been recognized
Forced migrant	Used to describe all those forced to flee, for whatever reason and whatever their legal status
Displaced person	Someone who has fled from their home, but remains within the same national territory
Exile	The condition of being forced to live away from one's 'home'
Exceptional leave to remain (ELR)	Until April 2003, a status granted to people whose claim for refugee status was not recognized, but who were allowed to stay in the UK on humanitarian grounds
Humanitarian protection	Replaced ELR on 1 April 2003
Immigrant	Someone who has moved to live in another country, whether as a refugee, or to seek work, for family, emotional or any other reasons
Economic migrant	Someone who migrates to seek work
Agent	Someone who helps an asylum seeker to get into another country, for a financial payment
Trafficker	Someone who exploits an asylum seeker, for continued financial gain – for example, by forcing them into prostitution or illegal work

immigrant

Both social policy and the media play a role in the construction of discourses of refugees and asylum seekers as 'other' and often use terms such as 'asylum seeker', 'refugee' and '**immigrant**' interchangeably: 'In its report ... of William Hague's speech on asylum policy, the Times referred to "**asylum seekers**" in its first paragraph; "**immigrants**" in its second; and "**refugees**" in its third' (Moss, 2001, p.48, original emphasis). Moss describes this 'confusion over the language' as reflecting 'our confusion over the issue itself'. However, a post-structural perspective suggests that such use of language reflects not confusion

Refugee

So I have a new name – refugee
Strange that a name should take away from me
My past, my personality and hope
Strange refuge this.
So many seem to share this name – refugee
Yet we share so many differences.

I find no comfort in my new name
I long to share my past, restore my pride,
To show, I too, in time, will offer more
Than I have borrowed.
For now the comfort that I seek
Resides in the old yet new name
I would choose – friend.

Ruvimbo Bungwe

Figure 4.5 'Refugee': a poem written in 2002 by Ruvimbo Bungwe, aged 9, from Zimbabwe (Source: Teichmann, 2002)

but important meanings which set up chains of connections. For example, such interchangeable use of terms strengthens the association between asylum seekers and 'undesirable' or 'illegal' immigrants.

This 'war of words' is important because 'beyond simple terminology, words constitute the strategic weapons taken up by politicians, association activists, social workers and intellectuals, who give them a new content according to actions and reactions' (Kastoryano, 2002, p.15). Thus supporters of the rights of asylum seekers and refugees often use the term 'refugee' much more widely than its narrow legal definition. In the library of *The Guardian* newspaper:

> Everyone gets put into a file called 'refugees', with the exception of high-profile individuals in well publicised cases who are seeking political asylum in the UK. The library has decided that the *term* 'asylum seeker' is bogus, rather than the bona fides of the claimant. Refugee organisations have drawn the same conclusion. There has been no obvious rush to rename themselves: the Asylum Seeker Council would not have quite the same ring to it.
>
> (Moss, 2001, p.48, emphasis added)

5.2 National identity and diasporic citizenship

National identity is frequently associated with country of origin and place of birth. This association created difficulties for many Jewish refugees in the 1930s who, like Lotte and Wolja, had to flee their country of origin. Despite the fact that he had his German nationality revoked and was stateless, the UK authorities viewed Wolja as 'German' because he was born in Berlin. In May 1940, when a German invasion was feared, many such people were deemed to be 'enemy aliens' and were arrested and interned, mainly on the Isle of Man. Wolja was interned as a German national whose loyalty to the UK was not absolutely certain. The letters between Lotte and Wolja at this time speak of her attempts to get him registered as 'stateless' and to secure his release. His letters express his anxiety about her health and safety and about his parents, now in Romania, his fears that he will be deported to Australia or Canada against his will, without her, and the injustice of his situation.

In one of these (unpublished) letters he asked her to find a solicitor:

> He should immediately call on Home Office and establish my non-German nationality. As my departure from here may occur very soon, he should apply for postponement of my departure pending decision of nationality question ... it is really a pity that I should waste my time in internment camps although I could do extremely useful work for this country. As the Authorities sometimes object to my having applied for naturalization in Germany, I want you to explain in reply: my parents came to Germany because of antisemitic persecution in their home countries, Rumania and Poland. Thus, in comparison, Germany before the national socialism appeared to me to be a refuge. Then I was persecuted in Germany as a Jew. That is the whole story. Thus there should be no reason not to allow me to continue my work, or some work, for this country. I hope you will succeed.

This letter illustrates starkly that national identity is not fixed or static, but a process which may involve complex negotiations. The Jewish refugees allowed in were those judged to be assimilable into the national culture by adapting to the 'English' way of life. The refugee organizations supporting the refugees advised them to be as invisible as possible, and never to speak German in public places (Kushner, 1994). In practice, Lotte and Wolja, like many other refugees, put down roots, made friends, found work and had children. Although the children became more or less 'invisible', Lotte and Wolja retained a sense of being viewed as 'foreigners' for the rest of their lives. This can be understood in terms of an analysis of the meanings of 'national identity':

> Nations tend to be imagined as racially and ethnically homogeneous ... If the nation is imagined as being made up of people said to be of the same colour and said to have the same ethnic origins, then all those who are defined as not meeting these two criteria can be constructed as being 'outside' the nation, as not rightfully a part of it.
>
> (Lewis, 1998, p.101)

This idea of racial and ethnic homogeneity was taken to an extreme in Nazi Germany, forcing Lotte and Wolja to flee because they were Jewish, even though 'Jewishness' had previously not been a central part of their identity. They were constructed as 'Jews' by a racist state, and had to construct themselves as 'Jews' in order to qualify as refugees and receive financial assistance from Jewish organizations in Germany and England. London (2000) describes the 'deal' that the British government did with Jewish communities in the UK to ensure that they would look after those refugees who were allowed in. Such a deal has a contradiction running through it. On the one hand, it depends upon a particular notion of ethnic belonging, and can be seen as one example of '**diasporic citizenship**': that is, one not premised on the boundaries of a nation-state. On the other hand, it also helps to maintain a hegemonic version of citizenship expressing a natural correspondence between a given state and its constituent population.

diasporic citizenship

The idea of a diaspora – a dispersal or scattering of a population – is a concept employed by postcolonial perspectives. It is used to 'capture the complex sense of belonging that people can have to several different places, all of which they may think of as home' (Valentine, 2001, p.313). The idea of 'diasporic citizenship' therefore challenges the assumption that there is a relationship between a particular group or ethnic identity and a particular territory. It recognizes that people have multiple identities that derive not only from place and ethnicity, but also from movements between different places, from historical relationships, as well as from religion, gender, class and so on.

Victor's relationship to being 'British' illustrates this idea of diasporic citizenship. For him, because of British colonial history, the UK was an 'imagined home'. But he also saw himself as continuing to 'belong' in Fiji. His great-great-grandfather was 'brought [to Fiji] by the British from colonial India in 1879 to toil on the sugar plantations as "overseas bonded labourer in exile"' (Lal, 1997, p.1):

> The racist coup also shattered my planned return journey from Oxford to Fiji, and forced me to travel down an unfamiliar road into exile. But, unlike my great-great-grandparents, I was filled with a belief that Fiji was (and still is) as much mine by 'right of vision' as it is mine by 'right of birth'.
>
> (Lal, 1997, p.2)

Brah's (1996) distinction between two notions of 'home' can help make sense of Victor's experience. The first is a sense of home as belonging to a nation:

> In racialised or nationalist discourses this signifier can become the basis of claims ... that a group settled 'in' a place is not necessarily 'of' it. ... In Britain, racialised discourses of the 'nation' continue to construct people of African descent and Asian descent, as well as certain other groups, as being outside the nation. ...
>
> ... the second ... on the other hand, is an image of 'home' as the site of everyday lived experience. It is a discourse of locality, the place where feelings of rootedness ensue from the mundane and the unexpected of daily practice. Home here connotes our networks of family, kin, friends, colleagues and various other 'significant others'. ... the social and psychic geography of space ... a community

> 'imagined' in most part through daily encounter. This 'home' is a place with which we remain intimate even in moments of intense alienation from it. It is a sense of 'feeling at home'.
>
> (Brah, 1996, pp.3–4)

5.3 Legal status and belonging

During the Second World War, Jewish refugees experienced great insecurity about their status, resulting in some cases in severe mental distress. Others 'chafed at existing conditions. Indeed, most refugees felt they had become part of British Society' (London, 2000, p.262). Being naturalized as British citizens was for many 'the milestone which established their settlement in Britain' (London, 2000, p.259).

Following the 2002 Nationality, Immigration and Asylum Act, prospective UK citizens were to be required to pass a test to demonstrate 'a sufficient understanding of English, Welsh or Scottish Gaelic' and a 'sufficient understanding of UK society and civic structures' and 'to take a citizenship oath and a pledge at a civic ceremony'; the stated aim was 'to raise the status of becoming a British citizen and to offer more help to that end' (Home Office Immigration and Nationality Directorate, 2003, section 1). The first British citizenship ceremony took place in Brent Town Hall in February 2004.

What would you include in such a test?

An advisory group which drew up proposals for the new 'Life in the United Kingdom' naturalization test, believed that the 'two senses of "citizenship", as legal naturalisation and as participation in public life, should support each other. In what has long been a multicultural society, new citizens should be equipped to be active citizens' (Home Office Immigration and Nationality Directorate, 2003, section 2).

Although they claimed that becoming British 'does not mean assimilation into a common culture so that original identities are lost' (Home Office Immigration and Nationality Directorate, 2003, section 2), their description of what is required to become an 'active citizen' includes ideas of a fixed British way of life, with references to 'we British' and to 'our history'. Becoming an active citizen is said to require as a beginning:

> practical and immediately useful knowledge of British life and institutions. ... If new citizens feel that such guidance is useful, many will want to go on to gain a deeper knowledge of our history, beyond that richer sense of national identity that comes from living in a country over the years and mixing with its settled inhabitants and other new citizens.
>
> (Home Office Immigration and Nationality Directorate, 2003, section 3)

The Joint Council for the Welfare of Immigrants (JCWI) suggests that these measures 'elevate the status of citizenship from a right to a privilege ... similar to admission to a private club where the applicant has to convince the existing members that their "face fits the mould"' (Joint Council for the Welfare of Immigrants, 2002, p.3).

Thus citizenship is constructed here as a particular kind of belonging, that of individual and social practices, articulated as practices of the everyday, with a moral dimension, about how 'we' ought to behave to one another. It reflects the generalized anxieties over multiculturalism and cultural identity that prevail in the UK in the early twenty-first century, to which postcolonial perspectives draw our attention. Valentine explains it in this way:

> transnational migration and diasporic cultures and identities have provoked fears that the boundedness and distinctiveness of individual nations' cultures are under threat, and that, as a consequence, so too is the nation state ... Across Europe legal and illegal migrants (particularly those who are non-white) are being identified as a threat to the economic and cultural well-being of nation states because they are regarded as a drain on the welfare state and as polluting national culture.
>
> (Valentine, 2001, p.314)

6 Citizenship and access to welfare

So far we have considered meanings of citizenship in terms of legal status, national identity and belonging. In this section we want to explore it in terms of 'access to welfare', recognizing that people who flee from their country of origin are likely to require assistance and support when they arrive. There is a long history of the state linking controls on access to welfare and control of migration since the 1905 Aliens Act (Lewis, 2003).

6.1 'Maybe you can look, but you cannot touch': asylum and restricting access to welfare

ACTIVITY 4.4

Look again at Table 4.1 in section 3. How would you describe the development of policy between 1993 and 2003 in terms of people's access to welfare services and benefits? It may be helpful also to look back at Chapter 1.

COMMENT

Successive pieces of legislation attempted to make it increasingly hard for people to enter the country, forcing them in many cases to try to get in illegally, to use agents to help them, or to resort to 'traffickers' (Table 4.2 describes the distinction between 'agents' and 'traffickers'). Their access to welfare benefits and services has also been systematically restricted, on the grounds that welfare acts as an incentive, or 'magnet', to make bogus claims for asylum in the UK. Many asylum seekers are detained on arrival in the UK, despite having committed no crime. Chapter 1 also indicated a process of the 'immigrationization' of access to some welfare benefits.

This successive removal of welfare services and benefits has had an enormous impact on the personal lives of people who have usually fled terrible circumstances in their country of origin, with dangerous and frightening journeys to get to the UK, which they saw as a place of safety. Such policies and practices affect the most ordinary everyday practices such as whether or not they are able to get enough to eat and somewhere to sleep. The uncertainty of waiting for a decision adds to the level of psychological distress experienced.

We can illustrate this by considering two of the most controversial policies introduced by the 1999 Act – dispersal and the vouchers scheme. Both policies were co-ordinated by a new government body, the National Asylum Support Service (NASS), through which asylum seekers were to be removed entirely from mainstream welfare services.

6.2 'No-choice' dispersal

Dispersal as a strategy aimed at resolving tensions, avoiding 'concentrations of aliens' and preserving 'ethnic balance' and 'cultural homogeneity' is not a new idea, but one proposed for the settlement of successive groups of refugees, and indeed immigrants, since the 1930s, and also used in the 1960s and 1970s in relation to housing and education (Lewis, 1998). The government's asylum dispersal policy of 1999, intended to 'ease the burden' of the south-east of England, was based on the identification of suitable 'cluster areas' which had, as Smith (2001, p.13) has noted:

- available accommodation;
- a multi-ethnic population or the potential to develop a multi-ethnic population;
- voluntary or community support structures already in place.

In practice, such aims were hard to realize. Many of the 'cluster areas' were in Scotland, and Glasgow City Council was the first Scottish authority to sign a contract (worth £101 million) with NASS to accommodate asylum seekers. Weekly buses brought people on a 'no-choice' basis from the south of England. However, the majority of asylum seekers were accommodated in Sighthill: 'one of the poorest areas of the city' (Ferguson and Barclay, 2002, p.2).

Dispersal to Glasgow had a negative influence on claims for asylum being upheld, with claims being rejected on grounds of 'non-compliance' (Smith, 2001). The timing and destination of the dispersal took no account of case deadlines or of the need to communicate with solicitors. Like other areas not used to large numbers of asylum seekers, there were very few immigration lawyers or translators in Glasgow. Yet all forms have to be completed in English, and all documents translated into English. Having been dispersed, all enquiries have to be made by telephone, which is much harder in a foreign language. Françoise's experience of dispersal, with her papers going to the wrong address and her appeal being turned down in her absence, is perhaps not uncommon.

The dispersal policy shaped the everyday lives of asylum seekers; they experienced it as a deprivation of human rights by cutting them off from friends, family and community. It conditioned the dynamics and circumstances of their relationships with others – strangers as well as friends and family. Many resisted dispersal, preferring to make their own arrangements or to return to London or the south-east, although this would make them ineligible for any welfare support.

Nevertheless, asylum seekers' experiences were contradictory. They were relieved to be free from the danger that had led them to flee and referred to the friendliness of the Glasgow people. However, there were high levels of hostility and racist attacks against them, culminating in Sighthill in 2001 in the murder of a young Turkish Kurd, Firsat Dag:

> Out of the horror evoked by such events, however, some good emerged ... One of the most moving and inspiring events of that time was the large demonstration into Glasgow town centre of asylum seekers, local Sighthill people and many others appalled by Firsat's murder under the banner 'Sighthill United Against Racism and Poverty'.
>
> (Ferguson and Barclay, 2002, p.2)

6.3 Shopping with 'vouchers'

ACTIVITY 4.5

The advice given to young asylum seekers, reproduced here as Extract 4.4, describes how the system of vouchers (see Figure 4.6) operated before it was discontinued in 2002 (other details of the scheme are given in Table 4.1). How might this have shaped their personal lives?

Extract 4.4 'How do I buy food and other everyday items?'

If you are being supported by NASS, you will receive vouchers so that you can buy food and essential everyday items. These vouchers are issued by a company called Sodexho. You will probably receive emergency vouchers when you first arrive, but later you will have to collect them each week from a Crown (main) post office near to where you are living.

You can use the vouchers only at selected shops. Your landlord can tell you the names and addresses of these shops in your area. Alternatively, look for shops displaying the Sodexho BUY-PASS symbol in their window. You will also receive £10 cash each week that you can use for travel costs and for purchases from any shop.

Shops will not be able to give you change from a voucher so make sure you get enough low value vouchers (they are available in amounts down to 50 pence) and try to spend up to the full amount.

(Darnbrough et al., 2001, p.10)

COMMENT

The advice did not explain that the total value of the vouchers was set at 70 per cent of income support, nor that vouchers, unlike other social security benefits, did not entitle people to other benefits or services such as reduced admission charges.

While shopping, an activity that most of us carry out automatically, asylum seekers were constructed as 'other':

> I feel we are marked in red because everyone knows we are refugees when we do our shopping by voucher. We feel humiliated at the checkout because when we give our vouchers, the cashier's attitude is usually really bad. Usually, when they tell us the total, they won't let us go back to pick up something for the change ... Other customers who are in the queue behind us ... often look at us in a very bad way, like: 'Look at this asylum seeker, they are here, they are buying things with vouchers and they are holding us up.' We try to be very fast and sometimes we end up making mistakes at the cash desk.
>
> (Fatma, quoted by Gillan, 2001, p.41)

This is a graphic illustration of the idea within Foucauldian post-structuralism that power resides not only in the state, but is dispersed throughout society through a range of human interactions and sets of relationships. In this instance, the 'power to humiliate sits behind the till' (Gillan, 2001, p.41).

The policy was criticized by all organizations involved with asylum seekers, by many trade unions and the British Medical Association, and in an Audit Commission Report (2000), for being inhumane and stigmatizing as well as bureaucratic and inefficient. In October 2001 the government agreed to phase out the scheme, but refused to return to providing cash benefits. Instead, asylum seekers would be housed in new reception and detention centres as these became available.

The 2002 Act further limited the access of asylum seekers to welfare, with even this limited support ending when they gained refugee status. Under Section 55, support was only available for those who applied for asylum 'as soon as reasonably practicable' after arrival in the UK, even though 65 per cent of people who received positive decisions had made so-called 'in-country' claims (Refugee Council press release, 19 February 2003). Refugee, human rights and homelessness organizations warned that it would leave 'in-country' asylum applicants literally destitute of the right to food or shelter. In contrast, the Home Office believed that 'if they have been staying off the streets and managing for the weeks, months or years before they claimed asylum, then there's no reason why they should not continue to do so' (Prasad, 2003, p.2). The way the policy was administered resulted in 'people ... being refused support despite applying within days, sometimes minutes, of arriving in Scotland. Refugees ended up having to sleep rough and go hungry simply because they were traumatised, did not know the procedures or spoke no English' (Scottish Refugee Council, 2003, p.1).

Here we have an example of the way in which such policies and practices are contested, in this case by voluntary organizations. In March 2003, following

Figure 4.6 The currency of citizenship denied

legal action taken by the Refugee Council and other organizations, the Appeal Court ruled that the implementation of Section 55 was unreasonable (Refugee Council, 2003a). Nevertheless, one newspaper reported that 'huddles of asylum seekers have begun visibly sleeping rough in central and south London ... They have had letters from the government denying them support, in effect leaving them on the street, where they have been setting up permanent "homes" – gathering cardboard boxes' (*The Guardian*, 18 August 2003, p.7).

The 2002 Act also introduced the development of a new type of large accommodation centres, which because of their size (housing 750 people), were to be sited in rural areas, in contrast to the original dispersal 'cluster areas'. Asylum seekers would only receive a small cash allowance, forcing them to stay at the centre for food and lodging, thus denying them such everyday practices as shopping and cooking. For the first time children were to be removed from mainstream schooling and educated within the centres.

Refugee organizations argued that the Act sought to maintain high levels of monitoring and surveillance of asylum seekers, through a system of induction, accommodation and detention centres. They feared that accommodation centres could easily become locked detention centres (see Figures 4.7 and 4.8 for a historical comparison), and that they would 'extend social division by ensuring that asylum seekers are effectively segregated from mainstream society' and 'become inevitable targets for racist attacks with barbed wire and security guards becoming a feature of these centres' (Joint Council for the Welfare of Immigrants, 2002, p.4). Many local communities campaigned against such centres in their areas, 'gripped by what ... [the] residents admit is "a fear of the unknown" ... They envisage men wandering their streets, skulking. They talk of threats to their children, of locking their doors, of terrorists. They admit they have no evidence for any of this' (*The Guardian*, 6 February 2003, p.11). Despite this opposition from refugee organizations and local communities, the Home Secretary was determined to press ahead with the centres, as they would 'ensure the application process is speeded up ... he also insists that the centres will ensure applicants do not drift away' (*The Guardian*, 20 August 2003, p.9).

Figure 4.7 British soldier guarding an internment camp for 'enemy aliens', Huyton near Liverpool, May 1940

Figure 4.8 Exterior fence of Campsfield detention centre, Oxfordshire, 1990s

7 Citizenship as 'participation in social life'

If 'citizenship, as social practice, is manifested by direct or indirect participation in public life, by both individuals and groups' (Kastoryano, 2002, p.143), then opportunities for asylum seekers and refugees to participate is crucial. Young unaccompanied asylum seekers in Milton Keynes (not one of the government's 'cluster areas') were very clear about what participation meant for them: '**secure housing, full-time education, special language training, friends and community support, leave to remain and a secure future**: "To learn English... To go to school... To marry an English girl... To learn about computers... To become a doctor... To be useful for the society"' (John et al., 2002, p.6, original emphasis).

Policies on vouchers, dispersal, accommodation and detention actively discouraged participation in public life. However, in 2001 the Labour Government gave an election commitment to assist the settlement and integration of refugees into UK society, though integration was only to be facilitated for people with refugee status or indefinite leave to remain in the UK, even though the greatest need for help is immediately after arrival. Thus, free English language classes were only available in England for people with three years' residence or refugee status (the situation is more flexible in Scotland, Wales and Northern Ireland). The education of children within accommodation centres has particular consequences for women and children, since involvement with schools is a good way of making friends and feeling part of a community.

Engagement in paid employment has long been seen as a key aspect of citizenship, both as a responsibility and as a right guaranteed by the state (**Mooney, 2004**; see also Chapter 2 in this volume). However, this opportunity has been limited for both asylum seekers and refugees, exacerbated by dispersal policies and removed entirely for asylum seekers by the 2002 Act. From Table 4.1 we can see that structural barriers to employment stem directly from immigration and asylum legislation, and asylum seekers themselves find it paradoxical that they are accused of sponging off the state but denied the right to work. At the time of the 2002 Act the government was also developing a 'Highly Skilled Migrant Programme' to encourage people with exceptional skills and experience to come to the UK to work. This had very little impact on those asylum seekers and refugees eligible to work, who have consistently found it hard to obtain employment. Most experience downward mobility, despite many of them being highly qualified in areas of serious shortage such as teaching and medicine. Discrimination by employers is seen as the main barrier to participation in work (Bloch, 2002). Many asylum seekers have been forced into the informal economy, working in unpopular jobs in catering, cleaning, building, farm labouring and food production. They are poorly paid, greatly exploited and further demonized for doing these jobs.

In a survey of 400 asylum seekers and refugees from five different communities, Bloch (2002) investigated the experiences of participation and employment of people eligible to work. Some of her findings are set out in Extract 4.5.

Extract 4.5 Participation and employment experiences of some asylum seekers and refugees eligible to work

- Most people had made new friends since arriving in the UK; this was important for participating in activities and feeling less marginalized. Women were more likely than men to have friends only in their own community. Kinship and community networks were very important; those who had moved had done so largely to be near family or friends or because of the existence of a community.
- Most people were literate in their first language and more than half were multi-lingual; most people's English language skills were not good when they arrived, but improved rapidly through language courses; access to language classes was harder for women with children.
- There was a low level of labour market participation even though 96 per cent had had formal education, 56 per cent had a qualification on arrival and 42 per cent had been working before coming to the UK; more men were employed than women, but in a much lower diversity of work than before coming to the UK; few people had professional jobs; most had poor terms and conditions of employment.

- Few people were studying or in training; this was due to insufficient language skills, not knowing what was available or they were entitled to, lack of child care or family commitments.

(based on Bloch, 2002, pp.1–3)

These findings spell out clearly some of the barriers to citizenship as participation in social life.

8 Knowledge and evidence

In this final section we consider ways in which 'knowledge' about refugees and asylum seekers is produced and reproduced through different kinds of research.

What kind of evidence has been used in this chapter?

We have used personal stories as evidence to support arguments about the mutual constitution of personal lives and social policy. The people in our stories all came to, or stayed in, the UK primarily because they saw it as a place of safety, not because of the welfare benefits or services they hoped to receive, and we have contrasted this with dominant discourses about (bogus) asylum seekers for whom welfare in the UK is said to act as a magnet. These dominant or official discourses, echoed by the media, focus on evidence, often described as 'facts', which is used to justify ever harsher procedures and removal of welfare services and benefits. A typical example, shown in Extract 4.6, is taken from a Home Office press release from February 2003; it presents the 'asylum statistics' for the final quarter of 2002. The government used these figures as a benchmark to measure its progress in meeting its declared target to 'cut asylum claims by 50 per cent' (Home Office, 2003).

ACTIVITY 4.6

Have a look at Extract 4.6.

- What might we learn from the data in this extract?
- Given the purpose of the figures as stated above, what implicit assumptions characterize this approach to obtaining evidence?

Extract 4.6 Some asylum statistics for the final quarter of 2002

The key findings of the publication of the 4th quarter statistics are:

- There were 23,385 applications for asylum in the 4th quarter of 2002;
- There were 85,865 applications in 2002 (estimated 110,700 including dependants). Since peaking in October at just under 9,000 there has been considerable progress, falling to 7,815 in November and 6,670 in December as the NIA Act [The Nationality, Immigration and Asylum Act 2002] began to come into force and the effects of increased security with the French reduced the number of illegal immigrants entering Britain;

- ...
- In 2002 8,100 (10 per cent) people were granted asylum, 19,965 (24 per cent) were granted ELR [exceptional leave to remain] and 54,650 (66 per cent) were refused asylum;
- A record number of failed asylum seekers were removed in this quarter (3,730). 13,335 failed asylum seekers were removed in 2002 – a record annual figure. ...
- NASS received 10 per cent fewer applications for support in this quarter (17,450);
- By the end of December 2002 37,810 asylum seekers were receiving subsistence only support and 54,070 were supported in NASS accommodation.

(Home Office, 2003)

COMMENT

We identified the following assumptions:

- Apparently neutral phrases like 'asylum statistics' mask the fact that the statistics imply that 'the real reasons' people want to come to the UK are to take advantage of the UK's 'lax' asylum laws and generous welfare state.
- 'Facts' always refer to numbers, which are assumed to be too high.
- The language of the statistics shown in Extract 4.6 gives no insight into peoples' experiences or the reasons for their applications.
- The term 'record number of failed asylum seekers' assumes that most of the claims were not 'genuine'.
- The idea of setting a target on a reduction in the number of claims is based on this same premise. It takes no account of the circumstances in the world that cause people to flee. Nevertheless, in commenting on the 'provisional figures for 2002' as 'deeply unsatisfactory' the Home Secretary referred to such world events, suggesting it was 'no surprise, with applications from Iraq and Zimbabwe accounting for nearly all the increase from 2001' (Home Office, 2003).
- The use of labels like 'asylum seeker' serves to homogenize people's experiences.

'Statistics' do not always support such dominant views. A counter example comes from a challenge by the Refugee Council to the association made between asylum seekers and 'terrorists' in early 2003, following the shooting of a policeman in Manchester. They refuted this association with their own 'facts at a glance' (see Table 4.3).

Table 4.3 'Facts at a glance'

22.8 million
the number of people who came to the UK in 2001 for stays of up to one year, including tourists, business travellers and overseas students
88,300
the number of asylum applications made in the UK during 2001
3
the number of asylum seekers being held under anti-terrorist legislation

Source: Refugee Council, 2003b, p.1

Research that is interested in the experiences of asylum seekers and refugees does not collect statistics, but uses qualitative methods such as interviews or focus groups. For example, Robinson and Segrott (2002) conducted interviews with 65 asylum seekers to understand the decision-making of asylum seekers. The choice of in-depth interviews as the research method arose from the researchers'

> beliefs about human agency and its complexity and rootedness in individual biographies ... this was the only way that the practical consciousness of the respondents could be explored, and the depth and quality of information that is needed be gained ... given the potential complexity of the decision making process.
>
> (Robinson and Segrott, 2002, p.8)

Recruitment of respondents, through contacts and organizations, was not straightforward. Not surprisingly, asylum seekers, whose status is still uncertain, may be quite anxious about participating in research, and wary of trusting anyone who seems at all 'official'. In particular:

> there was reluctance to participate in a study being funded by the Home Office, even though it was emphasized that this research was independent ... the Home Office's role was solely as funders ... The research met considerable suspicion about its motives, rooted in a belief that Home Office involvement in the project reflected a hidden agenda.
>
> (Robinson and Segrott, 2002, p.9)

People were persuaded to participate because the researchers gained their trust, partly through personal contacts, and partly through their credibility as researchers. In addition, the asylum seekers believed that they 'would have an opportunity to speak directly to the Home Office through this research' (Robinson and Segrott, 2002, p.10).

Robinson and Segrott found that people's overwhelming concern was to find a place of safety. Factors influencing their final destination included: their ability to pay for long-distance travel and whether they were dependent upon 'agents' who made the decision for them. If in a position to choose, they were influenced by having relatives or friends in the UK, the belief that the UK is a safe, tolerant and democratic country, previous links between their own country and the UK, including colonialism, and the ability to speak English or a desire to learn it. There was little evidence of prior knowledge of UK immigration or asylum procedures, of entitlements to benefits or availability of work in the UK. There was even less evidence that asylum seekers had comparative knowledge of how these varied between different European countries. Most wanted to work and support themselves during the determination of their asylum claim rather than be dependent upon the state.

Why do you think the Home Secretary did not draw on this research when interpreting the asylum statistics presented in the February 2003 press release?

Considering these findings alongside the statistical data and our personal stories, we can draw some conclusions about the production and reproduction of knowledge about refugees and asylum seekers through research:

- The terms chosen – for example, 'refugee' or 'asylum seeker' – themselves constitute discourses that convey meanings that reinforce or challenge dominant understandings. In the study discussed in section 7, Bloch (2002, p.1) used 'the term refugee ... to describe all forced migrants (that is refugees, people with Exceptional Leave to Remain, people with Indefinite Leave to Remain, asylum seekers on temporary admission and naturalised British and EU citizens who came to Britain initially as forced migrants), unless a distinction is specified'. By doing this she emphasized a common experience of forced migration, and implicitly challenged the negative meanings associated with statuses such as 'asylum seeker' that the Home Office uses.
- The relationship between researchers and researched, as well as the researcher's status and experience, have important implications for people's willingness to participate; this in turn is affected by the funding and the perceived, as well as the actual, purpose of the research.
- Quantitative methods cannot offer us information about people's individual experiences.
- Only through the use of in-depth qualitative methods can we obtain the kind of rich material that allows us to explore the interrelationships between personal lives and social policy.

9 Conclusion

In this chapter we have explored the mutual constitution of personal lives and social policy through an analysis of the implications of different aspects of citizenship on the lives of refugees and asylum seekers. We have seen that legislation, social policy and practice concerned with asylum have profound effects on personal lives. Crucially, we saw that the very words used to describe people, their access to welfare, rights to work, legal status and the procedures for becoming a British citizen all mark them out as different and 'other'. Immigration and asylum law and policy in the early twenty-first century are not based on ideas of universal human rights, but primarily on the premises of deterring people from coming to the UK, monitoring and surveillance of them while they are here, and removing them if possible. Importantly, we have seen the role of the voluntary organizations in challenging dominant discourses, policies and practices.

Different theoretical perspectives can help us to understand varying aspects of the relationship between personal lives and social policy, in particular the gendered and class nature of the relationship, the ways in which people have resisted or refused to identify with the subject positions offered to them, the anxieties provoked by claims to diasporic citizenship and the ways in which, through its citizenship proposals, the government has attempted to impose a dominant understanding of the nation/people.

Finally, we have seen how research can produce or reproduce particular kinds of knowledge about refugees, asylum seekers and citizenship. In order to explore the mutual constitution of personal lives and social policy, we need qualitative evidence that can open up and illustrate the multiple and contested ways in which people understand and represent their lives, evidence in which the experiences, feelings and emotions of those lives are articulated. That is why in this chapter we have made use of the personal stories with which we started. They gave us an opportunity at least to imagine people's circumstances and how they felt, to realize how different these experiences can be for different 'asylum seekers', and perhaps to empathize with them.

Further resources

A very useful overview of 'migration' can be found in Lewis (2003). A special issue of *Critical Social Policy* (2002, vol.22, no.3) on 'Asylum and welfare' focuses on refugees, asylum seekers and migration. Kushner's *The Holocaust and the Liberal Imagination* (1994) and London's *Whitehall and the Jew* (2000) provide comprehensive analyses of UK approaches to refugees in the 1930s. In such a rapidly changing area of social policy, up-to-date information and analysis can be found on various web sites: the Home Office Immigration and Nationality Directorate gives information about law and policy, as well as regular updates on statistical information (www.ind.homeoffice.gov.uk). Critical analysis of policy and personal stories can be found on the websites of the Refugee Council (www.refugeecouncil.org.uk), the Scottish Refugee Council (www.Scottishrefugeecouncil.org.uk), the Joint Council for the Welfare of Immigrants (www.jcwi.org.uk), and *The Guardian* newspaper (www.guardian.co.uk).

References

Audit Commission (2000) *Another Country. Implementing Dispersal Under the Immigration and Asylum Act 1999*, London, Audit Commission for Local Authorities and the National Health Service in England and Wales.

Bloch, A. (2002) *Refugees' Opportunities and Barriers in Employment and Training*, Department of Work and Pensions Research Report No.179, Norwich, HMSO.

Bloch, A. and Schuster, L. (2002) 'Asylum and welfare: contemporary debates' *Critical Social Policy*, vol.22, no.3, pp.393–414.

Brah, A. (1996) *Cartographies of Diaspora: Contesting Identities*, London, Routledge.

Crawley, H. and Loughna, S. (2003) *States of Conflict: Causes and Patterns of Forced Migration to the EU and Policy Responses*, London, IPPR.

Darnbrough, A., Kinrade, D. and Meegan, T. (2001) *How to Make a New Life in the UK: A Self-Help Guide for Young Refugees and Asylum Seekers*, London, National Information Forum.

Ferguson, I. and Barclay, A. (2002) *Seeking Peace of Mind: The Mental Health Needs of Asylum Seekers in Glasgow*, Stirling, University of Stirling.

Gillan, A. (2001) 'That won't do nicely' in Wollaston, S., Katz, I. and Williams, R. (eds) *Welcome to Britain: A Special Investigation into Asylum and Immigration, The Guardian*, June. (Originally published in *The Guardian*, 22 May 2001.)

Holden, K. (2004) 'Personal costs and personal pleasures: care and the unmarried woman in inter-war Britain' in Fink, J. (ed.) *Care: Personal Lives and Social Policy*, Bristol, The Policy Press in association with The Open University.

Home Office (2003) 'Asylum figures: tough year ends with early signs of progress from reform', press release, ref. 058/2003, 28 February, www.homeoffice.gov.uk/pressreleases.asp (accessed on 30 March 2003).

Home Office Immigration and Nationality Directorate (2003) *The New and the Old: The Interim Report for Consultation of the 'Life in the United Kingdom' Advisory Group*, London, The Home Office, www.ind.homeoffice.gov.uk (accessed on 28 April 2003).

John, A., Lindstrøm, C., Olszewska, Z., Williamson, K. and Zongolowicz, K. (2002) *Experiences of Integration: Accessing Resources in a New Society – The Case of Unaccompanied Minor Asylum Seekers in Milton Keynes*, RSC Working Paper No.10, Oxford, Refugee Studies Centre, University of Oxford.

Joint Council for the Welfare of Immigrants (2002) *Parliamentary Briefing: Nationality, Immigration and Asylum Bill*, www.jcwi.org.uk (accessed on 4 August 2003).

Kastoryano, R. (2002) *Negotiating Identities: States and Immigrants in France and Germany*, Princeton, NJ, Princeton University Press.

Kofman, E. and Sales, R. (2001) 'Migrant women and exclusion in Europe' in Fink, J., Lewis, G. and Clarke, J. (eds) *Rethinking European Social Policy*, London, Sage.

Kushner, T. (1994) *The Holocaust and the Liberal Imagination*, Oxford, Blackwell.

Lal, V. (1997) *From Reporter to Refugee: The Law of Asylum in Great Britain – A Personal Account*, Oxford, WorldView Publishing in association with the Refugees Studies Programme, Oxford University.

Lewis, G. (1998) 'Welfare and the social construction of "race"' in Saraga, E. (ed.) *Embodying the Social: Constructions of Difference*, London, Routledge in association with The Open University.

Lewis, G. (2003) 'Migrants' in Alcock, P., Erskine, A. and May, M. (eds) *The Student's Companion to Social Policy*, Oxford, Blackwell.

London, L. (2000) *Whitehall and the Jew*, Cambridge, Cambridge University Press.

McFadyean, M. (2002) 'Hard labour', *The Guardian*, 14 September, www.guardian.co.uk (accessed on 2 August 2003).

Mooney, G. (2004) 'Exploring the dynamics of work, personal lives and social policy' in Mooney, G. (ed.) *Work: Personal Lives and Social Policy*, Bristol, The Policy Press in association with The Open University.

Moss, S. (2001) 'Mind your language: asylum semantics' in Wollaston, S., Katz, I. and Williams, R. (eds) *Welcome to Britain: A Special Investigation into Asylum and Immigration, The Guardian*, June. (Originally published in *The Guardian*, 22 May 2001.)

Prasad, R. (2003) 'Pressure points', *Guardian Society*, 8 January, p.2.

Refugee Council (2003a) 'Section 55: latest news', *Xupdate, Newsletter for Supporters of The Refugee Council*, June.

Refugee Council (2003b) 'Facts at a glance', *Xupdate, Newsletter for Supporters of The Refugee Council*, February.

Refugee Women's Legal Group (1998) *Gender Guidelines for the Determination of Asylum Claims in the UK*, London, Refugee Women's Legal Group, www.rwlg.org.uk (accessed on 3 August 2003).

Robinson, V. and Segrott, J. (2002) *Understanding the Decision-Making of Asylum Seekers*, Home Office Research Study 243, Home Office Research, Development and Statistics Directorate, London, The Home Office.

Saiz, I. (2002) 'Crimes of hatred, conspiracy and silence', *In Exile,* September, www.refugeecouncil.org.uk (on-line magazine accessed on 4 August 2003).

Sales, R. (2002) 'The deserving and the undeserving? Refugees, asylum seekers and welfare in Britain', *Critical Social Policy*, vol.22, no.3, pp.456–78.

Scottish Refugee Council (2003) *Briefing: Changes in Law and Policy*, 26 March 2003, www.Scottishrefugeecouncil.org.uk (accessed on 3 April 2003).

Shaw, J. and Durkin, N. (2003) 'Unsafe countries, unlawful proposals', *Amnesty*, July/August, pp.6–7.

Smith, N. (2001) *Safe in Scotland?*, Amnesty Scottish Office, Amnesty International.

Teichmann, I. (2002) *Credit to the Nation: Refugee Contributions to the UK*, London, The Refugee Council.

Valentine, G. (2001) *Social Geographies: Space and Society*, London, Prentice Hall.

Weissbort, D. (ed.) (2003) *Iraqi Poetry Today* (guest editor Saadi A. Simawe), London, Kings College London.

CHAPTER 5

Citizenship: Rights, Belongings and Practices of the Everyday

by Gail Lewis

Contents

1 Introduction

In this book we have examined a number of ideas, debates and issues concerning citizenship in the contemporary UK in order to explore the relationship between personal lives and social policy. To help in this exploration the authors of the various chapters have utilized a range of theoretical perspectives, using their key concepts and analytic concerns to tease out some specific dimensions of the personal lives/social policy relation as articulated through questions of citizenship. The conjunction of different theoretical perspectives and particular dimensions or arenas of citizenship (the extension and consolidation of social citizenship in the aftermath of the Second World War; negotiation of the transition from primary to secondary school; and the struggles for rights and belonging engaged in by people seeking refugee and asylum status) has facilitated a complex approach to citizenship. It has enabled us to understand or conceptualize citizenship as multi-dimensional and a process rather than as a single status, designated through birth or naturalization and achieved once and for all. In a sense we have viewed citizenship kaleidoscopically, exploring some of its many configurations through particular analytic lenses and in particular concrete circumstances. If each chapter can be thought of metaphorically as representing one view through citizenship to the personal lives/social policy relation, the book as a whole has provided a more complex and layered picture of some of the ways in which citizenship mediates this relation. As a result, the aim of this book has been to demonstrate that:

Aims

- Citizenship is best conceived as a dynamic and relational process.
- The meanings of citizenship change over time and between different social groups.
- This fluidity is linked to inequalities in the distribution of social power.
- Relations of citizenship produce their own inclusions and exclusions, and the concepts of rights, belonging and practices of the everyday help us to excavate how and in what contexts inclusions and exclusions are brought about.
- Specific theoretical perspectives highlight different aspects of the relations and effects of citizenship.

Although presented separately, each of these points is intimately connected to the others and by now we hope that you have developed your understanding of some of the ways in which citizenship is one modality by which the personal lives/social policy relation is constituted and experienced. This final chapter will, therefore, take a few of the ideas that run across each of the previous chapters and consider how they throw light on the relationship between personal lives and social policy. The ideas are those of rights, belongings and practices of the everyday and we will consider how they have been used, but our emphasis is on exploring the specific inflection of these categories produced by distinct theoretical perspectives. Thus the main focus of this short final chapter will be a discussion of theory.

2 Interpreting the evidence: concepts and theories

As a field of study within the social sciences the academic discipline of social policy involves the identification, investigation and interpretation of certain kinds of social phenomena – that is, events, relations, institutions, procedures, entitlements, policies and discourses – that are relevant to the practices and professions of welfare and their study. At one level, to say this may appear straightforward and self-evident, pointing as it does to the notion of a cycle of enquiry which develops through a series of stages from evidence, through classification and on to explanation. In this sense the cycle of enquiry can be thought of as nothing more, or less, than a procedure by which to organize social investigation in a way that is systematic, transparent and coherent. There is, however, much more involved in this notion and it is worth us taking a little time to explore some aspects of this. Let us start with a general statement about theory. Theories can be thought of as frameworks of meaning-making and interpretation, the coherence of which depends upon the capacity of their key conceptual apparatuses to focus the analytic process in a way that is internally consistent. Don't worry if the ideas in this sentence appear quite complicated as we will discuss them further in section 2.2. For now you just need to understand that the strength of any given theory lies in the way in which it helps us to make sense of the world – that is, in its ability to provide a way of ordering experience and allowing for a convincing and consistent narrative about the character, relations among and effects of social phenomena.

2.1 Concepts

The beginning of this process of ordering, meaning-making and story-telling involves a process of conceptualization. Concepts are the basic building-blocks of all theoretical perspectives, and McLennan (1991) has suggested that they can be thought of in the following way:

- Concepts are a way of grouping phenomena into types or categories. In this they allow us to impose a degree of order upon an infinite array of 'things' – events, relations, items, experiences, individuals and groups, animals, etc. – that each of us confronts everyday throughout our lives. This 'order' is achieved by 'cutting up' the stream of things 'out there' into distinct kinds and categories.
- In this, concepts are representations of reality; they are neither exact copies nor transparent descriptions of it. They are a way of capturing 'in thought the structures and processes of reality itself. Concepts are all those signs, ideas, words and labels (= representations) which help to provide a "map" of reality for us' (McLennan, 1991, p.151).
- In so far as the classificatory groupings and their meanings are shared, concepts act as codes that facilitate communication.

To these general characteristics we must add two more points of profound importance. These are:

- As categorizations and codes, concepts are nevertheless provisional in that they are always embedded in specific historical and cultural contexts.
- Moreover, this historical and cultural specificity, together with the fluidity of meaning about any experience or social category, results in concepts being profoundly contestable and contested. Such contestation as to the meaning of any given concept arises in part from the effect of the specific theoretical framework within which the concept is being analytically deployed. In Chapter 2, for example, we saw two illustrations of contested meaning, one in the dispute between Bevan (1952) and Saville (1957/8) over the meaning of 'the welfare state' (section 2; Extracts 2.2 and 2.3), and a second in section 4.3 (Activity 2.5), where a clearly defined, but nevertheless singular conception of 'the personal' led to a particular textual reading.

So concepts, then, allow us to order and categorize real-world phenomena in ways that help us give meaning to these phenomena and establish a degree of shared understanding so that communication can occur. Nevertheless, because the same concept can be utilized in different theoretical frameworks, the meaning of any given concept is open to contestation. Such fluidity or imprecision of meaning suggests that social scientists, including those working within the academic discipline of social policy, should pay particular attention to a careful definition of what they see to be the scope and content of any particular concept.

Do you think that the authors of the preceding chapters in this book have paid careful attention to how they have defined the key concepts? What might be the effects of a failure to do so?

2.2 Theories

As mentioned above, theories are overarching, general frameworks of explanation that make claims to providing coherent interpretations about the causes, manifestations, effects and modes of connection between types of phenomena. They rely upon but are wider than concepts precisely because they attempt to *explain* rather than just group and define phenomena. If concepts are the tools with which to identify, order and classify phenomena and people – for example, into genders, classes, ethnic groups, sexual groups, and so on – theoretical perspectives dictate which concepts and which definitions of them should be used in social analysis. Indeed, specific theoretical perspectives dictate a particular ordering of concepts into hierarchies of greater or lesser importance. Or to put it another way, particular theories privilege some concepts and analytic or research questions over others.

Can you think of two or three examples of particular theoretical perspectives and the concepts they emphasize or privilege?

In Marxism, for example, with its concern to explore and analyse processes of capitalist exploitation and bourgeois rule, emphasis is placed on the dynamics of the capital/labour relation, and the very terms 'capital' and 'labour' act as tightly defined concepts that analytically group people into classes and provide a way of talking about what are seen in this perspective to be the essential characteristics of each class. The theory of Marxism, then, builds up to explain the dynamic of capitalist social relations by the use of additional concepts, such as 'exploitation', the 'forces of production', the 'relations of production', 'value' and 'surplus value'. In the context of our discussion here you do not need to know how these concepts are defined within Marxist theory, but you do need to understand that they are precisely defined terms which aim to classify certain social phenomena that are deemed essential to the formulation of an analysis or interpretation of capitalism (see **Mooney, 2004**, for an illustration of some of the ways in which a Marxist perspective can be used to explore the relationship between personal lives and social policy). Similarly, feminist theory (of all varieties) is concerned to understand and analyse both what it means to be a man or a woman and the many ways in which relations between men and women are constituted, organized and lived. To help such theoretical interpretation, concepts of 'gender', 'femininity', 'masculinity', 'womanhoods', 'patriarchy', 'the body' and 'sexuality' are among the conceptual toolkit that makes feminist thinking and theorizing possible (see Chapter 4 in this volume and **Carabine, 2004**, for examples of the use of feminist perspectives in analyses of the personal lives/ social policy relationship).

We can illustrate these ideas further by looking back over one of the chapters in this book. Take, for example, Chapter 3 where Helen Lucey uses a psychosocial theoretical perspective to analyse one key site in the mutually constitutive relation between personal lives and social policy – the period of transition between primary and secondary school. She identifies a number of features as characteristic of a psychosocial approach:

- A psychosocial perspective emphasizes the dynamic, relational nature of psychic and social life. It assumes that there are clear, though complex, connections between states of mind and individual, social, institutional and political life.
- In order to map those connections, a psychosocial approach brings concepts together that can take account of the *interior* processes of the human mind (to look at individual and group emotions) with those that relate to the *exterior*, public arenas of the social world (to examine structure and power).
- This approach assumes that *unconscious* as well as conscious processes come to bear on the everyday practices that make up personal lives and shape social policy.
- A psychosocial approach maintains that anxiety, and the strategies developed to defend against the difficult feelings that anxiety provokes, plays an important part in the construction of private, social and institutional lives.

- A psychosocial approach assumes that there are levels of our perception and experience that are deeply irrational. The privileging of rationality and reason in educational policy and discourses of citizenship denies important aspects of human experience.
- A psychosocial perspective on welfare policy maintains that public institutions embody contradictions that are inherent in the lives of citizens (Hoggett, 2003).

(Chapter 3, section 3)

Having identified the core features of the theoretical perspective through which she is developing her analysis and argument, Lucey explores the key concepts, drawn from psychoanalytic theory, that act to order and classify categories of internal or psychic phenomena. These provide a way for talking about and interpreting some of the actions and feelings of schoolchildren and their parents who are negotiating the process of school transition in the context of a specific policy universe.

Can you remember the key concepts that Helen Lucey identifies and how they are defined?

Thus we can see that concepts are tools for *organizing, naming* and *classifying* the information about the experience of school transition that Lucey (and others) generated through research, but that the theoretical position she adopts for the purposes of *interpretation* dictate which concepts and which definitions of them she uses, how she thinks about their relative importance and the relationships among them. As a result, we can see that, for Lucey, sociological concepts such as 'class', policy ones such as 'choice', or psychoanalytic ones such as 'unconscious' are not *on their own* sufficient to provide a more complete and complex *explanation* of the experience of school transition – and by extension, of the personal lives/social policy relation. For her, the achievement of such complexity requires an approach capable of capturing the dynamic 'between inner experiences of the self, to those of the family and group and out into the wider culture and institutions ... rather than treat them as separate fields of experience and therefore of enquiry' (Chapter 3, section 3.1; see also **Fergusson, 2004**, for an example of the various readings of the same phenomena that result from different theoretical perspectives).

We want now to use the ideas about theories and concepts outlined above to review further some of the ways in which the authors of chapters in this book have used particular concepts and theoretical perspectives to analyse citizenship and the mutually constitutive relation between personal lives and social policy. More specifically, we shall explore briefly how the concepts of rights, belonging and practices of the everyday have been deployed in the examinations of citizenship presented in the previous chapters and how the different theoretical perspectives used by authors inflect these concepts in particular ways. We will begin with the concept of rights but before doing so we can note that, as concepts:

- The three terms have acted as codes for certain kinds of phenomena:

  (a) 'rights' as a code for entitlements and a specific form of state/citizen relationship;

(b) 'belongings' as a code for forms of social, cultural and emotional inclusion (or exclusion) and connection (or disconnection); and

(c) 'practices of the everyday' as a code for the taken-for-granted, 'ordinary' ways of organizing living and relationships in networks of intimacy (families, lovers, friendships, etc.), workplace relationships, schools, hospitals or other public institutions, communities or other networks.

- Their meanings and remit shift according to the particular theoretical perspective within which they have been deployed.

3 Rights: the fluidity of meaning

The idea of 'rights' is, as we have seen from the previous chapters, central to questions of citizenship, reflecting as they do a particular relationship between individual and state, establishing entitlements to public resources, and indicating forms of belonging to national and other communities of identity and/or interest. The discussions of T.H. Marshall in Chapter 1 and William Beveridge in Chapter 2 illustrated the importance accorded to the notion of rights for citizens in the hegemonic intellectual tradition that underpinned the post-Second World War welfare state and the policy universe that organized the systems of entitlement to welfare services and benefits. This represented what Ruth Lister (1997, p.16) has called 'social–liberal notions of citizenship rights' and was seen as the expression of the new contract between state and citizen in which 'citizenship as an abstract status' endowed citizens with a right to make claims against the state. In this sense rights are conceptualized as a possession that individuals have. But in our discussions of the ways in which the unequal distribution of social power acts to make the rights of some individuals and groups more substantive than others (Chapter 1, section 2.1), and the ways in which increasing attempts to make rights of access to services conditional upon certain forms of behaviour (Chapter 1, section 3.1), we saw that the meaning of rights as a concept and as a lived experience shifts across time, as a result of specific ideological underpinnings of policy and according to social divisions and differentiation. We also saw the profound effect that inequalities in the distribution of rights have on personal lives. Such fluidity in the meaning of one of citizenship's key concepts has been illustrated in numerous ways throughout this book and you should ensure that you are able point to other examples and locate these shifts in particular contexts.

Thus in one sense, the concept of rights guides analysis as a descriptive category. For purposes of social analysis such description can be broken down into component parts which might involve the following steps:

1 description of types of rights – for example, to social security benefits, social housing, treatment under the National Health Service, legal representation, and so on;

2 description of the criteria by which such rights are attained and the procedures through which they are made tangible;

3 description of the categories of individuals and groups who possess such rights;

4 identification and description of the factors and processes that preclude some individuals and groups from fully exercising their rights (a division sometimes referred to as the distinction between formal rights and substantive rights);

5 exploration and description of any shifts in the nature and distribution of different kinds of rights.

We can reformulate these steps into a more general statement along the following lines. If we think of rights as an individual or collective possession we can use the term descriptively to identify the criteria upon which rights are accorded – for example, birth in a particular territory or procedure of naturalization, conditions of need, forms of behaviour – and we can also use it as a yardstick by which to gauge the distribution and experience of rights across distinct social groupings.

Given our statement in section 2.2 above about the impact that particular theoretical perspectives have on any concept, we can ask: what happens to the concept of rights when it is used as a category of analysis within a project of social investigation that has itself adopted a specific theoretical perspective? The first thing we can note is that where the concept of rights is deployed in a particular theoretical perspective it will be refracted through the lens of that theory's particular analytical concerns and priorities. Second, we can say that rights will be one in a chain of concepts, some of which may well be given greater emphasis or privileged as more fundamental. We can illustrate these points by referring back to the previous chapters.

We have already noted that in Marxist theory the central analytic concern is to explore (aspects of) the ways in which labour is subordinated to capital, seeing this (and the struggle of labour to resist such subordination) as the fundamental dynamic structuring all social relations. In the language of class this means that a Marxist perspective is concerned to analyse the processes by which exploitation occurs, and the working class (or proletariat) is conditioned to act in the interests of the ruling class (or bourgeoisie). Marxist theory places great emphasis on the role of the state, which is conceptualized as working in the interests of capital (not as standing above any specific sectional interest), but at the same time as being subject to the struggles of the working classes for their own interests. Thus in Chapter 2 we saw two examples of the kinds of theoretical interpretation of the welfare state that can emerge from Marxist theory. We saw the argument of Saville who claimed that the post-Second World War welfare state was more about maintaining the overall dynamic of capitalist social relations than about increasing redistribution of gross national product towards the working class. It was about instituting a kind of horizontal redistribution 'in so far as it was redistribution from one section of the working class to another, not from the rich to the poor(er)' and that this meant 'that the state compelled a certain kind of behaviour among the working classes – that is acceptance of savings (via national insurance)' (Chapter 2, section 2.1).

The idea that the welfare state was a means of producing a certain set of behaviours and dispositions was taken up further in the Gramscian notion of 'the ethical state' (see section 2 in Chapter 2) which, as you will remember, was defined in terms of the role such a state plays in constructing a certain set of values, sensibilities and identifications with state and nation. 'The ethical state', institutionalized in part in the welfare state, is, then, one key means by which the interests of the bourgeoisie are presented as the interests of all and thus labour is subordinated to capital. The effect of this analysis on the concept of rights is that they are no longer seen simply as a mechanism by which to accord entitlement and facilitate access to welfare services and benefits, or even to represent a relationship between state and citizen in which the state assumes a degree of responsibility for the well-being of its citizens. Rather, while these factors may have some social truth, rights in this theoretical perspective are also more formal than substantive and are one means by which bourgeois hegemony is effected.

ACTIVITY 5.1

Think back to Chapters 3 and 4 and identify the theoretical perspectives used by their authors. Can you see how the concept of rights is reinflected by these frameworks of analysis and explanation?

---

4 Belonging: forms of inclusion and exclusion

The multiple and uneven ways in which citizenship, as a relation and a process, constitutes and expresses forms of belonging has been a theme that all the previous chapters have addressed in some way. Having said this, the idea of 'belonging' is in many ways a more elusive and less precise concept than that of rights, despite the fluidity of meaning of the latter. Nevertheless, in Chapter 1 belonging was defined as:

> referring to those aspects of citizenship that designate, or prevent, membership in the polity and social body. 'Belonging' points to the associational and identificatory aspects of being a citizen – that is, to the ways in which we identify and associate *ourselves* and the ways in which *others* identify and feel associated with us.
>
> (Chapter 1, section 3)

We also drew on the work of John Crowley (1999) who has argued that belonging is a 'thick' concept facilitating analysis of processes of inclusion and exclusion, in part because it points to symbolic as well as material aspects of inclusionary and exclusionary processes. What the discussion in Chapter 1 also established was that the constitution of forms of symbolic and material belonging is profoundly unstable, shifting across social constituency, across the life-course, across the borders of nation-states and as a result of political and policy changes.

Esther Saraga's discussion of the shifting boundaries of citizenship that those seeking refugee or asylum status experience provides powerful examples of the constitution of belonging in relation to constructions of nation and ethnicity. She develops her argument through the use of a number of theoretical perspectives, although her main interpretive framework is that of post-structuralism, and she states her reasons for this selection of theories:

> The primary theoretical perspective through which these issues are explored ... is post-structuralism, because of its emphasis on the production of social meaning and the effects of such meaning or 'knowledges' on the experiences of different social constituencies. Post-structuralism is also used because this emphasis on meaning systems – or discourses – allows us to think about alternative or counter discourses through which opposition to dominant policy discourses may be presented. Forms of feminist and postcolonial theory will also be drawn on. Feminism alerts us to the impact of gender on the experiences of refugees and asylum seekers and how discourses of gender run through relevant policy. Postcolonial theory draws attention to questions of 'nation', its peopling, and national identity in colonial and neo-colonial configurations of power. It helps us to consider links between contemporary government approaches to refugees and asylum seekers and the generalized anxieties over multiculturalism and cultural identity prevailing in the UK in the early twenty-first century.
>
> (Chapter 4, section 1)

This conjunction of theoretical perspectives that privilege the constitution of meaning in general, in relation to gender and to national and ethnic identity, allows Saraga to explore the shifting dynamics of belonging and the impacts of this on the personal lives of people seeking refuge in the UK. What the emphasis on meaning leads to is an approach that uses concepts as a way of analysing and explaining the impact that discourses which claim to speak the 'truth' about individuals, groups, kinds of behaviour, and so on, have on people's experiences and social locations. In theoretical perspectives that privilege the production of meaning the names used to refer to particular groups, types of individual, conditions of need, behaviours or other social phenomena are seen as *constitutive*, as opposed to merely descriptive, of those social phenomena. In such perspectives it is not that there is no social reality, rather that how that reality is produced and what it means is a result of the effect of the power of discourse.

Thus in Chapter 4, we see that 'belongingness' is closely connected to the discursive effects of the allocation and distribution of rights of entitlement that are linked to the status of citizen. In addition, we are also shown how what it means to be a member of a national community, and movements in and out of national membership and belonging, constantly shift as a result of social and political developments. Saraga's four case studies illustrate this well but none more powerfully than the letter from Wolja to his wife Lotte, reproduced in Chapter 4, section 5.2. This example illustrates not only the ways in which social policies can help shape the personal lives of refugees, but also how

Wolja's national and ethnic identities were constantly changing as he attempted to seek safety through the acquisition of citizenship at first in Germany and then in England. In this he is seeking membership in a national community of belonging and there are echoes of this in Victor's story, while the poem 'Refugee', reproduced as Figure 4.5 in section 5.1, is eloquent testimony of the erosion of identity that can result for people when they are positioned outside the boundaries of belonging.

Chapter 4 also illustrates two further aspects of the ways in which social policies are implicated in the dynamic constitution of boundaries and identities of belonging. First, we see that membership of a minoritized ethnic group can itself be positioned by policy regimes as the 'passport' to a kind of subordinated belonging, as in the example from the 1930s when the UK government gave temporary residence to Jewish refugees 'only when the English Jewish community assumed all the costs of receiving and supporting them' (Chapter 4, section 4). Ethnic belonging, then, is not only constructed but is also differentiated from national belonging (Lewis, 1998) and the meanings of both act to hierarchically order different social constituencies. Thus we can see that, when embedded in a theoretical framework that emphasizes the production and effects of meaning, the concept of belonging can help us to identify the constructed, but nevertheless real, character of a range of experiences of citizenship and the different forms of inclusion in the social body and polity.

Second, by utilizing a postcolonial theoretical perspective to analyse yet another form or dimension – that of diasporic citizenship – we can see that not only are multiple identities and communities of belonging a common circumstance in an ex-imperial country such as the UK, but also that this multiplicity raises questions as to whether social policy and citizenship systems can accommodate such multiplicity. This is a question that has assumed increasing importance in the UK, and indeed across the European Union, as the discussion of the Government White Paper *Secure Borders, Safe Haven* (Home Office, 2001) in Chapter 1, section 3, illustrated.

ACTIVITY 5.2

Look back over the other chapters in this book. Can you think about how the concept of belonging has been used and what effect particular theoretical perspectives have had on its use?

5 Practices of the everyday: doing citizenship

In section 2.2 above we noted that particular theoretical perspectives privilege certain conceptual categories over others and that the same concepts take on a specific inflection in the context of different theoretical frameworks. While this is an important point to understand (as should by now be clear), we can extend it and say also that some conceptual categories are more compatible with some theoretical perspectives than others. This is because of the latter's central analytic concerns, the particular definition given to a concept and the assumptions about the nature of the social world that are embedded in the perspective. For example, despite numerous efforts in the 1970s to make the concept of exploitation amenable to feminist theorization of the social relations of gender – in what was known as the domestic labour debate – many feminists, including those who defined themselves as Marxist or socialist feminists, abandoned this attempt since the concept and language was too locked into a framework of interpretation that was seeking to explain relations of class rather than those of gender. As a result, the concept of exploitation was either dropped or added to a set of other concepts such as those of oppression and patriarchy. Similarly, those theoretical perspectives, such as Marxism or liberalism, that conceptualize ethnicity or sexuality as essentially natural, as opposed to constructed, categories, have difficulty in offering coherent interpretations of the ways in which these categories – and the identities linked to them – are profoundly social, cultural and indeed psychic phenomena.

How well equipped do you think a post-structuralist perspective is for the development of a coherent and compelling analysis of the state?

In many ways we can observe the same kind of variation in degrees of analytic 'fit' with different theoretical perspectives in relation to the concept of 'practices of the everyday'. This becomes clearer when we are reminded of the kinds of social phenomena this term relates to. In section 2.2 above we suggested that it be used as 'a code for the taken-for-granted, "ordinary" ways of organizing living and relationships in networks of intimacy (family, lovers, friendships, etc.), workplace relationships, schools, hospitals or other public institutions, communities or other networks'. In Chapter 1, a second element was added to this definition. It is stated there that the term practices of the everyday:

> refers to two overlapping but competing dimensions. On the one hand, there are the ways in which hegemonic discourses of citizenship have embedded within them ideas about the 'best' and most appropriate ways of organizing domestic, sexual, work or leisure activities. On the other hand, there are the actual practices of everyday life in these and other spheres of activity and how these might either be deployed in opposition to hegemonic conceptions and/or be the basis of claims for an extended or deepened citizenship.
>
> (Chapter 1, section 1)

Are you sure that you can see how the second definition extends the scope of the concept of practices of the everyday?

It should be clear that, as a social science concept, the term practices of the everyday aims at problematizing areas of life and experience that are usually taken for granted and at placing them on the agenda of social science research and analysis. The notion of 'the personal' is a powerful example of the ways in which some kinds of relationship and domains of experience are treated as self-evident and separated off from other areas of experience, and throughout this book we have been considering some of the ways in which citizenship as an aspect of social policy helps to shape the content of personal lives. In exploring this relationship you have also been engaging with a number of theoretical perspectives and so we are now in a position to consider briefly how compatible these different perspectives are with the concept of practices of the everyday and how they deploy it. Our aim here will be simply to indicate some of the ways in which different perspectives work with this concept. You should continue this line of thinking yourself by looking back across the chapters and developing the points raised below.

Perhaps unsurprisingly, those theoretical perspectives that have a central concern with analysing phenomena such as 'experience', 'identity' or how 'the self' is constituted and lived are more able to work with the concept of practices of the everyday than possibly are those perspectives that privilege analysis of social or institutional structures. Feminist and psychosocial perspectives fall within the scope of the former. In the case of feminist theory this is because one of its uses has been to explore how the concept of gender can be used to cast light upon some of the ways in which gendered assumptions embedded in policies – for example, the Beveridge Report of 1942 or contemporary asylum and refugee policy – and the practices of welfare professionals both shape the experiences of men and women and normalize or pathologize certain everyday practices. For example, in Chapter 2 we can see some of the ways in which the three Beveridge reports contained within them powerful ideas about what constituted appropriate forms of 'ordinary' or everyday practice in the welfare democracy that the UK had become as a result of the post-Second World War social reforms. And in Chapter 1, Extract 1.3 from the Government White Paper *Secure Borders, Safe Haven* provides further illustration of the links between constructions of normalized practices of the everyday and constructions of national and ethnic identity. These may not strike you as explicitly feminist, although you should look back at these examples to see how gender runs through them, but we can argue that, without the impact feminism has had in bringing to the attention of social science research questions of the intimate, the domestic and many other spheres of life designated as 'private', exploration of the links between personal lives and social policy would have been much impoverished.

Chapter 3, with its use of a psychosocial theoretical perspective, similarly illustrates well the compatibility of this interpretive framework with the concept of practices of the everyday. We see that these practices emerge out of and produce anxieties in schoolchildren and parents as they try to negotiate school choice and the policy environments underlying processes of choice. We also see how the development of state education was intimately connected with concerns to 'educe' (in the language of 'the ethical state' that we discussed in Chapter 2) a certain kind of subject who behaved in certain ways and upheld certain values.

These are just some of the examples of how authors have utilized the concept of practices of the everyday in different theoretical frameworks in an attempt to explain and illustrate the mutually constitutive relation between personal lives and social policies. No doubt you will have noted other illustrations and will have formed your own views about the utility of this concept, its degree of compatibility with different theoretical perspectives and what it can tell us about the personal lives/social policy relation. Whatever your conclusions, the main point is that you see how it works as a conceptual category and how it problematizes the taken for granted.

References

Bevan, A. (1952) *In Place of Fear*, London, Heinemann.

Beveridge, W. (1942) *Social Insurance and Allied Services* (The Beveridge Report), Cmnd 6404, London, HMSO.

Carabine, J. (ed.) (2004) *Sexualities: Personal Lives and Social Policy*, Bristol, The Policy Press in association with The Open University.

Crowley, J. (1999) 'The politics of belonging: some theoretical considerations' in Geddes, A. and Favell, A. (eds) *The Politics of Belonging: Migrants and Minorities in Contemporary Europe*, Aldershot, Ashgate.

Fergusson, R. (2004) 'Remaking the relations of work and welfare' in Mooney (ed.) (2004).

Hoggett, P. (2003) 'A service to the public: the containment of ethical and moral conflicts by public bureaucracies', paper to the *Defending Bureaucracy* workshop, St Hugh's College, Oxford, March.

Home Office (2001) *Secure Borders, Safe Haven: Integration with Diversity in Modern Britain*, CM 5387, London, The Stationery Office.

Lewis, G. (1998) 'Welfare and the social construction of "race"' in Saraga, E. (ed.) *Embodying the Social: Constructions of Difference*, London, Routledge in association with The Open University.

Lister, R. (1997) *Citizenship: Feminist Perspectives*, Basingstoke, Macmillan.

McLennan, G. (1991) 'The role of concepts', Block 2, 'Social structures and divisions', D103 *Society and Social Science*, Milton Keynes, The Open University.

Mooney, G. (ed.) (2004) *Work: Personal Lives and Social Policy*, Bristol, The Policy Press in association with The Open University.

Saville, J. (1957/8) 'The welfare state: an historical approach' in Fitzgerald, M., Halmos, P., Muncie, J. and Zeldin, D. (eds) (1977) *Welfare in Action*, London, RKP in association with The Open University. (First published in 1957/8 in *New Reasoner 3*. Reprinted in 1975 in Butterworth, E. and Holman, R. (eds) *Social Welfare in Modern Britain*, Fontana.)

Acknowledgements

Grateful acknowledgement is made to the following sources for permission to reproduce material within this book:

Text

Extract 1.3: Secure Borders, Safe Haven: Integration with Diversity in Modern Britain (2002) CM 5387. Crown copyright material is reproduced with the permission of the Controller of HMSO and the Queen's Printer for Scotland; *Extract 2.1:* Hall, S. and Schwarz, B. (1985) 'State and society, 1880–1930' in Langan, M. and Schwarz, B. (eds) *Crisis in the British State 1880–1930*, Department of Cultural Studies, University of Birmingham; *Extract 2.3:* Saville, J. 'The welfare state: an historical approach' in Butterworth, E. and Holman, R. (eds) (1975) *Social Welfare in Modern Britain*, Fontana; *Extracts 2.6 and 2.7:* Branson, N. (ed.) (1989) 'Hilda and Barney Lewis, and The Conspiracy Trial – Joyce Alergant', *The London Squatters 1946,* The Communist Party History Group.

Figures/Illustrations

Figure 1.1: personal property of Janet Fink; *Figure 1.2:* personal property of Gail Lewis; *Figure 1.3:* © Punch Cartoon Library and Archive; *Figure 1.4:* Rex Features Ltd and PA Photos Ltd; *Figures 2.1, 2.2 and 2.5:* © Hulton Archive; *Figure 2.3:* Solo Syndication; *Figure 2.4:* Val Wilmer; *Figure 2.6:* Canal + Image UK; *Figure 2.7:* Carlton Productions (Films); *Figure 2.8:* MGM; *Figure 3.1:* courtesy of Cheltenham Borough Council; *Figures 3.2 and 3.8:* Cartoon Stock; *Figure 3.4, clockwise from top left:* © Mary Evans Picture Library; Camera Press Ltd; John Bowlby (deceased); © Hulton Archive; *Figure 3.5:* © Icon Books Ltd; *Figure 3.7:* © Steve Bell; *Figure 4.1:* Crossing the River Gillo – by Mac Anyat, aged 17. From *One Day We Had To Run* – written by Sybella Wilkes and published by Evans Brothers Limited. Copyright © Sybella Wilkes 1994. All rights reserved. This image may not be reproduced, stored or transmitted in any form or by any means without prior permission of Evans Brothers Limited; *Figure 4.2:* front page *G2, The Guardian*, 1 May 2003 © Steve Caplin; *Figure 4.3:* Mahdi Muhammed Ali, translator Salaam Yousif (2003) 'Flight' in Weissbort, D. and Simawe, S.A. (eds) *Iraqi Poetry Today, Modern Poetry in Translation*, No.19, MPT, The School of Humanities, King's College London. © Modern Poetry in Translation 2003; *Figure 4.4:* Wiener Library; *Figure 4.5:* Bungwe, R. (2002) 'Refugee' in Teichman, I. (2002) *Credit to the Nation:*

Refugee Contributions to the UK. By kind permission of the Refugee Council; *Figures 4.6 and 4.8:* © *The Guardian*; *Figure 4.7:* © Hulton Archive.

Every effort has been made to contact copyright owners. If any have been inadvertently overlooked, the publishers will be pleased to make the necessary arrangements at the first opportunity.

Index